SONGS IN THE NIGHT

PERSON
TO
PERSON
BOOKS

1985

Palm Desert, California / Dallas, Texas

SONGS IN THE NIGHT

Vreni Schiess

SONGS IN THE NIGHT

Copyright ©1985 by Vreni Schiess

Person to Person Books
Palm Desert, California
Dallas, Texas

Library of Congress Catalog Number applied for

The Revised Standard Version. Copyright © 1952, 1971 by the Division of Christian Education of the National Council of Churches of Christ in the United States of America. Used by permission.

Cover photography by
  Herbert Lenzkes

Printed in the United States of America

Soli Deo Gloria

Be careful. You are about to begin an incredible experience in the Word of God. If you are undecided, read no more than two or three selections. Read any more and you will be caught up into a world of the spirit more vivid, more powerful, more real than you may be prepared for. If you are hungry for the Word of God, feast freely at the table set before you in these pages. For Vreni Schiess slices into the meat of the Scriptures and serves it graciously — seasoned with satire, blood, love, awe and great joy — just as it was prepared by its writers.

Her questions will strike below the belt, where you are the most vulnerable — where they will do the most good. Her earthiness may make you laugh or get angry or feel the blood rush to your cheeks, but it comes from being immersed in the earthiness of biblical language and culture. Her images are as clean and sharp as a surgeon's knife. And she knows where to make the lifesaving incisions, because she has felt the pain — and the healing — there, herself.

Carolyn A. Fritsch, Editor

P.S. You may find that reading the Scripture passage in context will give you added insight. For your convenience, the text reference is listed at the end of each selection with, in most cases, a suggested context after it.

Behold, I am doing a new thing; now it springs forth, do you not perceive it?

"Behold!" Let it sink in. Feel the weight of the word. Sense in it the Rock of Ages. Perceive in it the stumbling block. Consider the cornerstone ordained by the Lord of History. "Behold" is His claim on the beginning of this new year. It is both invitation and command to tune our hearing heart and exercise the gift of spiritual sight.

The discipline of consciously looking to God on this strategic day is not aided by our pleasantly undemanding wishes to have a "Happy New Year." Happy is the man whose favored team wins. Happy are they who muddle through yet another crisis-ridden year to emerge survivors.

"Behold, I am doing a *new* thing." New! "New improved" as in laundry detergent that suddenly comes in a brighter box and costs more? We have come to distrust the word *new* in a world of shifting values and power structures. New is often not safe. Our new inevitably turns old, tired, sour.

Behold the majesty and mystery of our God! In the beginning the earth was without form and void. And God said, "Let there be the delight of my creation." In the fullness of time He spoke again and said, "Let there be light." And in Bethlehem of Judea a baby was born.

Shall we perceive the new days ahead as heralding a year of doubt? Or shall we perceive them as ushering in the new year of the Lord's favor, the year of taking delight in our Lord?

Isaiah 43:19 □ *Isaiah 43:14-21*

My grace is sufficient for you, for my power is made perfect in weakness.

The countdown is on for a host of people on the annual collision course with their New Year's resolutions — the noble effort growing out of the niceness and not-so-niceness of the holidays. Expanded hearts and waistlines cause us to narrow down our faults — faults to be sacrificed on the altar of self-sanctification.

Not that we necessarily think of it that way. The decision to diet stems from tight clothes more than from tight thinking. Efforts to be more orderly don't have to be based on tidy theology. Who ever heard of scrubbing a bathtub to the glory of God? We no longer want to be thought of as sloppy, that's all.

We all yearn to be nicer, healthier, brighter, better. Who can quarrel with that? God doesn't. That's why He draws us to Him when we are bogged down in the guilt and despair of faltered efforts. And that's why He makes us scrub bathtubs to His glory when we have grown self-satisfied. But does He really want our paltry New Year's resolutions?

God is always after something more radical. Our will. The single-minded surrender of our will! Then grace becomes sufficient. Then at the foot of the cross God gathers to Himself a strong people.

2 Corinthians 12:9 □ 2 Corinthians 12:1-10

And we all, with unveiled face, beholding the glory of the Lord, are being changed into his likeness from one degree of glory to another; for this comes from the Lord who is the Spirit.

"Once upon a time . . ." Old myths die hard. Girl kisses frog and lo — instant royalty. Man embraces religion and lo — instant nobility of character. Myths are for kissing good-bye. Not only is the world still filled with frogs, but the church is jumping with them.

It is a sorry Christian myth that the ideal Christian life must be a victorious ascent from the Pit of Perdition to the Peak of Perpetual Perfection. Too bad our feet, so eagerly nimble to race up the trail of sanctification, are slowed by the baggage that must go along on the trip. The old Adam or Eve on our back makes for cumbersome mountain climbing.

God's glory is unlike man's glory — the flag-waving kind. God's glory is that of King becoming lowest of frogs. His Spirit alone enables us to apprehend and desire for ourselves this ultimate kingly glory. Natural man does not aspire to lowly froghood.

In that sense the Spirit-enabled Christian life is marked by descent, not ascent. It is characterized by the death and resurrection cycle. We move back and forth between Bethlehem and Jerusalem — the place where Christ is born and reborn in us to the place of confrontation where we are asked to lay down our life again and again.

This is the glory that comes from the Lord and makes for the radiant Christian.

2 Corinthians 3:18 □ 2 Corinthians 3:7-18

*He has put all things under his feet and has made him the head
over all things for the church, which is his body, the fulness of
him who fills all in all.*

We must beware of presenting the Christian life as a
cultural plus and the church as consumer-oriented in order to
attract believers. It is not so farfetched when we consider those
who actually shop for a church that caters to certain musical
tastes or offers diverse services, babysitting and traditional
among them.

We all have this thing about *our* church. There is pride of
ownership and satisfaction over the performance level. The
worship experience is gripping. The music an oasis in a wasteland of secular sound. We have people and programs for every
need. Won't you stop shopping and sign up with us?

Our church does not exist. Only *The Church of Jesus Christ*
does. It is not a structure, not an organization, not an appen-
dage to culture. It is not something we choose to belong to at
will. *Our* church does not bless us because of the collective
excellence of trained staff and carefully guided programs.

As *His* church, we are blessed because God has blessed us
in Christ "with every spiritual blessing in the heavenly places,
even as he chose us in him before the foundation of the world,
that we should be holy and blameless before him" (Ephesians
1:3-4).

Let empty pews call us to the emptiness of every heart that
longs for infilling and fulfilling through the sovereign Lord of
the Church.

Ephesians 1:22-23 □ *Ephesians 1:3-23*

Now to him who by the power at work within us is able to do far more abundantly than all that we ask or think, to him be glory in the church and in Christ Jesus to all generations, for ever and ever. Amen.

Our best religious thinking and asking is not good enough. We are afflicted with provincialism. We tend to pull things down to our level of comfort and reason. When our premise fits, we make it sacrosanct. Add to the great religions of the world our Important Religion of Pet Thought, complete with pet scripture to underwrite our presuppositions.

Today's prized individualist with his finely honed ability to think and act independently has no career advancement opportunity in the kingdom of God. "For my thoughts are not your thoughts, neither are your ways my ways, says the Lord" (Isaiah 55:8). That much was settled at least 2700 years ago.

Does that make God a stifler of creativity? Does He begrudge our probing of the mystery of who and whose we are? Quite to the contrary. With all His heart He yearns for us to understand and celebrate the greatest mystery of all. It is His invitation, yes, His imperative, that we become host and nourisher to His own Spirit within us. It is the same awesome Spirit that moved over the waters at Creation and raised Christ from His tomb. Does that not shock the petty provincialism out of us?

God does not offer the gift of His Spirit to enhance our intellect and emotions. It is for the purpose of His glory only. His "glory in the church and in Christ Jesus to all generations, for ever and ever." Will we "Amen" to that and get into His mainstream of purpose?

Ephesians 3:20-21 ☐ *Ephesians 3:1-21*

Look carefully then how you walk, not as unwise men but as wise, making the most of the time . . .

Making the most of the time. "Because the days are evil!" That spells trouble. Looks like the axe of judgment is about to pare our daily schedule. Less television. Less loafing. Less freedom as we are being fitted for the strait jacket of rigorous discipline.

Paul knows how to shock all right. ". . . but be filled with the Spirit, addressing one another in psalms and hymns and spiritual songs, singing and making melody to the Lord with all your heart, always and for everything giving thanks . . ."

We use time to *do* things. We chop it into units and race the clock to keep pace with the multiplicity of daily demands. Paul seems to say that we ought to celebrate time as that which allows us to become what we were meant to be. He does not equal time with the frantic allotment of parcels of our fragmented self. He speaks of wholeness at the core of our innermost being that naturally wells up in gladness.

It is the anchored soul that sings and flows with praise. A soul anchored in eternity where time is neither tyrant nor truant. If we are to make the most of the time we cannot simply get up 15 minutes earlier to give God the extra time we might have spent on sleep or breakfast. Our time for Him must be all of our time with Him. It is not a matter of scheduling, but being filled with His Spirit.

Ephesians 5:15-16 □ *Ephesians 5:1-20*

Return to your stronghold, O prisoners of hope . . .

We conceive of the new year as a launching pad. The pull of the unknown and undiscovered make it so. We sense the new frontiers of experience and the adventurer in us would have us go and claim them all. A fresh wind of enthusiasm fills our sail and we set out for the distant shore.

What if we find the sea becalmed outside the breakwater? What if we are ambushed a day's journey out of the fort? And what if doubt has us go in circles in the trackless wastes of the unknown? We quickly return to the safe mechanics of everyday life. There is balm in routine and sameness even though we mourn the ease with which we compromise our high hopes.

Let us not be deceived. It is God Himself who beckons us to step out decisively daily, regardless of season or sentiment. The choice is between stagnation and growth, rusting and risking. The challenge is still to follow Christ. He becomes our movable stronghold.

"'I will follow you wherever you go.' And Jesus said to him, 'Foxes have holes, and birds of the air have nests; but the Son of man has nowhere to lay his head'" (Luke 9:57-58). There is our true hope! No person or place or circumstance can willfully hold or delay Him. If we follow Him — who can hold us back?

Zechariah 9:12 ☐ *Zechariah 9:9-12*

For thou dost bless the righteous, O LORD; thou dost cover him with favor as with a shield.

Our lack of imagination is exceeded only by our indignation when life comes apart in unexpected ways in spite of the Christian veneer. We give lip service to the truth that the Christian life is unique in terms of redemption, not exemption. When the rug is suddenly pulled out from under our feet, we cannot help but feel let down. Of course.

Already God is blessing by allowing us to slide back and forth across the sharp edge of disappointment. He can take our honestly expressed emotions. He is willing to ride out the storm. So we have paid our Christian dues and still it did not buy immunity from life's ills. Does that make God our debtor?

When we are talked out and cried out — when, like Job, the fight has gone out of us, we too will come to say with him, "I had heard of thee by the hearing of the ear, but now my eye sees thee; therefore I despise myself, and repent in dust and ashes" (Job 42:5-6).

The specific privilege of the Christian life is never immunity, but intimacy with God. That's the shield of favor, the "steadfast love" of the Psalmist's praise. When we prize intimacy with our Lord more than we crave immunity from life's trials, He will often thrill us with the power of His supernatural intervention.

Psalm 5:12 □ Psalm 5

Then I said, "Here am I! Send me."

Is God calling us? Is that not His voice on the evening news? We recognize it in the moans of starving people; the shattering glass of the slums. We hear it in the shots and sobs and sirens of our sinful, suffering world.

The whole earth, it seems, is one big emergency calling for a squad of eager beavers to rush to its aid — Here am I! Send me! The whole earth is one huge crumbling dike of washed-out do-gooders — and how our thumbs hurt from holding back the leaks.

God must put to death in us the mistaken notion that the awful condition of the world determines our calling! The awesomeness of our relationship with God must do it.

If we are to be useful, we too must first see him "high and lifted up" and hear the emphasis of heaven's testimony, "Holy, holy, holy is the LORD of hosts; the whole earth is full of his glory" (Isaiah 6:3). Let us be confronted by that and with Isaiah cry out, "Woe is me!" Then God can close in on our own sinfulness and suffering. His personal touch makes for personal wholeness. Out of the internalized experience of salvation now comes the call to be broken and poured out for the needs of the world. "Here am I!" Christlike.

Isaiah 6:8 □ *Isaiah 6:1-8*

You believe that God is one; you do well. Even the demons believe — and shudder.

Faithless familiarity with faith! The church is still good at it. We seem to be born with a knack for religion. We love to enshrine our convictions in stout walls of stone and dogma. It is our attention to the trappings of the secondary that robs the primary of its vitality.

Because of our religious beliefs we go to a certain building on a certain day. There we corporately sing, smile and speak prescribed words at the discretion of a bulletin. The order of worship is Holy Writ. Now all those things are right and good if the things of God also make us shudder, weep, laugh, jump, and draw in our very breath with a sense of the sacred.

The natural tendency is to contain our faith within specified areas of our compartmentalized thinking and living. The distinction between spiritual and secular is held dear. Religious faith that manifests itself in the security of a familiar pew on Sunday is of the quantity kind. When crisis strikes, we frantically have to pray for more. If crisis lasts, we may well lose the little we had.

Righteous faith is the quality of being found in Christ. It contains all of us and all of life. It is eminently surprisable!

James 2:19 □ James 2:14-26

So Abram went . . .

Just like that. "So Abram went" and promptly went on to become Abraham, Enduring Sunday School Hero! And while his faith was imputed to him as righteousness, ours is just a bit strained. "Abram went" all right. Went down to Egypt to declare himself a coward and conniver. Went on record repeatedly as one afflicted with every human frailty, frustration and folly we have fallen heir to.

But Abraham kept going. Hemming and hawing, hoping and hurting, stumbling, stalling, searching for shortcuts to God's promises. This was no paragon of virtue, patriarchal aura notwithstanding. Imputed to him as righteousness was his essential faithfulness in his relationship with God — a relationship initiated, enabled and sustained by a covenant that put the burden of responsibility on God.

Will He do less for us? There is a Haran and Canaan in our life and God has said to leave the established and comfortable for the adventure of faith. The new covenant in the blood of the Savior says GO! The Pioneer and Perfecter of our faith says GO! A new faith chapter needs to be written today. Will the Abram in you and me go? Shall God be denied His heroes of the faith in our day and age?

Genesis 12:4 ☐ *Genesis 11:27-13:1*

If you have raced with men on foot, and they have wearied you, how will you compete with horses? And if in a safe land you fall down, how will you do in the jungle of the Jordan?

How indeed? The battlefields of the soul are not outwardly displayed. We can be locked into the most trying circumstances and the sympathy of the bystander is wasted, because we are moved and motivated by the inner joy of God's suffering servant. And a calm and uneventful outward life may belie the high drama of profound inner struggle.

Paul's letter to the Ephesians speaks of the "heavenly places." Dead through sin but alive in Christ, we have already been made to sit with Him in the heavenly places. As the church we are to make known the wisdom of God to the principalities and powers in the heavenly places. Are these "heavenly places" of ultimate confirmation and decisive confrontation not deep within our soul?

We worry about our capacity to meet future crises. Who can rehearse for the sudden shocks of existence? But the crisis moment is not necessarily the critical moment. The critical moment might have been weeks or years earlier when a battle of wills over a minor matter was lost or won in our deep inner heavenly places!

That's why we must allow God to press for supremacy in the common places of everyday life. That's why we must be found faithful in small matters. How will we do in the jungle of the Jordan? It depends on how we walk with God in a safe land.

Jeremiah 12:5 ☐ *Jeremiah 12:1-6*

And Jesus said to him, "What do you want me to do for you?"

Bartimaeus, "a blind beggar, the son of Timaeus, was sitting by the roadside" at the entrance to Jericho. In the deliberate detailing of his story, the gospel writer crystalizes essential truth.

Jesus is on His fateful journey to Jerusalem. A great multitude is marching along. The plot is thickening. History is in the making. The stage is being set. And there sits an unlikely prop!

The blind beggar, as must be his trade, is making a nuisance of himself. Only now he outdoes himself. "Jesus, Son of David, have mercy on me!" The self-appointed theologians in Jesus' crowd are annoyed. They have yet to understand the Son of man, but they are pro-God. And the cries of this noisy, lowly beggar do not fit their image of what God is all about. The crowd wants him silenced so they can march on.

"Jesus, Son of David, have mercy on me!" Authentic need has made a proper theologian out of Bartimaeus. Man's pressing private need is the touchstone of the gospel. It enables the personal encounter with the Savior. His response cuts to the quick, "What do you want me to do for you?" And then His healing touch of mercy makes for the meaningful Marching Society of Seeing Followers.

Mark 10:51 □ *Mark 10:46-52*

Now Jesus loved Martha and her sister and Lazarus. So when he heard that he was ill, he stayed two days longer in the place where he was.

That does not make sense to us. God's love does not fit our logic. The supreme Physician refuses to make the house call that might save a friend's life. He deliberately stays away in order for grief to come to pass.

God will not be put in a box. He will not tolerate our limited view of when or how He is to intervene. We must allow God to be God. Again and again He makes us drink the "wine of astonishment." We must stagger and fall from the lofty heights of human logic that runs counter to the designs of the Most High.

Christ's healing power had been amply demonstrated. His gift to Lazarus and the family of man was to be far more sublime. "Jesus wept"! Does that not deeply move us? The Son of God did not cheapen loss and grief by offering pious platitudes. The Son of man identified with us so fully that He was moved to tears. And did He not weep for Himself also as death's shadow tightened its net around Him?

In the triumph of Lazarus' resurrection we dare not miss the powerful lesson of his unbinding. "Lord, by this time there will be an odor, for he has been dead four days." Would we not rather dress up and play church than heed Christ's firm command, "Unbind him!" Who are we keeping "buried alive" because we won't do the unbinding?

John 11:5-6 ☐ John 11:1-44

Many of his disciples, when they heard it, said, "This is a hard saying; who can listen to it?"

God takes calculated risks with us. He is not after pampered pets or cuddly spiritual babies. We must grow up "to mature manhood, to the measure of the stature of the fulness of Christ" (Ephesians 4:13).

If He identifies with us, we must identify with His purpose for us. That means to "eat and drink Christ" until His nature is not only second nature to us, but our only one. There can be no half-breeds. So God undertakes to push us ruthlessly beyond our natural limitations. In vain we seek to understand Him. We are forced into unconditional surrender.

If there is heartbreak in this and there *is* — of the most exquisite kind — we must remember that God's own heart was broken long before ours. After the "hard saying" of having to eat and drink Christ, "many of his disciples drew back and no longer went about with him." What did that do to the Lover of mankind who came unto His own and His own received Him not? His emotions did not differ from ours!

God's calculated risk is that with Peter we will submit to His ruthlessness because we have no other choice. "Lord, to whom shall we go? You have the words of eternal life . . ." But out of the heartbreak of costly surrender does come blessed hindsight. In time our exultant heart will acknowledge Him as "God, my exceeding joy"!

John 6:60 □ *John 6:35-65*

But by the grace of God I am what I am, and his grace toward me was not in vain.

This is God's purpose personified, the paradox of selfhood exposed. When Paul was his old self — his own self — his peers cheered him and made him a leader. When his old self was crucified and he arose to a position of influence within the church, he frequently had to defend himself.

When Paul was weak for Christ's sake, he rated poorly compared with the "superlative apostles" who made a grab for power. When displaying strength in Christ's cause, he suffered ill repute because of alleged arrogance. To this day Paul's ego is being questioned. "I urge you, then, be imitators of me" (1 Corinthians 4:16). We are bound to take that with a grain of salt.

"Self" is in vogue at every level of society. Literature abounds with volumes on self-help to foster self-identity and self-love. Be your own self. Be good to yourself. Be God to yourself.

Oh, for the wisdom and courage of Paul to "flaunt" the crucified self! The church still has her moldmakers who pressure us to be conformers instead of transformers. There are still the dangerous cowards who seek to hinder us from places of confrontation by saying, "God forbid, Lord" (Matthew 16:22). Such stumbling blocks must be challenged by the sheer weight of rocklike authority, "By the grace of God I am what I am . . ." It must push others toward their appointment with Jerusalem.

1 Corinthians 15:10 ☐ *1 Corinthians 15:1-11*

Speak, for thy servant hears.

How can we know that the Lord speaks to us? We are rightly sceptical of the person who boasts of a direct line to heaven. Would it help if God spoke in a loud voice? In this day of traffic helicopters and bullhorns the voice from on high might trigger nothing more than a puzzled inquiry to the Police Commission.

The Old Testament is still the classical textbook to settle "Thus saith the Lord" questions. If the boy Samuel could learn to trust God, so can we. And the first lesson is precisely that: It is God's responsibility to make Himself heard and understood! Is the voice that accomplished Creation not qualified to communicate with man created in God's image? Let Him determine how best to get through to us.

May this "obstacle course" serve to dispel our anxieties: When God first called, Samuel was a sleepy child who "did not yet know the Lord." When Eli the priest perceived the nature of the calling, he instructed the boy to say, "Speak, Lord, for thy servant hears." Samuel promptly neglected to acknowledge the Lord's presence, repeating simply, "Speak, for thy servant hears." And afterward he was afraid to tell the vision to Eli.

The lesson is reassuring. If we are willing to be trained for the role of obedient servant, God can be trusted to do His part. "And Samuel grew, and the Lord was with him and let none of his words fall to the ground." God has things to say to His church today. Dare we become His hearing servants?

1 Samuel 3:10 ☐ 1 Samuel 3:1-4:1

And a young man ran and told Moses, "Eldad and Medad are prophesying in the camp." And Joshua the son of Nun, the minister of Moses, one of his chosen men, said, "My lord Moses, forbid them."

Personal contact with God must not lead to personality cult. The channel of grace must not be dammed up to become a reflection pool for our imagined greatness. God's contract with us is always signed with Christ's blood. No matter how exclusive the agreement in its application to our personal life, the purpose is always to manifest the inclusiveness of our Redeemer.

Moses staggered under the burden of being singularly God's man. The prestige of being the chosen one wore off to the point of anguish," . . . kill me at once, if I find favor in thy sight, that I may not see my wretchedness."

When Moses had come full cycle from ambition to agony, God's adequacy came through for him. Seventy leaders were called to be anointed with His Spirit. They would share in the task of being God's mouthpiece to the wandering, wavering nation. And now God's humor made a quick dent in the collectively shiny armor of these strutting Knights of the Kingdom.

They assembled eagerly, received the Spirit and prophesied briefly. And then "they did so no more." Meanwhile, back at camp, away from the power and prestige of Moses' inner circle, Eldad and Medad prophesied to their heart's content. Now Moses could afford to chuckle with God. "Are you jealous for my sake? Would that all the Lord's people were prophets . . ."

Numbers 11:27-28 □ *Numbers 11:1-30*

Never flag in zeal, be aglow with the Spirit, serve the Lord.

Never flag in zeal? The very thought is exhausting. Not one of us wants to be sentenced to a lifetime of "eagerness and ardent interest in the pursuit" of virtues uniquely Christian in character. We don't have Paul's metabolism.

Our zeal might flourish briefly with the appointment to some committee — our chance to take a crack at the church. But when novelty gives way to the drudgery of coffee-stained minutes; when despite the fires of enthusiasm nothing great gets off the ground, we flag down the nearest excuse to transport us back to the mediocrity from which we came in the first place.

Paul never said to get fired up in the explosive, fickle ways of idealism. We want to light up the sky, when a reliable flashlight is more what God has in mind. If that sounds dull, let us consider how the darkness of a cave is spectacularly relieved by the lighting of one single candle.

The injunction to maintain zeal makes sense only in conjunction with the Spirit-enabled life. The object is not to perform feats of human endurance, but simply to serve the Lord. While serving in Asia, Paul was so "unbearably crushed" that he longed for death. Yet, near the end of his life he testified, ". . . but one thing I do . . . I press on toward the goal for the prize of the upward call of God in Christ Jesus" (Philippians 3:13). That zeal can and must be emulated today!

Romans 12:11 ☐ *Romans 12:1-13*

So we do not lose heart. Though our outer nature is wasting away, our inner nature is being renewed every day!

Perish the thought that our modern "outward man" should still face "perishing." The cosmetics industry alone will not allow for such a disaster. But if worse comes to worse, we can exit the scene made into a very good-looking corpse.

The hallmark of the authentic Christian is self-evidencing congruity between the inner and outer person. If the heart is anointed with the oil of gladness, the Lord is also "the health of our countenance." But it would be folly to equate spiritual vigor with the Fountain of Youth.

Not only are we genetically programmed to "waste away," but the very rigors of Christian maturity can play havoc with our looks and health. Tears and tossings at night are not kind to the face. Hands knotted in prayer and knees glued to the floor do not make for a supple body. Gut-level wrestling may trigger migraines or ulcers. Fatigue from long vigil can make for thinness or fatness.

We do not owe the world an image of what the ideal saint should look or feel like. If there is a centerfold in the Book of Life it shows Christ sweating blood. Or Jacob limping, thigh out of joint. Or Job, covered with loathsome sores. So we get the picture — and do not lose heart!

2 Corinthians 4:16 □ *2 Corinthians 4:7-18*

All who make idols are nothing, and the things they delight in do not profit . . .

We agree heartily. Until we are shocked into discovering that "they" are us also! It is with the utmost of ease that the Christian relegates "idols" and "all they" to pagan societies of old. Or we condescendingly think of modern secular man who worships status or money. Enlightened Christians wouldn't be caught dead in such blatant heathenism. We live for Christian ideals.

Exactly. What is so different about ideals and idols? Are they not both images conceived by man? We strive for a host of ideals in the Christian realm. The ideal approach to steward-ship or missions. The ideal conditions to implement programs with the ideal person in charge. We have marriage ideals, child-raising ideals, old-age ideals. In our striving to achieve or live up to certain ideals, native literally to naivete, we must appear to God as primitive as the heathen does to us with his exotic strivings.

If we are to further the Kingdom in and around us, we must die to ideas and ideals and live to the person and reality of Jesus Christ. He did not come as ideal Man to foster a fellowship of ideal people. He came as the real God to dwell with real people!

We are all caught in the real needs of real situations. The reality of the person of Jesus Christ is sufficient for each. As our five senses unlock the reality of the natural world in which we live, so faith unlocks to the one alive in Christ the treasure of His resources. As our natural senses bring creation into personal focus, so faith puts us in personal touch with the highest reality — our Creator Himself.

Isaiah 44:9 □ Isaiah 44:9-20

We . . . take every thought captive to obey Christ . . .

We all long for spiritual highs that require no mental push-ups. We bemoan the pull of gravity that keeps our thoughts earthbound. Our shallow Christianity produces guilt that makes us fantasize about some future mental breakthrough that will boost us into an orbit of effortless God-consciousness.

But Christianity is not an intellectual discipline to start with! It is not a religion based on the teachings of Christ, which we must study religiously and distill into flawless dissertations. Christianity simply, sublimely, centers on the personhood of Jesus Christ. "I am the way, and the truth, and the life . . ." We cannot "master" Christ; He must become Master over us.

If we are to bring our thought life under the Lordship of Jesus, we must go from abstraction to action. The immediacy and intimacy of God does not come by mental process. The Holy Spirit is not connected to our ideas, but to the reality of Christ. The mystery of the Incarnation evades the reasoning power of our finite mind. In simple trust we affirm the presence of the living Lord within us. By an act of will we practice obedience to Him through action. It is in that process that God reveals Himself to us consistently.

Jesus, himself, warned of the passive thought life removed from the active reality of His life: "You search the scriptures, because you think that in them you have eternal life; and it is they that bear witness to me; yet you refuse to come to me that you may have life" (John 5:39-40).

2 Corinthians 10:5 □ 2 Corinthians 10:3-6

"As long as I am in the world, I am the light of the world." As he said this, he spat on the ground and made clay of the spittle and anointed the man's eyes with the clay, saying to him, "Go, wash . . ."

If we are serious about becoming the spiritual man after God's own heart, we are in for a surprise. God is more earthbound than we are. Embarrassingly so. He will do everything in His power to offend and alienate the latent religionist in us.

The religionist thrives on the poetry of spiritual language. "I am the light of the world" is right down his alley. He approves of the anointing as a recognized spiritual gesture. But common dirt and spit? O God — thou must be joking!

We dearly love the stories that pit the foolish Pharisees against our hero Jesus. It hardly ever dawns on us that the Pharisee is still alive and well — and kicking in us. And Jesus must still outsmart him. As of old, He will not give us the satisfaction of a theological argument, no matter how we bait Him. Jesus will go right on "impersonating" God in His maddeningly authoritative, incomprehensible ways and make fools of us along the way.

The mud-and-spit embarrassment will linger, because it will stare us in the face in the simple, trusting person who keeps insisting, "So I went and washed and received my sight." God will ridicule our religion until we enter into a personal relationship of simple trust and obedience with Him. Then He enlightens and broadens our view of the truly sacred.

John 9:5-7 □ *John 9:1-12*

Moses, Moses! . . . put off your shoes from your feet, for the place on which you are standing is holy ground.

How curious are we about the burning bush? If, like Moses, we choose to study the phenomenon more closely, we will first find "Vegetable Kingdom" in our Bible dictionary. From there we will backtrack to Hebrew symbolism. And all the while God is calling, "Moses, Moses!" until suddenly — forcefully — the truth confronts us: God is calling us!

The burning bush in our life can be any burning issue that simply will not go away. It might be an unfulfilled ambition, a recurring fear, a chronic doubt. If we have not consciously fueled it with the energy of our thoughts and will, we can safely assume that the God-confrontation in it has not yet taken place.

Now that we know, the issue must be faced. The heat is on. And suddenly we panic and want to run. We enjoy the sunshine of God's warmth on the surface areas of our life. But we dread the laser of His truth in the hidden recesses of our mind and emotions. We try to run from God and ourselves.

Take off your shoes, Moses! We, too, must be stripped of self-adequacy; deprived of the protective cushioning that fools us into side-stepping the thorny places of our life. Holy ground is thorny ground. Holy ground is the place where God pins us down — for good!

Exodus 3:4-5 □ Exodus 3

O LORD, why hast thou done evil to this people? Why didst thou ever send me?

Our decisive showdown with the ultimate I Am leaves us no choice but to affirm His absolute Lordship. Who can argue with the God of history, the proven Covenant God? Yet our earnest dialogue with Him — the good stiff argument even — is valid and fruitful. The more we are drawn out, the more the defenses come down. And God can move in for good. "The LORD . . . this is my name for ever."

When God pins us down and moves in "for good," He makes it plain that "LORD" is not ceremonial title, but authority in action. No longer is He merely a measure of sunshine, dappling our obscured life at our pleasure, but now He becomes the Refiner's Fire. His truth will illuminate the steps we are to take. His actions will fire our intellect and emotions. His passion will burn the chaff that hinders the developing friendship.

"Yes, Lord, I am yours!" Thus endeth the reading of the Burning Bush story. And do the "deliverers" live happily ever after? Of course not. Stripped of self-adequacy, we step out in the confidence of the Lord and the shock waves start rolling. The God of history is steering the course of nations. And what are nations if not simply people, some for and some against Him?

We are trapped in the furnace of affliction, forever in bondage to God. What has been set in motion cannot be reversed. "The LORD" — His actions are for ever! For good. How good? We too shall know when we get to the "mountain of God."

Exodus 5:22 ☐ Exodus 5:1-6:1

*For in him all the fulness of God was pleased to dwell . . .
making peace by the blood of his cross.*

Jesus Christ, Prince of Peace! We like catchy titles. It is
featured in bold letters on our Christian calling card. That's
how painlessly we hand out "peace," much like successful
businessmen exchange their cards. "Just do the will of God,"
the popular version says, "and you will always have marvelous
peace!" So why do "successful" Christians still go to pieces?

Why don't we talk more about the hell of acting out God's
will — and share the agony of it together? Christ's name is
Prince of Peace because He acted out conflict after conflict in
costly obedience to the Father. It wasn't until the Deliverer confronted His mountain of God — Calvary — that the peace of
God could be established. Reconciliation — peace between
Creator and fallen creation — is drenched in the blood of the
cross. How dare we throw it around so lightly?

We are peace lovers all right. "Do not disturb!" God calls us
to be peace*makers* and guarantees no peace except by the
blood of the cross. If in active obedience we follow the Savior,
every conflict of His will be ours also. Satan is sure to assault
us mind, body, and soul. Close friends and family will make
for the pain of torn loyalties. We, too, will know our betrayer
and taste the abandonment of Gethsemane.

Peace? Let us no longer bounce it off people like a cheery
campaign slogan. We must learn to say "Peace" as the gentle
password of those willing to enter into the camaraderie of
the cross.

Colossians 1:19-20 □ *Colossians 1:9-29*

And as they led him away, they seized one Simon of Cyrene, who was coming in from the country, and laid on him the cross, to carry it behind Jesus.

Luckless Simon! On vacation away from his home in North Africa, he expects to celebrate the Passover in Jerusalem. So close to his dream, why now the blunder? Why not slow his purposeful stride while viewing soldiers and rabble from a safe distance? Is he so engrossed in his thoughts that he does not notice?

Suddenly there is a rough yank on his arm and, as the crowd lets loose with a stream of obscenities, a bloodied cross-bar is thrust across his shoulders. Before his disbelieving eyes can fully take in the scene, the order to get moving is barked and he follows the pitiful figure of a condemned criminal. The folks at home will never believe this!

We feel for Simon as we picture the trauma of his accidental thrust into the main event of history. We would have gladly borne our Lord's burden, but it was not fair to the gentleman just coming in from the country.

Jesus must have briefly pitied the shaken stranger, but our sentimental thinking will not get us His sympathy. The purpose of the Calvary journey is not to glory in our martyrdom, but to fulfill God's strategy. Sooner or later our obedience will come to cost others also. But we are not co-regents with the King of Kings. We do not tell Him who can or cannot be thrust into the drama of our Calvary. We have neither the wisdom nor stomach for it!

Luke 23:26 ☐ *Luke 23:1-26*

So Ananias departed and entered the house. And laying his hands on him he said, "Brother Saul . . ."

When God's strategy is honored above personal sentiment, serendipities sweeten the results. Ananias had good reasons to call off his scary appointment with Saul. The palpable threat of persecution justified caution. Nevertheless, Ananias obeyed God at the risk of his life.

"And laying his hands on him he said, 'Brother Saul . . .'" Paul later recalled, "And one Ananias, a devout man according to the law, well spoken of by all the Jews who lived there, came to me, and standing by me said to me, 'Brother Saul, receive your sight'" (Acts 22:12-13).

Oh, that we would receive ours as well! It is so easy to applaud Ananias' courageous obedience and then shift the spotlight to Paul. But Ananias lived to freely lay down his life for Saul! We can see the necessity of dying to self or to God. But would our reserve, our churchmanship, our own ambition to carry God's name before influential people — would our pride permit us to greet Saul as a brother?

Ananias loved God and had allowed God to love him. Out of the deep, inner security of that mutual love flowed the gracious spirit that drew Saul into the caring fellowship of Christ's own. "Paul, an apostle of Christ Jesus by the will of God, and Timothy our brother. To the church of God . . . Grace . . ." Does Paul's style not reflect that first crucial meeting when God's will received glory through a grace-gifted brother?

Acts 9:17 ☐ *Acts 9:10-19*

When I came to Troas to preach the gospel of Christ, a door was opened for me in the Lord; but my mind could not rest because I did not find my brother Titus there. So I took leave . . .

Can this be Paul, the spiritual giant? In Troas he exercises his freedom in Christ. The freedom to falter, to be fully human; the freedom to decline a burden until the yokefellowship has been secured.

Woe to me if I do not have a yokemate in the gospel! I can do all things better in the companionship and corrective of shared strength! If God is to depend on us, we must learn to become interdependent. We picture the yoke as an oppressive device, but if we are Christ's own, we will come to cherish it as a high mark of His favor.

Christ's yoke is meticulously crafted and lovingly handrubbed to fit perfectly the contours of the wearer. Christ's yoke brings together under His care the weak with the strong, the mature with the inexperienced, the cautious with the adventurous, the nearsighted with the farsighted. Christ's yoke equalizes and emancipates. "There is neither Jew nor Greek, there is neither slave nor free, there is neither male nor female; for you are all one in Christ Jesus" (Galatians 3:28).

As disciples of Christ, Titus a Greek and Paul a Jew experienced the discipline and delight of His fusing of their diversity for His purpose, as well as their challenge and comfort. In Paul's eager longing for Titus we sense his need for emotional reinforcement. In Paul's letter to him we recognize the force of Paul's personality that would lend steel and verve to Titus' character and career. We can trust Christ for the yokemate who will complement us.

2 Corinthians 2:12-13

Remember me, O my God, for good.

To read Nehemiah in one sweep is an exercise in exhilaration. We are caught up in a spectrum of wholeheartedness that exudes energy. Nehemiah's terse exit line leaves us wondering. Did he get to sleep with his fathers along with the deluxe burial befitting God's passionate patriot? Or did his fathers refuse to sleep with him because he kept turning over in his grave? That's how deeply, how continuously he cared!

Cupbearer to the Babylonian king, he learns from fellow Jews of the sad state of post-exilic Jerusalem, as well as its dispirited survivors. The stage is set for him to step into the leader's role to rebuild the city and national morale. The drama involves a cast of thousands; the booing and cheering is spectacular also. In all this Nehemiah vigilantly plays to an audience of exactly one: God!

"Yea, I and my father's house have sinned." Having established that, he throws himself into his role, but when curtain time comes, he is not played out. "And I was very angry, and I threw all the household furniture of Tobiah out . . . So I remonstrated with the officials . . . Then I remonstrated with the nobles . . . And I contended with them and cursed them and beat some of them and pulled out their hair . . ."

Counterpoint to the theme of unrelenting people-pressure runs the theme of his abiding God-passion. "Remember me, O my God, concerning this, and wipe not out my good deeds that I have done for the house of my God and for his service." We picture Nehemiah's memorial service. What do the mourners and dignitaries remember most? It matters little. Nehemiah had played to God only and He remembers for good.

Nehemiah 13:31 □ Nehemiah 13

Would that you were cold or hot! So, because you are luke-
warm, and neither cold nor hot, I will spew you out of my
mouth.

That is decidedly unpleasant. We all have times when we
say, "This makes me want to throw up!" Only we don't. Christ
takes it one unpleasant step further: "I *will* spew you out of my
mouth." Not surprisingly, not even the most avant-garde artist
has ever depicted "The Nauseated Christ" in stained glass or on
canvas. No church would have it.

Perhaps it would serve the church well to congregate
around a body of stagnant water, made shallow and tepid by
the same blistering sun that makes people crazed with thirst.
Perhaps we should cup our hands and dip in and force the
liquid down our parched throat. Perhaps we should reel and
retch with the stark realism of the Christ of Revelation.

If the scenario is ghastly, it is hardly original. Just a short
time out of Egypt, Moses suffered the murmuring of his thirst-
crazed people. After three days of stumbling around in the
wilderness of Shur, they came to the water of Marah. Picture
the bitterness of discovering that it was undrinkable. Then God
showed Moses a tree to throw into the water and it became
sweet. (Exodus 15:22-25)

Is the cross not the tree that must transform the insipid
church of our age into the living water that will satisfy God
and the world He came to love so much? Art has produced
countless saccharin Christs. And the church has matched them
with like bodies. The Christ of Revelation cries, "Enough!"
Behold, He stands at the door. The Judge of the ages.

Revelation 3:15-16 □ *Revelation 3:14-22*

Therefore, my beloved, as you have always obeyed . . . work out your own salvation with fear and trembling . . .

Just one minute, please. We wish to back up 2000 years. The way we heard it we are home free! Does the Paul of Philippians wish to consult with the Paul of Ephesians? "For by grace you have been saved through faith; and this is not your own doing, it is the gift of God — not because of works, lest any man should boast" (2:8-9). Why, then, does our astute theologian throw a monkey wrench into our neatly defined doctrine of salvation? The proposed "workout" with fear and trembling strains our enthusiasm.

The trouble is that we like to quote Scripture the way insurance policies are sold. "The large print giveth, the small print taketh away." So we concentrate on the large print. The small print in Ephesians adds this important qualification, "For we are his workmanship, created in Christ Jesus for good works, which God prepared beforehand, that we should walk in them" (2:10).

In the redemptive act of Calvary we were saved from the wrath of God once and for all. However, we were not only saved *from* something, but also *for* something. Namely, to perform the good works which God prepared beforehand. This is the salvation we must work out "with fear and trembling, for God is at work in you, both to will and to work for his good pleasure."

Salvation is not a historical parchment signed with Christ's blood, to be treasured in the National Archives of our faith. We are called to be the living document and contemporary validity of that signature! We are to live single-mindedly to our Author's intent. Do we begin to sense our need to work this out with fear and trembling?

Philippians 2:12 □ *Philippians 1:27-2:18*

It is a fearful thing to fall into the hands of the living God.

Some say that cleanliness is next to Godliness. So we take our daily shower and read our daily Scripture. And when we come to this kind of verse it is like accidentally discovering a lump on our body. The soapy hand, already flying on, in sudden shock comes back to the skin with the cryptic sensory message. While the hand feels, the mind races. Cancer! Twice shocked, the hand flees and the mind summons every trick to play the deadly game of denial.

"It is a fearful thing to fall into the hands of the living God." Immediately the mind conjures up images of primitive fire-and-brimstone preaching. We have seen the ravages of sick religious excess where the fear of God is made the focus of the believer. We will have no part of it. God is love!

Armed with a pair of sharp scissors, we would love to edit Scripture to our undying comfort. But the needed surgery must always take place in the living tissue of our own being. We must dare to expose our troubled self to the cold surgical light of the Spirit's scrutiny. We must allow God to skillfully excise and hold up for testing what we seek to repress. The Christian who loves God and himself will give up the deadly game of selective believing in favor of spiritual regeneration and wholeness.

It is a tragic thing to profess allegiance to the living God and not know the fear of having fallen into His hands. Unless we have wrestled with the fear of God, we cannot know grace. And where grace does not pervade every fiber and tissue of our being, we are dead to the mind and heart of the living God!

Hebrews 10:31 ☐ *Hebrews 10:19-39*

The law and the prophets were until John; since then the good news of the kingdom of God is preached, and every one enters it violently.

We envy the person with the dramatic conversion experience. He won't have to squirm when sooner or later the question is asked, "How did you become a Christian?" The squirmer has always been one. His family has always gone to church. Thank God His Word shakes us out of the nominal Christian delusion. No one is born a Christian! Christ says matter-of-factly that we must enter His kingdom violently. Satan puts up a fight!

Nicodemus discovered the agony of pride that wanted God's kingdom on more gentlemenly terms. But God's holy standard could only be met through death to self and new life in Christ. Wisely, our Lord spoke of God's wind that blows where *He* wills. Rebirth comes at His initiative. But we can aid God's love by moving from secret cringing to open confessing of pride and fear. Like Nicodemus we may have to wrestle with the birth process.

Perhaps we must consciously enter into the womb of God's mercy and in ancestral memory regress back to the innocence of the beginning. We must thrill to the strong, joyous heartbeat of our oneness with God in Eden. Our body must tense with the lust for equality. Our flesh must crawl with the horror of suddenly exposed genitals. Our nostrils must fill with the smell of warm blood as slaughter takes place to cover our nakedness. The need to cover it must follow us from the shut gates of Eden down through the ages.

We have tried to cover it — with our goodness, our awards and degrees, the church affiliation. But it is all foreign matter to mercy and the womb contracts again and again to expel it.

We squirm in the birth canal. There is blood on our nakedness. We dimly perceive a figure writhing in agony. There is gasping for breath. Suffocation. Darkness. Stunned silence. And then the piercing cry of the newborn: His blood set me free! I am covered with grace! I am at peace!
Luke 16:16

Sing to the LORD a new song . . .

Of course! Let someone from the worship committee suggest it to the music director. Let him confer with the choir. Let the choir secretary submit a list of new songs to the worship committee chairman. Let him discreetly approach the business manager. Let the business office draw up a membership-giving profile. Let everybody send a memo to everybody. Let an all-staff conference conclude on the note that new songs pose headaches.

Of course! The financial backbone of the church comes from that age segment where the mind narrows to the tune of the expanding waist. We cannot risk their displeasure with a new song. There is a vocal minority of guitar enthusiasts and they will sing any new song with gusto. But that would alienate those who helped pay for the new organ. So help us, it is not easy to sing a new song to the Lord.

Off course! The new song has nothing to do with music or artistic mode or method of accompaniment. The new song does not come from the mind of composer or lyricist. The new song issues from the heart of God. It is His gift of realized grace. The new song is in parenthesis on the page of our familiar hymnal: "Were you there when they crucified my Lord? (Were you there?)" When we have been there, we will sing our new song!

We are on course when our actions begin to speak what the tongue routinely sings: "When I survey the wondrous cross on which the Prince of glory died, my richest gain I count but loss and pour contempt on all my pride. Were the whole realm of nature mine, that were a present far too small; love so amazing, so divine, demands my soul, my life, my all."

Psalm 149:1 ☐ *Psalm 149*

And when they began to sing and praise, the LORD set an ambush against the men of Ammon, Moab, and Mount Seir, who had come against Judah, so that they were routed.

Hard things sometimes do come in the proverbial threes. If in doubt, look grim anyway. Why should the Christian break into cheers when he is about to reach the breaking point?

Oh, for grace to enable us to take God by His word! The Psalmist, familiar with the threat of disintegration from within and without, testifies boldly, "He sent forth his word, and healed them . . ." (Psalm 107:20). When we need healing from the bruising impact of mounting pressure, the tested Word of God brings relief. His prescription of praise is the antidote for grimness of soul and circumstance.

As for Judah of old, our purpose is to inhabit our promised land and establish the lordship of God in it. When our position in this is endangered, we are not to ask the debilitating questions of the "Why" and "Who is to blame" kind. Jehoshaphat's rallying cry must be ours also, "O LORD, God of our fathers, are thou not God in heaven? . . . We do not know what to do, but our eyes are upon thee."

There is no greater gift to the embattled soul than this grand assurance: Be still! The battle is the Lord's! At this crucial point our praise is not yet a glad emotion, but an act of will and exercise of trust. And make no mistake: It is not our feeble impulse of cooperation that unleashes the undeniable power of God, causing our pressures to self-destruct. His free love motivates Him! His love sets us free. And in the released floodgates of praise we discover the "spoil" of the unsearchable riches of Christ.

2 Chronicles 20:22 □ 2 Chronicles 20:1-30

He brought me forth into a broad place; he delivered me, because he delighted in me.

What is heaven on earth? To the skier it is powdered slopes; to the angler, a stream glinting with trout. To the lover it is the ecstasy of a lingering embrace; to the mother of young children it may mean a quick nap. But true heaven on earth is to know the delight of the Lord.

Delight is the essence of His love fully savored. It is to embrace with God in the mutuality of unconditional love. Delight is the exquisite intimacy of the Garden of Eden. Delight is the Song of Solomon unblushingly written on the heart: "I am my beloved's, and his desire is for me."

God's desire in Creation was to delight in us. From sheer pleasure we were made in His image, because all He had made was "very good." Why then do we barely allow Him to love us? Did Christ die in vain? We once were God's own and we sold ourselves into the slavery of Satan. God redeemed and restored us to our position as His rightful possession — prized beyond our wildest imagination! This God who flung the galaxies into the vast reaches of space, who clothed earth in her beauty and commanded wondrous creatures to inhabit her, did this God not stoop to the depths of dying to reclaim His right to delight in us uniquely?

Why deny Him His right and pleasure? On the night of her wedding does the bride bring to bed her china? Does she regale the groom with tales of her family's prominence? Or does she come yielded in body and soul to learn the delight of a bonding that exceeds all bonds and affections? For us to love God is not only to live the disciplined life of the disciple, but also the delighted life of the dearly desired!

Psalm 18:19 ☐ *Psalm 18:1-19*

Come, I will show you the Bride . . .

The church as the Bride of Christ captivates our imagination. Brides and showmanship in the church have a long-standing tradition. We love showing off. Stand back, dear God, and applaud our pageantry! Listen to the majestic music. Notice the meticulous attention to detail. Feast your eyes on finery of dress and decor. Take pleasure in this the Bride's hour. Brush her cheek with a fond fatherly kiss.

God *is* keenly interested. His Son is heir to a kingdom. He requires an exceptional Bride. Because His love is undying, the union is destined for all time and eternity. Much is expected of the Bride. God's high standards are not rooted in the shifting sands of time. His scrutiny must go beyond our obvious showmanship. How does God view the Bride of our day?

To some extent she is largely ceremonial — a walking-down-the-aisle-on-Sunday tradition. In some quarters she has remained virginal. The cross has not penetrated and faith has not been reproduced. In some ways the Bride has become an "old dear," a relationship comfortably grooved and intimacy no longer attempted. To a large extent the romance of redemption has diminished into the regimented institution of which some derisively say, "So who wants to be committed?" The Father is visibly concerned.

"Come, I will show you the Bride, the wife of the Lamb." This is what we must see: The Bride after God's own heart rejoices in her Lord's passion. She gives birth to a living hope. Clothed in humility, she washes the feet of the world. Grace adorns her. She delights in being the apple of the Father's eye. Oh for us, this day, to respond afresh to the Lamb's wooing!

Revelation 21:9 □ Revelation 21:9-27

When Noah awoke from his wine and knew what his youngest son had done to him, he said, "Cursed be Canaan; a slave of slaves shall he be to his brothers.

The story of the Great Cover-Up has us puzzled. As poor Ham tells it, here is what happened: "Dad was real pleased with his vineyard. When he tasted that first wine he got carried away. The Old Man actually passed out and slumped to the floor. What a sight! He didn't wear a stitch and I didn't want him to catch cold or wake up with a stiff back. So I had my brothers throw a blanket over him. So what's the big deal? Instead of thanks, why do I get kicked out?"

Why indeed? Because ever since the Fall the Fig Leaf Mentality prevails and God must insist that it makes for the curse of separation. Noah needed to come to in an acute state of discomfort and make an honest assessment of where he had slipped before God. He needed to stand stripped before Him until His forgiveness would clothe and restore him to dignity.

Noah remembered the days preceding the Flood, when "the LORD was sorry that he had made man on the earth, and it grieved him to his heart" (Genesis 6:6). With sudden horror he realized a chilling truth. Ham had treated his father's fall from grace in a conspiratorial manner that violated God's renewed trust. First he made it into a bit of delicious gossip. Else why tell his brothers? Then he instigated the cover-up as a first step toward his own intended practice of hiding from God. Ham's subtly corruptive influence had to be stopped cold in its track. Hence the curse of slavery.

God's people must heed Noah's warning. How quickly we say, "We are all sinners" and let it go at that. That line must become the lifeline of confession and cleansing. Otherwise it becomes a line of deception that will ensnare us and corrupt the body of Christ.

Genesis 9:24-25 □ *Genesis 9:20-28*

But as one was felling a log, his axe head fell into the water; and he cried out, "Alas, my master! It was borrowed." Then the man of God said, "Where did it fall?"

The thriving fellowship of Elisha's followers necessitated the building of enlarged quarters. So they went to the river and felled logs. And when the teamwork was slowed because of the mishap with the axe head, the prophet was equipped to deal with the crisis. He cut off a stick from some "miracle wood," threw it into the water, and it drew the axe head to the surface. The relieved worker retrieved it and work could be resumed.

How gracious of God to prevail on the Old Testament writer to preserve this marvelous story for the generations to come. We who actively desire church growth and underwrite it with our own labors of love and money and service, will treasure Elisha's gift of insight.

God delights in enlarging our vision and footsteps. To our church of today He emphatically says, "Enlarge the place of your tent, and let the curtains of your habitations be stretched out; hold not back, lengthen your cords and strengthen your stakes" (Isaiah 54:2). God is utterly for us and equips us with His own tools of the Holy Spirit.

When growth is hampered and building slows down, we tend to redouble our efforts and push on by sheer willpower. Don't, says Elisha. Think back instead and locate the place where you lost God's power. Take what you have appropriated from Calvary's tree and throw it into the water of clarification. It will draw to the conscious surface the evidence of how God's tool was misused or handled carelessly. Repent! Give thanks! Go on with power!

2 Kings 6:5-6 □ *2 Kings 6:1-7*

Bless the LORD, O my soul; and all that is within me, bless his holy name!

That is a tall order. "All" that is within me is not fit to bless His holy name! If our soul is to be pressed into the ministry of adoration, we had better do some house cleaning in there. So we sweep up the garbage and stuff it into the hidden recesses of our mind and emotions. And then we give Him our cleaned-up act. Bless the Lord, O my soul — on Sunday!

On Monday we are dragging. On Tuesday we suffer from lower back pain. On Wednesday we quarrel. On Thursday we are vaguely depressed. On Friday we are frantically active. On Saturday we have not gotten anywhere with anything or anybody, or so it seems to our nagging self. But on Sunday — praise God for Sunday — we will take a couple of hours if it kills us, and we will bless the Lord!

"Bless the LORD, O my soul, and forget not all his benefits, who forgives *all* your iniquity, who heals *all* your diseases, who redeems your life from the Pit, who crowns you with steadfast love and mercy . . ." Our soul is plainly instructed that what is released into God's holiness will receive His crowning touch of wholeness. What we hide from Him will increasingly hurt us.

Why do we play games with our Lord? While we foolishly hide and reshuffle our private not-so-nice sins, we blatantly display arrogant pride and the poison of our ill-fated self-rule. God doesn't want our glib Sunday compliments. He wants to complement all of our life with His grandeur and grace.

Psalm 103:1 ☐ *Psalm 103*

For we have not a high priest who is unable to sympathize with our weaknesses, but one who in every respect has been tempted as we are . . .

"I know just how you feel!" We are rightfully dubious about shallow professions of sympathy. Yet, we are touched by the sincerity of the kind soul who gives our hand a quick squeeze when we are hurting. He or she far exceeds in maturity and popularity the Christian backslapper who says to leave everything to the Lord and everything will be just fine and dandy. With that kind of sympathy we can bleed to death right under the person's nose.

Life is constantly dealing in surprises. Some we handle better than others. Taxes, illness and death come to us all. No matter how traumatic, those lend themselves to sharing with others. In that process strength and comfort is gained all around.

Some surprises are shockers. What of the sudden attraction to a shapely neighbor? What of the drink that unexpectedly has become a necessity if we are to survive our job? What of the bruise inflicted on the baby's flailing arm when his crying enraged us? What of the time we borrowed money from petty cash and before we could quietly replace it, someone else had been accused of stealing? Add to the list of "Christian surprises" the habit of shoplifting and the horror of incest. Picture every evil known to mankind and try saying, "I know just how you feel." We either become judges or liars.

Jesus "knew all men and needed no one to bear witness of man; for he himself knew what was in man" (John 2:25). Will we believe Him? Or will the cross in vain have visited on Him the wretched pain of our private hells? The hurters and healers in the church must touch base at Calvary before we can legitimately feel for each other.

Hebrews 4:15 ☐ *Hebrews 4:14-5:10*

And he said to him, "Truly, truly, I say to you, you will see heaven opened, and the angels of God ascending and descending upon the Son of man."

Here is a spiritual geography lesson. As the people of life's ups and downs, we picture heaven up. Our language reflects the upward trend of all that is favorable. Things are looking up. Thoughts are uplifting. Hopes are raised. The sky is the limit. When things don't go well, we are literally downcast.

When we are weighted down by life's cares, the thought of a haven above can fly away as quickly as a child's carelessly held balloon. God understands. He does not say cheer up, but be of good cheer. Calm down. Heaven is down as well as up. If we are too down to look up, let us look to the "down under" resources and ministrations of heaven. Jesus declared open season on heaven from whence angels "ascend and descend."

That is a curious way of putting it. Did the gospel writer merely mean to go back and forth? John, with his obvious gift for word illustrations was surely not careless here. When he puts "ascending" first, he is making a point. Heaven, after all, is not a distant space colony. Heaven does not come to a crashing halt as it encounters the earth's atmosphere or outer crust. Heaven is the Lord's all-encompassing habitation.

A geologist may scratch his head, and so may we, but the Psalmist had understanding. "For he will give his angels charge of you to guard you in all your ways. On their hands they will bear you up, lest you dash your foot against a stone" (Psalm 91:11-12). If at times we are not up to face heaven, why not look for its messengers of comfort and cheer down where we are? Our Lord, the Most High, made His message down-to-earth.

John 1:51 ☐ John 1:43-51

O Daniel, I have now come out to give you wisdom and under-standing. At the beginning of your supplications a word went forth, and I have come to tell it to you, for you are greatly beloved . . .

We are all specialists in the service of our divine King. Each specialty has its own occupational hazards. Daniel, seer of visions and interpreter of dreams — "ten times better than all the magicians and enchanters" serving the Babylonian king — made no bones about his.

"As for me, Daniel, my spirit within me was anxious and the visions of my head alarmed me . . . my thoughts greatly alarmed me, and my color changed . . . And I, Daniel, was overcome and lay sick for some days; then I rose and went about the king's business; but I was appalled by the vision and did not understand it."

No matter whether we serve God with our mind or tongue or hands or feet, as His greatly beloved we are eminently quali-fied to receive the astonishing ministrations of heaven. Of his speedily dispatched messenger Daniel says, ". . . while I was speaking in prayer, the man Gabriel, whom I had seen in the vision at first, came to me in swift flight . . ." The man Gabriel! No scary otherworldly apparition to one alarmed by the visions of his head. In swift flight! Clear recognition of God's loving, supernatural intervention.

That gives us courage and comfort to expect much from the Most High, when in His service we are pushed out on limbs from which there is no backing down. But we cannot cry help from the heights of position and achievement. "While I was speaking and praying, confessing my sin," says Daniel, God dispatched the divine messenger. All of heaven's resources are ours to claim on that basis today!

Daniel 9:22-23 □ Daniel 8 and 9

If you continue in my word, you are truly my disciples, and you will know the truth, and the truth will make you free.

How pleasant it is when the things of God fall into place. When rigorous testing has produced victorious trusting and there is tangible evidence of God's favor, the victory is sweet indeed.

Thoughts and feelings rush together in impetuous expressions of praise. There follows the realization that the experience of grace has permanently deepened our faith. From this flow the tears of consecration and the praise that nerves our will. All of our life must become an instrument of praise — with all the stops pulled out!

No sooner said and the deepened faith adventure begun than God will do the one predictable thing we never get used to. He will promptly jam the machinery so freshly lubricated with the oil of gladness. In one deflating swoop of overpowering authority he reduces the mighty instrument of praise to a mousy squeak of protest: Lord, what went wrong? One moment we are blazing a trail to glory, the next we have sputtered to an ignominious halt.

In this we are no embarrassment to God. His job is to unsettle us the moment we settle down. We always want to settle down to our particular corner on truth, or to a security of mind or circumstances. The Perfecter of our faith must press His advantage while we are still tender with our recent growth. Resolutely He must reduce us to abject spiritual poverty to prepare us for the next enriching growth cycle. As the Master Builder of His kingdom He must hold us to the rigid standard of His word — and an apprenticeship shaped solely around it.

John 8:31 □ John 3:31-47

Come to him, to that living stone, rejected by men but in God's sight chosen and precious; and like living stones be yourselves built into a spiritual house, to be a holy priesthood . . .

To fully grasp the significance of the spiritual house and holy priesthood, we must go back to Calvary. "And Jesus uttered a loud cry, and breathed his last. And the curtain of the temple was torn in two, from top to bottom" (Mark 15:37-38). "It is finished!" To the old Israel it was a death cry. Never again would the Spirit of God dwell in her man-made holy of holies. The priesthood had failed — fattening itself on power and prestige, instead of yielding the fruit of righteousness.

"It is finished!" The awesome act of redemption was completed; the ultimate sacrifice of the unblemished Lamb of God performed and never to be repeated. A new breed of priests was to be called. The church — the called out — would emerge as the new Israel chosen to show forth His glory.

When the resurrected Lord returned to His broken and dispirited disciples, He spoke peace to them and laid the groundwork. "As the Father has sent me, even so I send you." And then — catch the drama, remember the torn veil — He breathed His first! "And when he had said this, he breathed on them, and said to them, 'Receive the Holy Spirit . . .'" (John 20:21-23).

How often we ask God to bless our church! We really expect Him to sneak by one night during the week and touch the building with His magic wand. By Sunday we expect new life in every stony-faced person sitting stiffly in their pew. When we expect God to breathe life into the institution of our church, we court the icy blast of condemnation. When we allow Him to breathe life into us personally, His church comes alive!

1 Peter 2:4-5 ☐ *1 Peter 2:4-10*

In the days of his flesh, Jesus offered up prayers and supplications, with loud cries and tears . . .

If we are to touch the hearts of men, we must be touched by the heart of God. If others are to know Christ, we cannot mouth His teachings. Our heart of stone must become a heart of flesh and beat with the conviction of His compassion.

We know the passion of our conviction that the world is going to hell. Immorality and crime have come to every neighborhood, robbing every person of the innocence and peace of mind of former days. No wonder we make the church into a Christian country club complete with the golf course of "green pastures" and the swimming pool of "still waters." Once saved, we really know how to play it safe.

From a world awash in sorrow we have retreated into the ark of the church, hoping to float over the troubled waters of our time. But God did not call us out to be Noahs, but Christs. Mark opens his gospel account with a keen observation. "In those days Jesus came from Nazareth of Galilee and was baptized by John in the Jordan" (1:9). Why did He who came to baptize with the Holy Spirit receive for Himself the baptism of water? He identified with the sinner! From the moment He stepped into the river He publicly got Himself into the hot water we are all in.

If the priesthood of believers is to become the bridge over troubled waters, we must so identify with Christ that His passion becomes ours. When have we last offered up prayers and supplications with loud cries and tears? And when and how have we laid down our own life that others might know the resurrected Christ through us?

Hebrews 5:7 □ *Hebrews 5:1-10*

If any one thirst, let him come to me and drink. He who believes in me, as the scripture has said, "Out of his heart shall flow rivers of living water."

Bottled water is big business in this fussy age. Bottled anything is big business. Bottled sunshine. Bottled smog. The bottling principle works like a charm on a sated, gullible public. Sand on the beach is sand. Sand in a bottle is chic, witty and an artistic statement. Even if it is all a joke, there is no harm in laughing all the way to the bank.

God is not amused when the church goes into the bottling business. We have no right to run a medicine show that sells the elixirs of our denominational persuasion. We bottle our programs and preachers and push them in the marketplace — as if the things of God related to an emporium instead of an empire encompassing eternity.

God's bottling principle works in reverse! He is after the uncorked Christian — willing to be poured out as a sacramental wine, balm for wounds, and living water for man's thirst for eternity. But we cannot give away that which we do not possess. If with our lips we attest to the mighty power of God, but have not personally experienced it, we are guilty of "holding the form of religion but denying the power of it (2 Timothy 3:5).

Oh for the church to develop the kind of eternity thirst that has us corporately crying out for living water! Oh, for us to be consumed by abject need to know the infilling power of the Holy Spirit! Oh for the church to celebrate the joyous abandonment of a contagious people set free from fear and reserve! Oh for the church to spill itself out into the highways and byways of this parched land!

John 7:37-38 ☐ *John 7:37-52*

*For the creation waits with eager longing for the revealing of
the sons of God . .*

It may come as a revelation that we are the temporal land-
lords of God's creation! "The earth is the LORD'S and the fulness
thereof, the world and those who dwell therein . . " (Psalm
24:1). As the body of Christ we are supposed to take charge!

In song we thank Him for the beauty of this earth. We are
the twice-blessed visitors to our national parks. We love trees
and gentle breezes that chase the poison from the air we
breathe. But mention *ecology* and God's people become a
political people guided by personal bias. We think of student
and protest movements and — if sufficiently provoked, we let
a bumper sticker express our personal view.

Ecology is the study of *home* — our earthly home away
from the eternal one. From the time our primal parents sold out
to Satan, creation itself was put into bondage to decay. Picture
a fine mansion from which its owners are forced to leave. Put
in transients and tenants who lack pride of ownership and
watch the place deteriorate. But "our place" has known the visitation of a Redeemer! How can the redeemed of the Lord
engage in name-calling and coining of slogans, and miss creation's sublime longing for the revealing of the sons of God?

Some men and women can in good conscience take opposite stands in environmental controversies. Creation does not
eagerly await our pat answers or dictatorial directives. It
eagerly awaits the Miracle of Bent Knees. Knees bent in prayers
of repentance and reaffirmed loyalty to the divine Landholder.
Knees bent, perhaps, in the priestly act of picking up litter. Not
once or twice, but for a lifetime, if that is our personal
revelation!

Romans 8:19 ☐ *Romans 8:18-27*

I call heaven and earth to witness against you this day, that I have set before you life and death . .

"It is a matter of life or death!" Sirens scream out the message or perhaps the voice of a ham operator coolly conveys it. An emergency calls for immediate response. We quickly move out of the way or jump in to help. Law and moral conviction compel us to opt for life in life-or-death matters.

Tragically, the same does not necessarily apply to the life that Paul calls "life indeed" (1 Timothy 6:19). Moses had witnessed the spiritual "mass suicide by vacillation" that was commited by the generation of Israelites he had led out of Egypt. Singly or in groups they repeatedly shrank back from God's wooing and warning, until His wrath leaped out at them and consumed them.

No wonder Moses declared a permanent state of emergency at the close of his ministry. Choose life, he implored, and made clear that such choice would demand decisive obedience day after day. The prerequisites to life — loving God, obeying His voice, and cleaving to Him — could not be accomplished by mere mouthing of creed or holding fast to intellectual conviction. They had to be acknowledged at the gut level of immediate response and action.

Our bodies are marvels of automation. We draw the breath of life unthinkingly. In contrast, our soul lives by hard choice. It must be muscled by the exercise of will, fleshed out to the dimensions of God's highest purpose. Again and again it must pant for breath and cry out for the oxygen of the Spirit. It is a matter of life or death!

Deuteronomy 30:19 ☐ *Deuteronomy 30:11-20*

In the wilderness prepare the way of the LORD, make straight in the desert a highway for our God.

That was clearly John the Baptist's assignment! We prefer to be meandering brooks in verdant valleys, bubbling pleasantly in the established flow of inspiration. That is why God periodically removes us to the desert places of the spirit — to dry us out and set us straight.

When we assess the sobering reality of our unexpected predicament, the first impulse is to straighten ourselves out. If suddenly our God seems light-years away, we will do anything to bring Him back. Frantically we go dig in the past and resurrect every fault and failure known to our inner heart. Round and round we go — questioning, dismissing — dabbling in discouragement and consternation. We finally choke on the blinding dust that is raised from our churning in circles of futility.

When we are bone-dry and bleached from the scorching heat of our hopeless introspection, the gentle dew of heaven settles on our understanding. "Remember not the former things, nor consider the things of old. Behold, I am doing a new thing; now it springs forth, do you not perceive it? I will make a way in the wilderness and rivers in the desert" (Isaiah 43:18-19). Perplexity turns into fresh perspective and praise abounds.

When called to be strategic channels of God's power, we cannot detour our life around secondary loyalties. The decisive reorientation to Christ's "I am the way, and the truth, and the life" is best accomplished in the stark desert setting, where the familiar landmarks of our faith are non-existent. Here the radical nature of our new creation in Christ wells up from the fathomless depths of eternity's purpose. Blessed are we when we bless God for dealing "creatively" with us!

Isaiah 40:3 □ Isaiah 40:1-11

Or what king, going to encounter another king in war, will not sit down first and take counsel whether he is able with ten thousand to meet him who comes against him with twenty thousand?

The thought of first sitting down in a coldly calculating manner to count the cost of discipleship offends us. We prefer to take our cue from Sunday's pep rally, "Stand up, stand up for Jesus, ye soldiers of the cross . . ." In those ennobling moments of shared enthusiasm we are ready to swagger all over creation to conquer it for Christ. If the church is to be a movement to the future and not a monument to the past, we must move!

Because we have not sat down in that coldly calculating manner first, the church is lukewarm with half-baked disciples. The cross is our favorite adornment, the external focus of the free gift of salvation in which we rightly rejoice. But costly discipleship demands that the cross be embedded in our life as a thorn in the flesh — a chronic irritation to the internal tissue of our natural inclinations — a pain that will manifest itself daily.

"If any one comes to me and does not hate his own father and mother and wife and children . . . yes, and even his own life, he cannot be my disciple." We know how to tone down that line lest we ruin our essential sales pitch that God is love. Yet it is precisely that unheard-of love that demands that we sit down and face it realistically.

"I came not of my own accord, but he sent me." That is what is plainly written on the blood-stained face of Him who coolly conducts our discipleship interview. Are we able to keep our eyes on that face and then go against the natural grain of things for the rest of our own life? We are not able. But if we are willing — in the face of that ultimate reality — His own obedience will enable our faithfulness.

Luke 14:31 □ *Luke 14:25-33*

Thou hast caused lover and friend to shun me; my companions are in darkness.

Our picture of servanthood is mercifully blurred at first. We view God as a gentleman employer. The idea is to wear white gloves. We are to be a cut above the common worker, a bit more disciplined and moral. In time we hope to become as polished and valued as the family silver, with the prestige rubbing off on those nearest and dearest to us.

The rub comes in unexpected ways. When God chooses to honor our basic commitment, He has no choice but to conform us to His image of the honored servant. It calls for drastic transformation. Eternity is on the march in our inner being and irrevocably erodes our temporal disposition.

Slowly, people think of us as becoming more religious. As a private indulgence it is considered harmless. But woe if the growing inner passion leaps out in sparks to ignite God-passion in those around us. Unless hearts have been readied by the Holy Spirit, nothing more than heated objection or cool disdain is coming our way. Normal life is ruined. Guilt and despair take turns assaulting us. We learn to identify with Christ who from the time He was twelve made a career of being difficult with family and friends.

The process hurts. It violates our own sense of ethics. We planned to have our high-class servanthood discreetly worked into the existing frame of our middle-class life, enhancing all and inconveniencing no one greatly. Instead, we find our servanthood modeled on Christ who emptied Himself and became obedient unto death. Part of our dying comes from those nearest and dearest who sense the shadow, but cannot grasp the substance of our personal cross. It is a sorrow we must leave with God.

Psalm 88:18 □ Psalm 88

If I say, "I will not mention him, or speak any more in his name," there is in my heart as it were a burning fire shut up in my bones, and I am weary with holding it in, and I cannot.

Ah, the pathos of the lovesick adolescent! Witness the anguish of unexpressed ardor, the ecstasy of encouraged affection. We grin and bear it with a mixture of tenderness and embarrassment because we remember . . . Oh, for the mystery of hormones, the misery of tension that turns a peaceable household into an ammunitions dump! In time, thank goodness, the rigors of romantic love abate. If domesticated love seems dull at times, it is decidedly kinder all around.

The New Testament writers speak of babes in Christ and the mature in faith. A chapter about the Christian's "awful adolescence" should have been specifically included and so labeled. We plunge into it when the growth spurts we have been longing for catch us by surprise.

Suddenly expelled from the relative ease of our childhood, we find ourselves drifting in uncharted waters made treacherous and exciting by our bursting self-awareness. The distant shore of maturity seems lined with stolid Christianity of which we want no part. Furiously we paddle water, buoyed by our delicious rebellion. Madly in love with God, we are hazardous to those around us. In time He pulls the plug, rescues us from the ensuing mire, and establishes our trek through maturity. And everybody heaves a sigh of relief.

Except for the Jeremiahs of the faith! The Jeremiahs whose intense awareness and rebellion against sameness are harnessed by God for His own purposes. The Jeremiahs who try to conform and cannot. Be tender to the weeping prophets of our day. They cannot outgrow their lovesickness!

Jeremiah 20:9 □ Jeremiah 20:7-18

Then Samuel took a stone and set it up between Mizpah and Jeshanah, and called its name Ebenezer; for he said, "Hitherto the Lord has helped us."

The "stone of help" is crucial to our spiritual journey. As the landscape of our faith expands, we need to establish landmarks. They remind us of God's faithful interventions. They also stand as our points of no return.

The sincere Christian inevitably gets bogged down in the mistaken notion that he must somehow first "arrive" before venturing forth with God. But Scripture is adamant in hammering home truth; God is not interested in our product, but only the process. He declines our goodness and works with our weakness. The venerable heroes of the faith had more than feet of clay. They committed murder and adultery. Peter, after three years of intimate exposure to Jesus, slipped into the role of cursing traitor with astonishing ease.

But somewhere along the line Peter had come to grips with the divine claims of one Jesus of Nazareth. Based on the rock-like conviction — Yes, Lord, you do forgive sin and enable new life! — the early church took shape at Pentecost. Let us curse, if we must, the garbage of our humanity that seems to demean the journey to glory. God will not cringe, but be outright delighted if we allow Him to turn it into fertilizer along the way. Our Ebenezer might well be a compost heap!

We must periodically search out the things that diminish our witness, and declare them boldly in the presence of our Lord. He will discard what needs to be discarded. And He will charge with positive energy the hindrances chosen to be redeemed for His glory. Here we now set up our Ebenezer, the memory stone that celebrates God's goodness. Then we press on in the transforming power of His grace. The exhilaration of such process will cure our hankering for a product which cannot be on this side of eternity.

1 Samuel 7:12 ☐ *1 Samuel 7:5-17*

But Moses' hands grew weary; so they took a stone and put it under him, and he sat upon it, and Aaron and Hur held up his hands . .

Here is a makeshift prayer meeting to delight the saint who is catching on to the robust flavor of authentic faith. We tend to reduce prayer to a soft-spoken ritual — a neatly packaged something sent ahead to insure good fortune. We use tired old phrases in time-honored sequence and expect the formula to be the workhorse that will pull the freight train of our faith. There is nothing like a rousing emergency to explode myths and focus truth.

"All the congregation of the people of Israel moved on from the wilderness of Sin by stages . . " We had better shake our pious image of a neatly choreographed movement of the graceful people of God. Moses trudged back and forth between two million grumblers, malcontents, pregnant women, whiny children, shuffling seniors, and possibly some straggling rock hounds.

At Rephidim the faint and weary stragglers of whatever persuasion were attacked by Amalek. Moses, who shortly before passed to the front of the people to deal with a water crisis, now had to rush to the rear. After conferring military leadership on Joshua, he hiked up a hill to watch and intercede for him. We marvel at his stamina. What a joy to watch this harassed, robust man of faith go into action, motioning Aaron and Hur to use common sense and lend him a hand. How God must have delighted in responding to the vigilance of His faithful servant.

Prayer is neither engine nor caboose, but sturdy track laid across the rugged frontiers of our faith. It is the breath and heartbeat of our relationship with God. It is the robust exercise of friendship. It is the means by which we stay in love with God and each other!

Exodus 17:12 □ *Exodus 17*

And the angel of the LORD appeared to him and said to him,
"The LORD is with you, you mighty man of valor."

We all have times when we feel like a small cog in a huge
machine — locked into circumstances beyond our control. No
matter what the source of our chafing, God is the great Liber-
ator still. The sixth chapter of Judges is a Magna Carta of sorts
for the insignificant person.

To fully appreciate Gideon's amazing encounter with liberating grace, the background must be dramatized. After the
conquest of Canaan, Israel turned traitor and worshiped the
native fertility gods. Punishment came through the marauding
Midianites who reduced Israel to a miserable hiding existence
in the mountains. Caught in the crossfire of deadly culture
clash, Gideon found himself startled by God in the furtive,
humbling act of having to thresh wheat in a wine press.

"The LORD is with you, you mighty man of valor." Gideon
must have spun around to see who else was with him! "And the
LORD turned to him and said, 'Go in this might of yours and
deliver Israel from the hand of Midian . . .'" The classic
response? I am a nobody coming from a family of nobodies.
You came to the wrong address, God! And then, in the very
process of trying to convince God of his timidity, Gideon confirmed the boldness God had initially affirmed. As a result we
later come to one of the most thrilling statements in all of Scripture, "But the Spirit of the LORD took possession of Gideon;
and he sounded the trumpet . . "

God's people are still caught in the conflict of syncretism.
God plus the gambling with good luck. God plus the daily hor-
oscope. God plus our personal success formula. The Holy
Spirit longs to clothe Himself with you and me. The trumpet
needs to be sounded afresh. "The Lord is with you, you mighty
man and woman of valor." Shall we not thrill to the mighty
truth that God believes in us and will validate His personal
affirmation?

Judges 6:12 □ *Judges 6:11-18*

And Joshua said to them, "Do not be afraid or dismayed; be strong and of good courage . . "

Where have we heard that line before? Does Joshua sound like a broken record? Maybe so, but the music is sweet just the same. It sounds a theme of hope that we must add to our repertoire of faith; God tirelessly picks us up until we become a boost to others. It was Joshua's military genius that catapulted him to fame, but God established and exalted him. Out of the exultation of his remembering heart flowed the tested words of encouragement to others.

Immediately before commissioning Joshua to lead Israel into the Promised Land, Moses told the people, "Be strong and of good courage . . . for it is the LORD your God who goes with you; he will not fail you or forsake you." Then he summoned Joshua and carefully repeated, "Be strong and of good courage . . . It is the LORD who goes before you; he will be with you, he will not fail you or forsake you; do not fear or be dismayed" (Deuteronomy 31:6-8).

After the death of Moses, Joshua must have tensed with trepidation. No doubt he suffered his worst attack of cold feet. Immediately God wrapped him up in His warm affirmation, "I will not fail you or forsake you. Be strong and of good courage . . . Have I not commanded you? Be strong and of good courage; be not frightened, neither be dismayed; for the LORD your God is with you wherever you go" (Joshua 1:5-6;9).

Do we get the touching picture — the rhyme and reason of repetitive sound? God acts like a solicitous nursemaid to a military hero, patiently reciting the ABCs of trust to him as often as needed! How much more will He honor and encourage our feeble efforts to lead the people of our lives into the land of promise!

Joshua 10:25

When Jesus saw him and knew that he had been lying there a long time, he said to him, "Do you want to be healed?"

Is Jesus mocking thirty-eight years of suffering? Of course the man wants to be healed. Why else would he be camped out on Invalid Row by the pool of Bethesda? If we marvel at our Lord's seeming insensitivity to the obvious plight of the lame man, we had better watch out. Jesus is about to fix His penetrating gaze on us, the hale and hearty, and ask the same disturbing question, "Do you want to be healed?"

We are positively speechless with protest. Which is just as well, because presently we are hypnotized by a look of infinite pity on Christ's face and as we see what He sees, we recoil with the recognition of our own lameness. Yes, we are lame and blind and paralyzed, members of the crippled Body of Christ still encamped near the living water of the Holy Spirit! Why have we not only tolerated our crippled condition, but subtly shifted blame for not gaining access to stirring spiritual power for unencumbered living?

"Do you want to be healed?" The truth is, we are not sure. We are so used to our life of limitations that we don't rightly know what we are missing. Besides, we take pride in managing as well as we do. There is comfort in company where the fine edge of accountability is conveniently blurred. Mostly, we are scared to death of the life-changing immersion in the Holy Spirit! Why trade the known for the unknown — the shelter of our personal portico for a wide-open world of risk?

"Rise!" Our Lord can no longer tolerate the atrophy of His church. The decisive first step must be taken. We either go forth in the power of the Holy Spirit or we shall die inch by inch of tragic terminal regret. There is work to be done in this world and we have run out of excuses.

John 5:6 □ John 5:1-9

Therefore lift your drooping hands and strengthen your weak knees, and make straight paths for your feet, so that what is lame may not be put out of joint but rather be healed.

We bear testimony to the mystery of the Trinity in a most intimate way. It is our trinity of body, soul and spirit. As long as there is no challenge to the inherent harmony, we function in the intended integrated manner.

The theological challenge to this mystery does not come from religious sophisticates, but from pain. Pain that appears out of nowhere, like a distant eccentric relative, and comes and goes at whim. Pain that rings the doorbell and runs, making us wonder if the nuisance is masterminded by mere mischief or the mighty Mafia. Pain that thumbs its nose at aspirin and prayer.

This peculiar pain — is it messenger or message? — does not seem to indicate pathology, but in its nagging recurrence actually creates dis-ease. We are plagued by doubt, tormented by anonymous accusers. The body is suspicious of the mind. The mind resents the innuendoes. The soul is searched for secrets. Pain takes to center stage as a puppet manipulated by the wires of our tension. In our effort to control and comprehend we become disjointed and disabled.

To this debilitated Christian the writer of Hebrews seems to say, "Heal yourself!" Don't exercise your imagination, but exercise your salvation. One is eccentric, the other centers on God's established integrity of character and purpose. Let go of symptoms, lay hold of our completeness in Him, through Him, and for Him. The "straight paths" are in His tested Word. The lifted hands and strengthened knees affirm His abiding presence. Let Him own the pain and mystery of our being. In the messenger and message of the Good News we already own His wholeness.

Hebrews 12:12-13 □ *Hebrews 12:1-13*

When we heard this, we and the people there begged him not to go up to Jerusalem. Then Paul answered, "What are you doing, weeping and breaking my heart?"

Paul had his face set like a flint toward Jerusalem and his unfolding martyrdom. The outpouring of sympathy at Caesarea, a mere fifty miles away, must have rained like hammer blows on his brave heart. In exhorting his friends to honor God's sovereign plans, he was forced to relive the wrenching emotions of his one-way commitment. In countering their resistance, he had to fight doubly against the rising fear in his own frail flesh. The tearful "Don't go!" was a dubious, cowardly gift to Paul who needed to be fueled with faith in step with his own.

We cannot fault his friends for using the Holy Spirit's testimony of suffering as a brake instead of boost. "Fools for Christ" need occasional protection from themselves. Beware of the person who maps out his own martyrdom with seeming ease. In trying to save someone else's skin, we are building safeguards for our own, of course. But the harsh facts of Paul's hard lesson remain to this day.

It is easier to suffer heartbreak at the hands of God whose motives arise unselfishly out of His ultimate, all-encompassing good. For great trials He supplies extraordinary comforts. The partnership of suffering is suffused with eternal glory. The time comes when we have no quarrel with God's highest purpose for us. In His service we become single-minded.

If the vitality of the Book-of-Acts church is to be recovered in our time of history — and it must — it only follows that our cherished personal God must be allowed to reign as the sovereign Lord of history. In His service we become expendable. And those who would deny Him break our heart from selfish love!

Acts 21:12-13 ☐ *Acts 21:7-14*

What I did not steal must I now restore?

God's truly meek people are fighters at heart. Innate tenderness is complemented by like toughness. Free in Christ beyond measure, they are firmly bound to Him as prisoners. Theirs is not docile submission in drab, neutral shades of dull, but the fire and ice of character put at His disposal in joyous abandon. The meek look deceptively ordinary. They have an astonishing capacity for sticking out like a sore thumb — and hurting commensurately.

The mighty meek do not mind baring their shrinking soul. They are not adverse to human comfort. They know that shared blunders and hurts make for superb mortar in cementing relationships. So why do the meek often strike us as the prima donnas of the faith — so very prickly to the touch?

The meek are living paradox — Exhibit A of every seeming contradiction that is apparent in Scripture and brought into harmony only by the dynamics of the Holy Spirit. The meek need to cry, but they abhor coddling. They seek to be understood, but decline analysis based on human sympathy. They hunger for personal affirmation, but ultimately insist on confirmation of self-denial. The meek are maddeningly simple and forbiddingly complex. They really get sore when piously told to "let go and let God." A spiritual Band-Aid for spilled guts? Never!

In truth, the blundering, blubbering meek do fare wondrously well in the presence of God. He owns the fire and ice, the irritating blend of contradictions that so often make for trial. Imprisoned in His arms, we are gladly granted the belligerent ranting session that exhausts and exhilarates us and we feel His embrace tighten. Thus lavishly loved, we go forth in the freshly chastened and crystallized might of His meekness.

Psalm 69:4 □ *Psalm 69:1-5*

Let us know, let us press on to know the Lord; his going forth is sure as the dawn; he will come to us as the showers, as the spring rains that water the earth.

"Let us press on to know the Lord." It sounds like a grim pitch for Christian adult education. With Hosea it was a glorious case of spring fever — of freshly falling in love with God and His people. Spring fever dated ca. 710 B.C. and catchable still!

It is the miracle of a man frosted by duty and suddenly bursting forth in tender green shoots of delight. His whole world explodes into freshness of hope. Tears turn into spring rains. The seed of God will surely sprout and in time yield the fruit of right relationships. Let Hosea's magnificent spring fever entice our duty-dulled senses.

Ordained by God to suffer the ordeal of an adulterous mate in order to convict Israel of her harlotry, Hosea's soul knew the wintry desolation of love grown cold and hard. Choked by the hopelessness of his entrapment, he must have fled outdoors one day and greedily breathed in the balmy spring air. From the barrenness of his hardened heart he must have looked to the countryside eager to spring into bloom. In the faithful going forth of the sun he must have warmed to God's tireless going forth on behalf of His people. Out of Hosea's singing, sobbing heart welled up the gentle tears that are spring rain to our barren faith.

To know God from duty and grim determination is to know Him as a stern taskmaster. To know Him from deep inner need and delight is to acknowledge Him an eager and exciting Lover. "Jesus, lover of my soul, let me to Thy bosom fly . . ." What if we had a mad spring fling and made that the catchy slogan to encourge ongoing Christian education!

Hosea 6:3 □ *Hosea 5:1-6:3*

Rejoice always, pray constantly, give thanks in all circumstances; for this is the will of God in Christ Jesus for you.

This spiritual prescription smacks of cod liver oil. There is something fishy about the cheery admonition to rejoice always, when in fact we are getting stuck with the will of God. We remember the parental pep talk delivered to us upon entering school — with FUN splashed in bright colors all over the canvas of our imagination — only to discover that we were slapped with a life sentence of tough discipline for the crime of being blissfully ignorant.

In the same vein we think twice about this invitation to delight, when in fact rejoicing turns out to be a complex discipline centered on the formidable will of God. The will of God, all pious pretensions aside, is every bit as popular as a parent's curt "Because!" when pressed to the limits by a youngster's favorite sport of asking "Why?" The full line, "Because it is good for you in the long run!" is fraught with gloom. The long run implies a short leash.

In this crucial verse Paul is depriving us of a favorite game that we practice to perfection in our spiritual childhood. We like to make noble distinctions between faith and feelings. We play "faith" with the same earnestness that children play "grown up." But when things go naturally well — and rejoicing and thanksgiving well up naturally — we have no quarrel with our feelings. Depending on mood and circumstances we hop and skip on this railroad track or that, vaguely visualizing an eventual destination because the tracks run parallel.

Paul interrupts our games by blowing the shrill whistle of an approaching freight train. The will of God is about to bear down on us and neither faith nor feelings can halt the momentum of His sovereignty. God's arbitrary "Because it is good for you!" consolidates faith and feelings into tough fiber that handles all of life in the strength of His redeeming love.

1 Thessalonians 5:16-18

If thou triest my heart, if thou visitest me by night, if thou testest me, thou wilt find no wickedness in me . . .

This kind of challenge is apt to put some snap into a slackened Christian life. We who know how to tie God into our busy routines as just one more obligation — rendering Him harmless in the process — do we dare let Him out at night, knowing the laser of His truth might pierce our sleep when we least expect it? It seems foolhardy to give up blissful oblivion for an extended exercise in accountability.

A gift to be prized, sleep nevertheless makes for a poor hiding place. Ragged and raw from exposure to punishing circumstances, David longed to lose and hide himself in God alone. "Keep me as the apple of the eye; hide me in the shadow of thy wings." This is not the cry of a foolhardy braggart, but of a man intimately acquainted with the comfort and counsel of his God. Supreme confidence in the Lord's righteousness made him suggest the nighttime visitation.

When hounding needs make us crave the soothing ministrations of the night, we hope for a convenient blackout that magically produces wholesale resurrection by six o'clock next morning. That kind of optimism wears off as quickly as the morning coffee. Perhaps a nighttime visit of the Lord would shed light on our daily walk with Him.

If by faith we have appropriated Calvary's atonement, and if His steadfast love has taught us to keep short accounts, we can boldly welcome His light in our shadowy night. In Christ's righteousness are hidden forever the memories of our wickedness. In the exquisite intimacy of His comfort and counsel we discover a resurrection that will unflinchingly stand the test of time and temptation. The boldness of our night will transform the blandness of our days because He keeps us as the apple of His eye!

Psalm 17:3 □ Psalm 17:1-9

*From now on, therefore, we regard no one from a human point
of view; even though we once regarded Christ from a human
point of view, we regard him thus no longer.*

"From now on, therefore . . . " This signals a point of no
return, but it is not a fixed point in time. Paul implies the tense
drama of spiritual surgery when God pioneered the procedure
allowing Him to permanently tap into the jugular vein of his
will. Again and again Paul must deliberately bleed to death in
order to receive a blood transfusion of the Calvary type.

"From now on, therefore . . . " is not a dictatorial declara-
tion, but a concession to unprecedented vulnerability. Paul
goes on to preach the new creation in Christ and culminates his
appeal with the uncompromising, "We beseech you on behalf
of Christ, be reconciled to God." That is the offending line that
leads to crucifixion.

From now on, therefore, this singular reconciliation must
be preached afresh. The modern Christian, as did his counter-
part in antiquity, wants just enough God to be reconciled comfortably to his circumstances and relationships. We press Him
into service as enhancer of life and celebrate the essence of such
enhancement by the extraordinary setting and conduct on
Sunday mornings. It is all froth to the substance of funda-
mental truth that we must be reconciled to God to a depth that
can be measured by the cross only.

From now on, therefore, we must rejoice over the wretch so
alienated from society's norms that he prizes reconciliation to
God above everything. And we must mourn for our good, religious friend who does not live in the shadow and glory of the
cross. This unnatural reversal in our assessment of relationships seems so grossly unfair, so terribly hurtful, that only the
most drastic of blood transfusions can save our life lived for
Christ alone!

2 Corinthians 5:16 □ *2 Corinthians 5:11-21*

God is spirit, and those who worship him must worship in spirit and truth.

Toss this piece of meaty advice into the Christian arena and watch the gladiators of the faith go to work on it and each other. Man is born with the need to worship and the mode of it can actually become our object of worship. Traditionalist and innovator are bound to clash; cathedral lover and nature enthusiast will surely contend.

But the real goad is in the abstraction of language. It almost contradicts the character of Christ who became flesh to give us a handle on God. We strain with all our intellectual might to compress Him further still; to render "spirit and truth" into concrete teaching that can be mastered eventually. What made the woman at the well catch on so rapidly that — amazingly — "Many Samaritans from that city believed in him because of the woman's testimony, 'He told me all that I ever did'"?

The high-noon encounter between Savior and sinner was way over the woman's head in terms of theological discourse. The "living water" left her mystified. Her spiritual capacity centered on religious history and landmarks. But she took the "gift of God" at face value because Truth Incarnate could not be denied. Truth is not wisdom drawn with the cup of imagination from the well of opinions, but Jesus Christ in person.

Now as then, Savior and sinner need to converse and confront at the well of salvation. We need to taste the cup of the new covenant in His blood. When we accept the gift of God at face value because He freely accepts us "as is," we too will realize that He alone is worthy of worship. Then "worthship" will no longer mean a place or program or conceptual presupposition, but the actualization of God in Jesus Christ, as personified by the Holy Spirit. No matter how frail our intellectual grasp, His mighty hold on our grateful heart makes for worship pleasing to Him.

John 4:24 ☐ *John 4:1-41*

*But Peter said, "I have no silver and gold, but I give you what I
have; in the name of Jesus Christ of Nazareth, walk."*

Wall Street might not quite see it this way, but without
question this is the most relevant "precious commodity" quote
of this confused day. If every Christian were gripped by the
excitement and promise of it, the world could witness a gold
rush of astounding proportions. Any investment in the "Acts
of the Holy Spirit" pays off beyond our wildest imaginings.

Why such fuss over one lame man's healing? Ah, but that
was only the foregone conclusion to the transaction of faith.
The high point of the lesson comes earlier. As we accompany
Peter and John to the temple, we carefully avert the eyes of the
lame beggar. God knows we feel sorry, but just the same we
would rather lick Easter seals and endure junk mail than look
the handicapped straight in the eye. Our compassion is tainted
with guilt which makes us vaguely resentful.

We certainly don't expect Peter to give the beggar more
than a cursory glance, lest he be late for prayers. But here he
does this astounding, contrary thing! "And Peter directed his
gaze at him, with John, and said, 'Look at us.' And he fixed his
attention upon them, expecting to receive something from
them." What a novel approach to the persistent problem of
peripheral people seeking to burden us!

"Look at us." What if we allowed the needy world to
interrupt us on our way to church? What if our voice rang out
with such clear hope and conviction that transfixed expectation
would complete the circuit of faith that makes for miracles?
What if a fresh Pentecost were to translate the people of God
into a fresh chapter of the "Acts of the Holy Spirit"? What if we
asked and our faith investment paid off? Look at us. In the
name of Jesus Christ let us rise to the challenge!

Acts 3:6 ☐ *Acts 3:1-10*

The kingdom of heaven is like leaven which a woman took and hid in three measures of flour, till it was all leavened.

Why the prosaic emphasis on yeast, when the subject of homemade bread lends itself to such poetic exploitation? Our kingdom of heaven is like a clever Disney replica of a turn-of-the-century bakery — with a not-so-romantic twist. Grandma's Homemade Bread Shoppe secretly connects to a fully computerized ten-acre factory, from where a fleet of trucks carry the assembly-line loaves to a larger public still.

Silly? Perhaps we should take a sober look at our institutional church with its penchant for putting up a homey front amidst the ever burgeoning sophistication of our electronic age. No practice of deception is implied, only our exercise of resourcefulness. But the basic resource of the kingdom of heaven must be living organism, not lustrous organization.

That is why Jesus stresses the mystery of lowly yeast. Yeast is a living organism that dictates to the breadmaker, whether the kitchen is of soot-covered vintage or stainless-steel efficiency. The baker is forced to cooperate with the subtleties of three-thousand-plus billion cells per pound of yeast. Such baking requires as much patience as time, and above all a heightened sense of awareness. At its best it is a labor of love.

The kingdom of God is His labor of love in our midst. The leaven of the Spirit is hidden in the hearts of His people. Today we are called afresh to a heightened sense of awareness, but also to the humble art of patient waiting. When the full measure of willing hearts has been leavened, the fire of the fresh Pentecost will fully energize the body. Then we shall rise to power as the kingdom people who find favor with those who hunger for the true Bread of Life.

Matthew 13:33

No distrust made him waver concerning the promise of God, but he grew strong in his faith as he gave glory to God . . .

When the great Plowman of Eternity furrows our soul for the planting of great promise, we must trust Him for the inherent life force of the seed. Earthbound clockwatchers that we are, we soon concentrate on surface realities and lose sight of our future appointment with God. But He is diligent in cultivating the circumstances that aid the ripening of His promise. Perhaps we cooperate best by burying our nose in the seed catalogue of His living Word, and studying the pictures that already prove God as faithful nurturer of promise.

Concerning His covenant with Abraham, we are indeed part of the picture. As heirs of a righteousness attributable to God alone, we need to take to heart the caption that stresses Abraham's cooperation. The quality of his faith and conviction was directly related to his practice of giving glory to God.

To be in one's glory is to be caught up in a state of keen appreciation. When privately and publicly we acknowledge God as the source of our satisfaction, we give Him the glory. But it is more than an occasional round of applause. It is the persistent practice of the presence of God as Creator and Sustainer. It is the disciplined training of our faculties to recognize His providential hand in the minute details of our life. It makes for the dedicated acknowledgement of such awareness and appreciation.

The ordinary life infused with His glory becomes the extraordinary life transfused with His power. Whether we live to see the full implementation of God's great promises or not we are keenly satisfied to live in the fulfilled dimension of the classic prophetic utterance, ". . . the will of the LORD shall prosper in his hand; he shall see the fruit of the travail of his soul and be satisfied" (Isaiah 53:10-11).

Romans 4:20

If any man would come after me, let him deny himself and take up his cross daily and follow me.

Jesus says it so matter-of-factly. The passage evokes the rhythm and momentum of habitual, purposeful walking. No fancy footwork needed; anybody can heed the call. While He speaks of essential lifestyle, we entertain notions of exotic behavior — like giving up sweets for a forty-year Lent.

When first we encounter Christ's unsettling challenge, we are forced to rearrange some mental furniture. Before long the whole house of our life begs revamping. We start with a good spring cleaning. Old habits are swept out, shining convictions polished to perfection. Cheered by our display of discipleship, we settle into the comfort of our self-begotten renaissance. Alas, old habits and familiar patterns — like kids and dogs — will sneak back in and track dirt across our sterile sanctification. When we limp after artificial perfection, the Christ of our intellectual projections and sentimental attachments will not save us from falling spectacularly.

"Follow me." Forget for now the little habits — form the one big habit of looking straight to Christ! How does a baby learn to walk except by walking, looking to the example and encouragement of the parent. We do not ban him to his playpen until he has mastered textbooks on anatomy and Olympic competition. It is just as absurd to try to reason out the great challenge of Christ in the vacuum of conceptualized thinking that harps on the theme, "If only . . ." His "if" is practical: "Follow me."

To follow in the steadying rhythm of Christ's footsteps takes constant exercise of will to identify with the Master to the exclusion of all lesser loyalties. The daily cross speaks of the repeated tension of costly confrontation. But the daily exercise of Christ's companionship makes for the momentum that carries us from one death-and-resurrection cycle to the next.

Luke 9:23 □ *Luke 9:18-27*

I rejoice at thy word like one who finds great spoil.

We are lucky to find a quiet moment or two to gulp down our daily Scripture portion — the spiritual vitamin pill that is part of the recommended daily regimen of the dutiful Christian. But unless we learn to read the Bible for "fun and profit" in our recreation time, we miss out on the delight of discovery that prompted the psalmist to address 172 verses of this 176-verse psalm to God alone — in singular praise and thanksgiving for His sustaining Word.

How does one progress from duty to delight? We must immediately dismiss the notion that the psalmist had an obvious advantage because of his own literary bent. Archaic language or outdated settings are of no consequence either. The Word of God is undeniably contemporary in any tongue or culture. He is the same yesterday, today, and tomorrow. Man's abject need of God transcends the ages as well. The Holy Spirit testifies to both.

It was raw need of survival, not affinity for fine literature, that drove the psalmist into the sacred writings of his day. Hounded by enemies and haunted by the anarchy of his own heart, he clung to the objective, incorruptible standard of God's Word. Within the boundaries of His sovereign precepts he discovered the steadfastness of His boundless love.

Duty and discipline may mark us a serious Christian, but if the Word of God does not draw us beyond our meager routines, we are spiritually comatose. A vital love affair with Christ makes for a vital love affair with His book. The dullest pages, filled with the seeming trivia of bygone ceremonial practice, come alive with the absolute integrity of our God who tabernacles with His people that we might know His love and live by His power. Why the quick pep pill when His Word makes for a banquet? When will we sit down and really feast on it?

Psalm 119:162 ☐ *Psalm 119*

And the word of the LORD came to me, saying "Jeremiah, what do you see?" And I said, "I see a rod of almond." Then the LORD said to me, "You have seen well, for I am watching over my word to perform it."

"The word of the LORD" — would His prophet recognize it today? What if we borrowed his eyes and viewed the contemporary scene? We cannot help but be awed by the prestige and popularity of the Bible. The nation's bookshelves are bulging with handsomely bound and illustrated editions.

"Jeremiah, what do you see?" A people singularly blessed, yet curiously powerless — "functional illiterates" awash in a sea of print. A nation intellectually astute, but not vibrantly alive in the intimacy and immediacy of God's "performing" word.

Long before John coined the phrase, "And the Word became flesh . . ." Jeremiah's flesh had become word. He would readily understand the play on words. The "rod of almond" (*shaqed*) and "watching" (*shoqed*) are exactly that. And what else did Jeremiah see? A boiling pot, baskets of figs, a potter at work . . . In the natural settings and circumstances of his fleshly existence, the prophet perceived the performing word of God and rendered it into the idiom of his day, assured — by obediently living it himself — that it would prevail. Living in exclusive communion with the Communicator, he skillfully expressed the inclusive heart and emotions.

Awed by the Bible glut of this land, Jeremiah would surely remind us of the awesomeness of God's "language" evident not in print, but in power. Lest we forget, by His spoken word creation came into existence! That same inherent power is poised on our bookshelves. We might let it gather dust, but God is watching over His word to perform it. That awe-ful truth will grip us sooner or later.

Jeremiah 1:11-12 ☐ *Jeremiah 1:1-12*

It is written, "Man shall not live by bread alone, but by every word that proceeds from the mouth of God."

Jesus was led into the wilderness for the express purpose of encountering the Tempter. Does the solitary fast of forty days and forty nights imply rigorous preparatory discipline, or a deliberate descent into a compromisable state of weakness with which we can and must identify?

Christ was not thrust into the public eye until the age of thirty. Surely the man who discoursed with scholars and theologians as a boy of twelve did not require time out for the honing of his debating skills. True to His unique calling, the Savior stripped Himself of His adequacy and put on our fleshly vulnerability. When the beguiling words of the Tempter fell on His ears, He had exactly one recourse open to Him, "It is written . . ." Unable to trust Himself, He trusted the inherent power of the word of God.

The eloquent author of the Sermon on the Mount simply quoted from Deuteronomy, and Satan — as fine a Bible scholar as there ever was — countered with Psalms, expediently editing his material. Where Christ wielded the sharp sword of the living Word, Satan fumbled with a make-believe dagger. Rhetoric was no match for relationship. The sword pierced straight to the "division of soul and spirit, of joints and marrow . . ." (Hebrews 4:12), to Satan's original line as immortalized in Eden, "Yea, hath God said . . .?"

Matthew 4:4 □ Matthew 4:1-11

But thanks be to God, who in Christ always leads us in triumph, and through us spreads the fragrance of the knowledge of him everywhere.

In the night watch of the embattled soul, when the dimly flickering flame of faith casts a ghostly pall on our wounded hopes and dying dreams, the dread of ongoing contest looms forbiddingly large. In the shadowy comings and goings of our dark hour we perceive the whispering of enemy and defector, and the strange familiarity of their bearing haunts us.

To the Christian determined to muster a militant spirit at all cost — in order to get on with the business of life's conquest — Paul presents a disarming thought. Picture yourself a captive, not a captain! Be nothing more than a captive in the victory parade of Christ the Conqueror. Walk in humble submission. Spot the crown of fresh flowers pressed on Him by the jubilant crowd. Savor the mood of adoration. Surprise yourself with an approving smile. This is much more than a review of ancient Rome's military glory — it is liberating truth.

Where Christ is the Captor, we in turn become captivating. Drink in the fragrance of the victor's crown. Vividly relive His claim to fame. Pay tribute to His courage. Acknowledge that you were made one of His own. Describe your startlingly new life. Express the surprise of your satisfaction. Live in a state of "hero worship." Unconsciously we thus become "the aroma of Christ."

How wise of Paul, who knew the stench of inner battle-fields, the musty odor of starkly real prisons, to exercise his faith and ours by keen observation and vivid imagination. For all who strive so conscientously to communicate Christ, there is no greater release than capitulation to the lovely truth attending this loveliest of Paul's phrases: Prisoners of Jesus Christ, we are perfumed with "the fragrance of the knowledge of him!"

2 Corinthians 2:14 □ *2 Corinthians 2:14-16*

Then they ran and fetched him from there; and when he stood among the people, he was taller than any of the people from his shoulders upward.

This is not mother's tea party where darling Junior, freshly tall and contemptuous of adoring ladies, must endure their gleeful little shrieks as they proclaim his emerging manhood. This is Israel — with Saul fresh out of cowardly hiding — on the very threshold of ill-begotten monarchy!

To get at the biting irony, the towering tragedy of this scene, it helps to consider the ominous closing lines of the Book of Judges. "In those days there was no king in Israel; every man did what was right in his own eyes." Delivered from slavery to exercise highest freedom under God, they turned libertarian, declaring every home a castle and every man his own king. Across the drawbridge of tolerance entered envy, greed, lust, contempt, confusion. Chaos of heart and mind ignited conflict at home. Spiritual and moral bankruptcy spread like wildfire across the land.

Samuel, passionate judge and prophet, called Israel to her identity as God's unique people, chosen to be a light to the nations. They crowned his life's work by clamoring for a "real" king to ape the nations around them. And God, willing to risk His faithfulness against the people's folly, relinquished His visible kingship to Saul — whose name means "asked for." With his public proclamation at hand, he literally had to be asked for.

God declares Himself sufficient still to be the Sovereign of heart and history. Our folly, too, He will heal with His faithfulness. But there is a price to be paid when in competition with the world we aggrandize what we proclaim right for us. The sovereign rule of God providentially excludes the right to self-determination because it brings on bondage of towering proportions.

1 Samuel 10:23 ☐ *1 Samuel 10:17-24*

Rejoice greatly, O daughter of Zion . . . Lo, your king comes to you . . . humble and riding on an ass . . .

At the rate crowned heads of state have toppled in this century, the only royalty left standing will soon be the kings and queens of chess — a distressing thought to incurable romantics. A similar disenchantment awaits the Christian who adores his King enthroned on popular appeal.

If only we could say to our nation: Rejoice greatly! Your king comes to you with such political acumen and personal charisma that a powerfully united citizenry is about to redis-cover the pleasures of patriotism and world prestige! Or to our neighborhood: Your king comes to you proclaiming a perma-nent block party in celebration of his cures for crabgrass, graffiti and barking dogs! If only we could herald to ourselves: Your king comes to you with such pizzazz that your life will turn from soap commercial to box office sensation.

Of course we are entitled to fond expectations as promoters of the everlasting kingdom. But while we plot grand schemes, the King arrives at the scene of our triumphant preparations — "humble and riding on an ass." It does not square with our image of Rolls-Royce-powered royalty! And so we had best remove from the road He means to travel our updated agenda so enthusiastically spread out for Him.

This enduring King of Kings does not encourage lofty ambition, does not call us to be creme de la creme. Poised on that ordinary donkey He makes a proclamation requiring no pageantry, no prime-time television coverage. "Be salt," He begs and rides on — into all of our ordinary life to anoint it with the nobility of His caring heart. Rejoice greatly! Your king comes to you to play with your baby; to car pool with you; to bless your tuna sandwich; to help pick out paint at the hard-ware store . . .

Zechariah 9:9 □ Zechariah 9:1-10

My soul magnifies the Lord, and my spirit rejoices in God my Savior, for he has regarded the low estate of his handmaiden.

It was Mary's glorious privilege to be the mother of our Lord, but we do her a disservice if we enshrine her "Magnificat" in the magnificent past of Christ's historical incarnation. If we put it under glass in isolated museum splendor, we mummify Mary and rob her of the gift she means to bestow on us in the very bloom and essence of her life.

"Magnificat mea anima dominum . . ." The measured rhythm of solemn church language does not match the hum of a Palestinian household. The Magnificat sings and flows with fifteen Old Testament quotations. It follows that Mary grew up in a home where the sacred writings formed an integral part of ordinary life. Mary's personal and spiritual profile shows no repression from a so-called patriarchal religion. Her Magnificat was spontaneous "woman's talk" in response to Elizabeth's spirited welcome. This "handmaiden" was magnificently alive and confident in her Lord before she received into her womb the world's Savior.

Perhaps Mary's personal legacy to us is not her biological partnership in a mystery that eludes our understanding. Her gift lies in her radiant faith that sprang from the heart of God. Within the intimacy of her abiding before God Almighty she was shaped to expect great things of Him — and so was led to bear testimony to His humble partaking of our very humanity.

It is so easy in this day to seek inspiration at our finger tips. (Dial a prayer; turn on a cassette; switch to radio or TV; drive to church.) What if we looked to our soul? With all His heart God still longs to clothe Himself with our flesh, think through our minds, love and empathize through our emotions. The miracle and majesty of His incarnation awaits us afresh. Oh, for your soul and mine to magnify the Lord!

Luke 1:46-48 □ *Luke 1:46-55*

And Joshua . . . sent two men secretly . . . as spies, saying, "Go, view the land, especially Jericho." And they went, and came into the house of a harlot whose name was Rahab, and lodged there.

Here is a bit of biblical embarrassment that needs editing. At stake is not only the imminent possession of the heavily promoted Promised Land, but also God's reputation. This, then, is the morally inspired version of what happened:

And Joshua recalled the scary memories of his own spy career. His fellow Israelites had nearly stoned him in tribute to his bravery. Dismissing the past in blind faith, Joshua decided to push ahead with the new intelligence mission amidst full public disclosure. In honor of his trust God led the spies straight to the home of a man named Reuben Righteous. He and his family of secret believers held an all-night prayer vigil while their guests stretched out in the master bedroom. As a result no one in wicked Jericho wised up to sneaky Israel. The devout man later signed on as an army chaplain.

There is just one hitch. God is not the ten-foot-tall incarnation of our highest idealistic thinking. As the sovereign Lord of history and all creation He could well afford the "wising up" of jittery Joshua who sent his spies secretly to prevent another demoralizing effect on his volatile charges. But what of Rahab — prostitute, liar, betrayer of her own people? She lodges like raw herring in our throats.

What if God really reserved His gift of faith and revelation for those strictly deserving it? In Joshua 2:12 Rahab pleads for Israel's mercy, having herself "dealt kindly" with the representatives. The Hebrew word is *hesed* — more commonly used to indicate God's mercy and steadfast kindness to Israel herself. Access to the Promised Land can never be through our paltry goodness. The true "highway to Zion" always cuts straight across the heart of God and is hewn out of bedrock of His sovereign *hesed!*

Joshua 2:1 □ *Joshua 2:1-21*

Jesus said " . . . no one comes to the Father, but by me."

This is the line that separates the good from the bad. The "bad" say Amen! The "good" — you and I — hem and haw. The trembling sinner recognizes it as Christ's foremost inclusive statement. To the trembling saint it sounds so radically exclusive that he has trouble reconciling it to the world he must co-exist with. Our rapidly shrinking world invites tolerance.

Thanks to modern marvels of communication the farthest reaches of earth congregate in our living rooms. Amazing diversity becomes evident as microphones and cameras examine every "kindred, every tribe on this terrestrial ball." *National Geographic* deepens our appreciation of exotic peoples and colorful customs. Primitive religious rites are pictured to arouse cultural interest, not convert-zeal. Naked heathens no longer offend us. Today's African warrior sporting a frivolous T-shirt pains us as a betrayer of his heritage.

Our freedom of religion renders us similarly ambivalent. Although we abhor cults and are suspicious of the more vocal brethren among ecumenicals, we gladly exercise responsible citizenship. In all this we court a dilemma that explodes with this key verse. We cannot convert all people to our First Church of the True Believer — and we cannot consign all outsiders to hell. And so we hem and haw and hope to God that somewhere at Road's End there is a makeshift place where the unenlightened get a quick chance to cram for finals, and hopefully squeak by!

Why such a mad obsession when we can have a magnificent one? Why seek to fully possess God's mind on the fate of a billion unknowns when all He seeks is to possess you and me fully! And how can He possess us fully unless we empty ourselves of all claims to adequacy? When He becomes way, truth, and life incarnate in us, this shrinking world will expand afresh with the saving grace and knowledge of mankind's Redeemer.

John 14:6

So Pilate, wishing to satisfy the crowd, released for them Barabbas; and having scourged Jesus, he delivered him to be crucified.

Pilate went down in history as a political coward. Jesus endured cross and tomb to rise and reign as Redeemer forever. But what of Barabbas who disappeared into the mob? He might slip back into the present to jolt our calm acceptance of history's most infamous plot. Barabbas has evidence of surprising complicity. But first the gospel writers' assessment of him: John says, "Now Barabbas was a robber." Luke elaborates, ". . . a man who had been thrown into prison for an insurrection started in the city, and for murder." Mark agrees fully. Matthew sums up, "And they had then a notorious prisoner, called Barabbas." Before writing off the fellow completely, we had best examine a historical footnote that says his full name was Jesus Barabbas. Matthew 27:17 would then read as follows, "Pilate said to them, 'Whom do you want me to release for you, Jesus Barabbas or Jesus who is called Christ?'"

The secret is out regardless. Barabbas means "son of the father." We are caught with a subtly symbolized transfer of identity. The guiltless Son of the Father went to Golgatha; the guilty son of the Father went free. "Barabbas" is our brother in Christ. Cloaked in anonymity he roams the world far from eternity's rest because guilt hounds him. He needs to be told the arresting news. "Death in the family. Last will and testament read.You are chief heir. All is forgiven. Come home and claim it!"

Will Barabbas respond? He might if we give him our own name for surety. Are we not Barabbas also? Could we not catalogue our rebellion against God? Set free by the suffering of the Son of the Father, let us trace back the brotherhood of man to Barabbas who stood in for us when Pilate satisfied the crowd. We need healing of the notorious pride that sets us apart.

Mark 15:15 □ *Mark 15:1-15*

But Jesus did not trust himself to them, because he knew all men and needed no one to bear witness of man; for he himself knew what was in man.

The chicken was fork tender and the hostility such that it could be cut with a knife. Only moments before the room had been tingling with happy anticipation. Approving eyes followed the speaker as he strode to the lectern. He flashed the ladies his best boyish grin and each took him to heart as if she alone had wiped his nose and nurtured him to such exemplary manhood.

When the church women's catch of the season began to speak, he caught them off guard. "We are all no damn good," he announced breezily, and from sweet little old lady to starch community pillar they all gasped. There issued a whirlwind of hot indignation that was checked only by the thinnest veneer of cool politeness. His Amen signaled their Good Riddance Forever. Perhaps the young man of conviction was led to a prison ministry — or learned language suited to ladies' luncheons.

The real shocker comes when the Word who became flesh "and dwelt among us, full of grace and truth" turns on us with the double-barreled blast that He did not trust Himself even to believers, "for he himself knew what was in man." And then the very thing that was "in man" — in every single one of us — got nailed to a cross for all the world to gawk at. So dark was our crime against God, so hatefully hidden, that the sun could not bear the shock of revelation and earth itself was plunged into our darkness of soul.

Why does the Savior shock us into self-revelation? Is it not that He might better reveal Himself? Knowing firsthand what we are like, the Son of man put His trust in God alone and was content to love us. To trust God alone is to know protection from bitter disappointment. To love people in the power of His self-revelation is to invite esteem of the highest order for all concerned.

John 2:24-25

There is therefore now no condemnation for those who are in Christ Jesus.

Paul's classic self-portrayal in the preceding chapter — "Wretched man that I am!" — finds its triumphant climax in this thundering text that has thrilled Christendom from the day the challenge was delivered. Paul dares us to go from applause to application, from intellectual thrill to internalized truth.

Context is crucial to deep understanding. "I do not understand my own actions. For I do not do what I want, but I do the very thing I hate. . . . I delight in the law of God . . . but I see in my members another law at war with the law of my mind and making me captive to the law of sin which dwells in my members. . . . I of myself serve the law of God with my mind, but with my flesh I serve the law of sin."

Where Paul speaks law, we think magic. "Thanks be to God through Jesus Christ" becomes a formula designed to automatically trip a spiritual gadget that will charge us with immunity from inconsistency. What if the sin of gluttony — our love of food — has saddled us with unwanted flesh? The law of the mind says, "Diet!" The law of the flesh counters, "Eat and cheat!" We discover that the most famous "wretched dilemma" passage in Scripture is not eclipsed by a triumphant, "There is therefore no struggle, no failed pinch test for those who are in Christ Jesus!" In truth there is abyssmal failure with ample forgiveness. Now look in the mirror and dare to love yourself through the eyes of the Redeemer. Pride, not flesh, distorts the image.

We do not win the battles of the flesh by grim self-denial. We cannot redeem ourselves. God abhors our earnest self-rehabilitation programs, but graciously invites the daily surrender of pride and confession of need. Until the Christian is sold on that law, Christ cannot redeem. Rehabilitation can never take the place of redemption.

Romans 8:1 □ *Romans 7:7–8:1*

And I am sure that he who began a good work in you will bring it to completion at the day of Jesus Christ.

And just exactly what makes Paul so sure? Even as the Philippians are commended for their partnership in the apostle's life work, various remarks in this highly personal letter hint at petty jealousies and personal ambitions sure to hamper any good work.

Tellingly, Paul addresses his remarks to "all the saints in Christ Jesus . . . with the bishops and deacons." Brilliant theologian, planter and nurturer of local churches, Paul is speaking to the laity. Reverends and doctors of divinity are within hearing range, but not the primary target of his exhortation

To the key church worker — you and me — Paul writes from Rome; prisoner not of Caesar but of Christ. Bound, yet free as never before, he outlines a strategy for confidence that needs to undergird every "good work." Good work is not successful churchmanship orchestrated by professional "overseers." Good work is not a project, but a process. It is the process of sanctification which God initiates in us and carries through to completion. We are the good work — His patient labor of love.

As a true statesman of God, Paul is burdened for the church at large. A true lover of Jesus Christ, Paul enables a homesick Epaphroditus to go home; entreats a Euodia and Syntyche to work out their problem with the help of other individuals. But Paul, terminal prisoner of powerful Rome, pins his hope for the church not on key people or pilot programs, but solely on the person of Jesus Christ — who "being found in human form humbled himself and became obedient unto death." For this reason we can be sure that every good work proceeds beyond good intentions and dismal failures. God purposes, persists and perfects. Do we project that freedom to "all the saints in Christ Jesus" who struggle through their "partnership in the gospel from the first day until now?"

Philippians 1:6 □ *Philippians 1:1-11*

Finally, be strong in the Lord and in the strength of his might. Put on the whole armor of God . . .

Why not slip into something more comfortable? There are pious platitudes and popular formulas that promise immunity from life's disturbances. Thoughts of armor conjur up images of young David drowning in King Saul's clanking coat of mail. We would rather wing it than suffer the discipline of a rigid Christian dress code.

Imprisoned in Rome, Paul had ample time to study the function of military dress. Backed by Caesar and his empire's might, headquartered at the very seat of power, the praetorian guard did not sport leisure wear. Skilled in the art of defense, their manner of dress advertised constant vigilance.

Ironically, when the "powers and principalities" hostile to God invade our own time and space, we frantically bark out orders for heavy ammunition and run like mad from one crumbling rampart to another. If David looked ridiculous in his initial monster-like gait toward Goliath, think how pathetic we must appear to "the spiritual hosts of wickedness in the heavenly places." We were never meant to slug it out with these, only to "fear not, stand firm, and see the salvation of the LORD" (Exodus 14:13).

Dressed essentially for defense, we are to constantly exercise our focus on Him who equips us with the helmet of salvation. It does not indicate our rank or allegiance, but signifies our unmerited gift of divine favor. But lest we think that such an "honor guard" is mostly ornamental, Paul reminds us of "the sword of the Spirit, which is the word of God." It is the offensive weapon that slashes away at pious platitudes and popular formulas that dull our senses to the wonder of God doing battle on our behalf always. "The battle is the Lord's." Shall we not honor His might by wearing His armor gladly?

Ephesians 6:10-11 □ *Ephesians 6:10-20*

For the mountains may depart and the hills be removed, but my steadfast love shall not depart from you . . .

How easily we forget that God's love is rooted in eternity. We forget that it is a grand and stubborn love that does not want to be domesticated, does not want to be measured by our shallow experience or timid expression.

God's love is not marshmallow at the core of life's struggles, is not the frosting on top of worldly success. God's love is not invitation to the easy chumminess of those who make a fetish of religious informality. God's love cannot be immortalized in works of great art or literature. God's eternal love eludes the limitations of our finite mind.

Faith enables us to taste God's love, but only faith that has been to hell and back can begin to fathom the faithfulness of a God who cannot deny His character. Faith needs to take serious Isaiah's graphic illustration of love rooted in eternity. His prophetic vision of cataclysm ushering in the birth pangs of the new heaven and earth must explode in us the myth that God's business is to be nice when in fact He must be holy. His love in us must not create niceness, but holiness, and this urgently so because we are destined to inhabit eternity with our Maker.

As we survey the house of our life with its accumulation of cherished knickknacks and niceties of our religion, what would we allow God to shake or cataclysmically remove until we would question His love? If God will level mountains to fix our attention on His eternal love, shall we not flee the house of our own fixed order and fling ourselves on Him alone? God's love is stern in its stability. It will stubbornly hold and keep us — and present us in Christ "without blemish before the presence of his glory with rejoicing" (Jude 1:24).

Isaiah 54:10 ☐ *Isaiah 54:9-17*

But many of the . . . old men who had seen the first house, wept with a loud voice when they saw the foundation of this house being laid, though many shouted aloud for joy; so that the people could not distinguish the sound of the joyful shout from the sound of the people's weeping . . .

"This house" was the temple being built in post-exilic Jerusalem. The "first house" was Solomon's Temple, reduced to rubble by Babylonian rampage some fifty years earlier. With the new foundations in place, a festal service of dedication was held. And so the joyful shout went up — and weeping of such magnitude that its sound matched the shout fully.

Why such tears? Did those old men mourn the haunting splendors of a bygone era? Did their brokenness acknowledge God's righteous judgment? Was God pleased, we wonder, that the triumph of the new temple was tempered by tears of reserve? Is not outwardly focused church building an exercise in Solomonic "vanity"? Tellingly, the new temple lay "desolate" some fifteen years later. Enthusiasm for its completion had peaked with the great shout. The weepers won.

God always has the last word. He spoke through Haggai, His first post-exilic prophet. Haggai noticed luxury homes of imported wood, yet a curious lack of prospering among God's people. He prompted them to wholeheartedly rebuild the temple, promising unprecedented splendor for "this house." His call to moral housecleaning was secondary. (There goes our notion that a chastened church must swear off "building" mentality.)

Haggai discerned that failure had led to futility which denied a great future. With the grand monuments of the flawed past wiped out, the "paneled houses" symbolized a lesser grandeur tied timidly to fleeting personal moments in time. The movement of God was frozen in guilt. The restored sanctuary visibly demonstrated God's forgiveness and confidence in a future bright with His glory. God builds up His people still. Let the joyful shout triumph as we rebuild the church of this age on the foundation of Jesus Christ!

Ezra 3:12-13 ☐ *Ezra 3:8-13*

Cry aloud, spare not, lift up your voice like a trumpet; declare to my people their transgression. . . . Yet they seek me daily, and delight to know my ways, as if they . . . did not forsake the ordinance of their God . . .

The prophet is describing "Mother's Day" in heaven. If a mother could only have her children's obedience, they would never have to bother with Mother's Day spectaculars fashioned from cardboard or financed by dad's allowance. When on Mother's Day her brood bickers over who does what chore — with marginal effort expecting maximum effect — our Queen for a Day is ready to check into a motel. How much more she would rather enjoy the giver than gifts and gestures dictated by custom and commercialism.

Does God not sound like a grieved parent who can no longer tolerate the carelessly perpetuated inconsistencies in His growing offspring? Isaiah speaks scathingly on the Lord's behalf, "Bring no more vain offerings; incense is an abomination to me. New moon and sabbath and the calling of assemblies — I cannot endure iniquity and solemn assembly. Your new moons and your appointed feasts my soul hates; they have become a burden to me, I am weary of bearing them" (Isaiah 1:13-14).

God plainly does not covet our religious fascination with Him, nor appreciate our taking delight without taking into account His essential character and desires. This God abhors the role of ceremonial figurehead to satisfy our whim for rituals and guilt-reducing exercises. He does not seek our adoration apart from "worship in spirit and in truth."

Authentic worship of God leads to stewardship on behalf of the poor, the oppressed, the hungry, the naked, the widowed and fatherless. The Son of God states it simply, "Truly, I say to you, as you did it not to one of the least of these, you did it not to me" (Matthew 25:45).

Isaiah 58:1-2 ☐ *Isaiah 58*

I had heard of thee by the hearing of the ear, but now my eye sees thee; therefore I despise myself, and repent in dust and ashes.

There is no greater joy than intimacy with God. There is no deadlier trap than to presume that easy familiarity will get us there. Woe if we call Him "The Man Upstairs" and bank on a grandfatherly disposition. Woe if we picture Him a blessing machine activated by our goodness. Woe if we treat Him as cosmic cop who walks his beat in our precinct exclusively.

Job's ordeal serves as a stark reminder that every private assumption about God is a grievous presumption sure to be blasted sky-high. Consider how we handle crisis. The initial shock of helplessness is bound to throw us on God without much delay. We grudgingly grant Him the right to allow or even engineer crisis. We really buy the theory that suffering benefits the soul, especially when the concept of grace has never descended from head knowledge to gut level, where guilt feeds as a parasite.

When crises become chronic, our Rock-of-Gibraltar faith splits and turns into a swarm of gnats that buzz off everywhere in search of plausible causes. Like Job we leave no stone unturned to establish our blamelessness, which in time leads to our chipping away at God. We try every approach to prayer, consider everybody's pet prescription from the Bible, and when God still won't budge — not even when we are fighting mad — we cannot help but suffer violent disillusionment.

Was Job disillusioned about God? Of course. Before we can truly know Him we must see Him as He is, utterly devoid of illusions. God must be God. He owes us no explanations, no solutions, no rewards. We must repent of using Him. But when — by his gracious forbearance — we see Him as He really is, the adventure of knowing Him intimately has gloriously begun.

Job 42:5-6 □ *Job 42:1-6*

He said to them, "But who do you say that I am?"

What a rough spot to be in. We have walked with Jesus, watched Him in every imaginable and unimaginable situation, have broken bread with Him, have loved Him. And one fine day — for no obvious reason — He stops dead in His tracks, turns on His heel, and looking us straight in the eye of our soul, asks briskly, "But who do you say that I am?"

Is He fishing for compliments? Is He leery of the Gallup Poll? Have we unwittingly displeased Him? Are the pressures getting to Him? Is He enforcing some kind of loyalty oath? "But who do *you* say that I am?" We have watched Him heal, so we could call Him physician. Or teacher. Lover of children and parties. Loner. Revolutionary. Therapist. Preacher. Visionary. Authority figure. Our mind is exploding with titles and names and attributes, but the tongue simply sums up, "You are the Christ, the Son of the living God."

His enthusiastic blessing, "For flesh and blood has not revealed this to you, but my Father who is in heaven," almost embarrasses us. We have seen no blinding light, heard no thunder clap, have not felt great emotion or brilliance of mind. Why would our simple reply cause such fireworks?

"From that time Jesus began to show his disciples that he must go to Jerusalem and suffer . . . " Jesus now walks with intimates ordained and equipped by His Father! The excitement unfolds in the fact that Jerusalem suddenly is no longer a pilgrim's Dream City, but the disciple's code word for confrontation and obedience unto death. When we duly protest because the rock of our faith is but a pebble, we are really rocked when Satan gets a blasting. It is indeed a rough spot where God nails us for the incomparable adventure of intimacy with Him. But in going before us, the Son of the living God will exalt every valley, make low every hill, and the rough places "plain."

Matthew 16:15 ☐ Matthew 16:13-20

Take my yoke upon you, and learn from me; for I am gentle and lowly in heart, and you will find rest for your souls.

Here is a sales pitch out of sync with today's high-powered hustlers of good news on television and elsewhere. Imagine, no money to send, no books and tapes to accumulate, no seminars to sign up for and no rallies to cheer on. Imagine joining a prestigious organization dedicated to the fine art of living. Instead of riding herd on underlings with slick brochures and quotas thrust at them, the chairman of the board abandons his oak-paneled office, exchanges natty suit and tie for our kind of work clothes — and then comes to work and play and live with us, patiently modeling the perfect approach to life.

So mind-boggling is the concept that it behooves us to scrutinize such a man well. If he means to stick closer than our own skin and last a lifetime, he can be neither overbearing nor easily discouraged.

Jesus is disarmingly honest. He does not proclaim "Rest for Weary Souls" in glossy letters and bury the word "yoke" in the limited warranty clause added in fine print. But when He matter-of-factly introduces the yoke as prerequisite for satisfying teamwork, He does not glorify stoic oxen who dully plow straight furrows. His yoke signifies the discipline of instruction in the companionship of God's own Son. The Gospels sing out His singular capacity to serve and succor the weak.

The rested soul is one deeply centered on the perfect will of God. It need no longer concern itself with one of Christianity's most eccentric questions: how to find or do the will of God. Yoked with Christ, we cannot miss the mark. Is He not God's perfect will incarnate? His meekness is the natural result of being centered in His Father's love. A rested soul is gentle, having become unassailable.

Matthew 11:29 ☐ *Matthew 11:25-30*

Will any one of you, who has a servant plowing or keeping sheep, say to him when he has come in from the field, "Come at once and sit down at table"? Will he not rather say to him, "Prepare supper for me, and gird yourself and serve me . . . "?

"The apostles said to the Lord, 'Increase our faith!'" That is the curious context of this tough text that will undo our pretext. How can any good news for modern man contain such grating anachronism, "So you also, when you have done all that is commanded you say, 'We are unworthy servants; we have only done what was our duty.'" We cannot miss the immediate illustration either. Jesus healed ten lepers and only one, a Samaritan at that, came back to thank Him.

Is Jesus not out of step with the times? Has He not heard of labor reform and social justice? After work should the servant not enjoy a hot shower and meal, and be invited to watch cable TV in the family room? Pass him the pretzels, too.

"Increase our faith!" We buy the mustard-seed theory and scratch our head at the mulberry-tree mystery. How can a tree uproot and transplant itself? Sensing that the mystery will come unglued in our own lap, we pretend that Jesus is talking way over our head. But Jesus patiently models the debasement of the dutiful, devoted servant who after a hard day's labor "girds" Himself to serve. It means to dress for the occasion, to play the part to the hilt.

"Increase our faith!" After tending the sheep in the day of His flesh, Jesus by nightfall prepared for the Passover of His broken body and shed blood. He girded Himself with a towel and washed the disciples' feet. Uprooted from heaven's natural majesty and transplanted into our unlikely existence, He modeled the fruit of obedience. Has He not stirred and enlarged our faith in God? If we exalt this Christ, His own humility will elevate our servanthood from duty to delight.

Luke 17:7-8 □ *Luke 17:1-19*

Consider the lilies of the field, how they grow; they neither toil nor spin; yet I tell you, even Solomon in all his glory was not arrayed like one of these.

Consider the winsomeness of Jesus Christ, how He unwittingly betrays a keen eye for the superb simplicity of God. Would the Queen of Sheba have logged 1200 miles on camelback to feast her eyes on the grain fields of Palestine so exuberantly dotted with the loveliness of a common flower? In his opulent day Solomon made silver as common as stones, but Jesus commends neither his tailor nor interior decorator.

Christ's expertise with glory predates His observations as historian and naturalist by measureless time. He knew of a glory which He had with the Father "before the world was made." This discriminating Son of man took time to stoop over a common field flower and exalt its glory. We sense His child-like pleasure of discovery. We need to imitate it.

Christians can be among the worst ingrates when it comes to God's splendor lavished on common creation. We range from grossly indifferent to spiritually aloof, unless we are the consummate camera buff who bags sunsets and floral specimens for Show and Tell — which involves lens, shutter speed and novel filter use, but no unmitigated delight in the ungilded lily.

The next time we read "environment" and automatically think carcinogens, let us practice our prerogative of being fellow heirs to Christ's glory. What splendor can we recommend to our Queen of Sheba? The idea is not to look religiously for God in every stalk of grass, but to let down our spiritually done-up hair and luxuriate in His common grace. Some call it smelling the roses. We might call it re-considering. Consider the spider web instead of thoughtlessly obliterating it. Consider the superb simplicity of its structure. Could Solomon's Syro-Phoenician-inspired architecture have matched its glory? Where is that now?

Matthew 6:28-29 □ Matthew 6:25-34

She has done what she could; she has anointed my body beforehand for burying.

We dare not miss what Mary did. Two days before the crucial Passover Jesus sat at table in Bethany and the contemplative sister of Martha and Lazarus "came with an alabaster flask of ointment of pure nard, very costly, and she broke the flask and poured it over his head." She was promptly castigated by the hard-nosed in His company for wasting stuff which "might have been sold . . . and given to the poor." Because of Christ's affirmation the fragrance lingers and the question remains: How does our contemplation of His life manifest itself?

Back in the heyday of our Lord's popularity a groundswell of excitement swept all kinds of people to their feet, and they followed the Galilean in an ominous dust cloud of mixed motives and private agendas. When Martha hosted her reception for Him, she fairly blustered with the importance of having landed the social catch of the season. How could Mary not show off her date nut bread and help fuss over the guests? Her sister sat quietly at the Lord's feet "and listened to his teaching."

Doing the same two days before Passover, His teaching suddenly became fleshed out in Mary's mind. The Son of God must go to Jerusalem; His body must be broken and His blood shed for the redemption of many, especially Mary. Her response? She broke and poured out her most prized possession in symbolic acknowledgement of His imminent sacrifice. While His well-tutored disciples still entertained mixed motives and private agendas, Mary believed her Lord. He greatly honored her for that.

At the nerve center of our relationship with God must be the stark fact of His redemptive death. Unless our faith in Jesus Christ delivers us from the zeal of the do-gooder, we are idealists doomed to disillusionment. Will we anoint our Savior with the fragrance of our broken self-will and poured-out soul?

Mark 14:8 □ *Mark 14:1-9*

So the soldiers came and broke the legs of the first, and of the other who had been crucified with him; but when they came to Jesus and saw that he was already dead, they did not break his legs.

"The Old Rugged Cross" is not sweet-old-hometown-USA legacy. The crucifixion demands to be reviewed in the light of Jewish history. John highlighted in his interpretive gospel the Jewish roots of the cross. "Behold, the Lamb of God, who takes away the sin of the world." Mosaic writings had established that no bones of the Paschal lamb must be broken. Of the mystery of Christ's naturally hastened death John writes triumphantly, "For these things took place that the scripture might be fulfilled, 'Not a bone of him shall be broken.'"

Significantly, the cross in God's heart was actualized long before it was externalized on Golgotha. From the day He slew an animal to cover the nakedness of Adam's and Eve's trespass to the day Christ wore our nakedness on the cross, God wove redemptive analogy into the fabric of Jewish history. The Jews were not groomed as cosmic pets, but as His revelation to all nations. In His sovereign plan, Egypt's land of Goshen was not simply a concentration of enslaved Jews, but a womb where Israel's distinct identity could be nurtured and the Passover Lamb introduced.

In Jesus, the Light to the nations became perfectly incarnate. Behold, the Redeemer: "It is finished!" His supernatural work of redemption accomplished, Jesus dismissed His spirit and His body was found lifeless. "For this reason the Father loves me, because I lay down my life, that I may take it again. No one takes it from me, but I lay it down of my own accord" (John 10:17-18). He died deliberately, only to rise likewise — for you and for me.

John 19:32-33 □ John 19:28-37

Thy way was through the sea, thy path through the great waters; yet thy footprints were unseen.

We want our God big enough to ward off bullies and small enough to fit into our thinking; holy enough to fit the desirable-member profile of our church and benign enough to blend in with real life. We like a predictable God. In truth, He is eminently predictable. Why, then, the paradox of the God-forsaken Christian, the predicament of the Psalmist, "I think of God, and I moan; I meditate, and my spirit faints. . . . Are his promises at an end for all time?"

When real life has eroded our comfortable image of the predictable God, we begin to fathom the bleak mood of the disciples after the crucifixion. Bleakness is dull resignation to a life ruled by unending routine, but robbed of reason. With Jesus dead, His intimates seemed sentenced to a life of haunting memories. Thank God they did not have emotional strength to found the church right then and there, or we would have a historical precedent to function as memorial rather than marching society.

From the day His divinity was revealed to His followers, Christ predicted His death and resurrection. If cross and empty tomb have not yet become the bench marks of our faith, we have little right to be the church and no power to revitalize its witness. Pentecost was nothing more than "the exclamation point to the Resurrection!"

Our God is big enough to reduce all of man's recorded history to a mere comma in the annals of eternity. He is small enough to be welcomed as a baby. The Psalmist looked back to Exodus in order to march forward again. We look back to the mysterious hiatus between Good Friday and Easter in order to measure God's predictability in relationship to His essential character. In Jesus Christ every hope has an eternal home.

Psalm 77:19 □ *Psalm 77*

Now on the first day of the week Mary Magdalene came to the tomb early . .

We have Easter down pat. Could there be a new twist to the story? What if it served up Easter ham and a retrospective on Eve and Eden? Jesus will vouch for the truth.

Gospel writer John is the "Easter ham." Watch him show off as he describes the race to the empty tomb. "Peter then came out with the other disciple, and they went toward the tomb. They both ran, but the other disciple (John) outran Peter and reached the tomb first . . . Then the other disciple, who reached the tomb first, also went in, and he saw and believed; for as yet they did not know the scripture, that he must rise from the dead." While all this "me first" male strutting is going on, the female lead in the unfolding drama quietly slips into place. Mary stands weeping outside the tomb. What compels her to stick around?

Jesus cast seven demons out of Mary of Magdala. Seven suggests a "totality" of bedevilment which called for radical deliverance. No wonder her tears mesh with tenacity. Peering once more into the tomb, she finds herself spoken to by a sympathetic angel. Turning around in shocked confusion, she thinks she sees the gardener. "Mary," Jesus says tenderly; and wild with joy she fairly flies at her Rabboni! Gently the Teacher draws back from her embrace and speaks of His ascension. It is the prerequisite of Pentecost and the miracle of the intimacy and immediacy of God unfettered by time and space — available to every man and woman in Christ.

God walked in Eden's garden to teach joyous intimacy between the sexes and with Himself. Bedeviled Eve in naked terror fled from His voice. Eden's angel communicated terminal separation with his flaming sword. In the garden of Easter the deadly order was reversed. Mary typifies Eve's redemption. The first Adam could not help her. The "last Adam" Jesus Christ was able — and still is. This last Adam healed John of his need to be first. In Easter's Eden God's men and women initiate the fellowship of the forgiven.

John 20:1 □ John 20:1-18

First of all you must understand this, that scoffers will come in the last days with scoffing, following their own passions and saying, "Where is the promise of his coming?"

Peter had his scoffers labeled and lambasted. Do we? What do we make of his conclusion that God is "not wishing that any should perish, but that all should reach repentance?" Scripture is good at such tension. The Bible is mirror more than road map, always pressing for fresh self-examination.

All right. Today's scoffer doesn't buy Christmas. To him it makes dollars and cents only. We cannot spring Easter on him. "He is risen." Indeed! How much water does the once-a-year proclamation hold with death, doubt and despair as rampant as ever. The Shroud of Turin does not help. The scoffer might side with testy old Calvin who was as content as the gospel writers to let "the linen cloths lie . . ."

It matters little to the scoffer that history is divided into B.C. and A.D., or that "dark" Africa is fast becoming the foremost Christian continent. The thin veneer of Western civilization is barely holding back the jungle of urban violence. Europe's grand cathedrals are lifeless shells afflicted with industrial pollution. America's congregations suffer the pinch of inflation and the plague of consumerism that shops for creature comforts more than for courses in how to lay down one's life.

Let not the scoffer's arrogance bring out our own. There, but for the grace of God, go I! The scoffer, nailed painfully to the narrow scope of his passions, must surely have a remnant of instinct for the historic miracles of Easter and Pentecost. Adrift and helpless against the shifting sands of time, could he not be a candidate for the hope of Christ's return in glory? In the tension between scoffer and saint, we can either give as good as we get; give in to our brand of cynicism; or give ourselves away afresh in creative risk-taking. Christ did not blast the scoffing thief on the cross. He blessed the one who reached repentance through His obedience. If we scoff at radical obedience for our Christian life, we have no right to scorn scoffers.

2 Peter 3:3-4

Sir, we wish to see Jesus.

The request is polite and to the point. These Greek Jews who had traveled to Jerusalem for the Passover stepped into a hotbed of rumor and speculation. Lazarus had been raised from the dead; Jesus rode into the city and was hailed King; the religious establishment was plotting to kill both. Caught up in the ferment of the day — unable to get an unbiased opinion — these devout Greeks sought to see for themselves.

Scripture is silent on their reception, but eloquent in Christ's terse reply to Philip and Andrew who acted as go-betweens. "And Jesus answered them, 'The hour has come for the Son of man to be glorified. . . . If any one serves me, he must follow me . . .'" Overwhelmed by His own sense of urgency, He then speaks the heart-rending line, "Now is my soul troubled."

It may well be troubled still. The inquiring Greeks are still with us and more than ever they hunger for a personal introduction to Jesus Christ. They have seen the slogans on our Christian T-shirts and bumper stickers, listened to our jargon, browsed through our tapes and jewelry symbols. They have considered our slick invitations to crusades and "Bring an unchurched neighbor to the Super-Sunday-Extravaganza." They have endured our impeccable smiles and awkward back-slaps.

"Sir, we wish to see Jesus." All right, I welcome you into my own life. I will take you into my hurts and hopes, strengths and weaknesses. I will take you into my relationship with the Father. I will give you the courtesy of a willing ear and the empathy of a hearing heart. I will take greater time still in deep silence before my God, and in faithful intercession that your hunger might be satisfied. I will be a witness to His glory and power, and dare you to become Christ's own disciple!

John 12:21 □ *John 12:20-36*

Now I know in part; then I shall understand fully, even as I have been fully understood.

What a pity that we become so familiar with a text that it loses its punch. Feed "1 Corinthians 13" into the Christian computer and out comes "The Love Chapter, of course." Poor material for soap operas where jealousy and resentment are joyously honed to a fine art for invigorating people's lives and loves. "Love is" and "Love does" a number of things that give us fits just the same. Unable to practice such love, we romanticize the text and love it for its poetry.

If we are to get fresh perspective on familiar text and fossilized thinking, we must allow the Holy Spirit to restore Paul's own humanity for us, to put us on common ground. We have an unfortunate tendency to eviscerate the saints of old when in fact they were men and women "of like nature with ourselves" and eminently capable of displaying it.

Notice how the author of the love chapter ends his letter, "I, Paul, write this greeting with my own hand. If any one has no love for the Lord, let him be accursed." What if our pastor told some of us to go to hell? What happened to the love that hopes all things and is never rude? Did Christ damn people for not loving His Father or did He woo them to His very dying day?

It is all right to embrace the poetry of the love chapter, if we also grasp the practical, obvious truth. God through Paul is not cataloging our failure potential, but is disclosing His very own astonishing love for us. The crowning glory of such disclosure is summed up in "I have been fully understood." Savor that! We all ache to be fully understood. Who else could give us that unspeakable assurance but the true Author of the whole love story Himself. When we are fully loved and understood, we receive power to become effective lovers.

1 Corinthians 13:12 □ 1 Corinthians 13

Say to Hezekiah, "Thus says the great king, the king of Assyria: On what do you rest this confidence of yours?"

It takes a swashbuckling Sennacherib to peel back the protective layers of our psyche to expose the character of our innermost being. Glory be if Christian Swashbuckler steps forth and rises to the occasion! Horror of horrors if Joe C. Churchgoer (C. as in chicken) is found cowering in there.

Joe C. Churchgoer dislikes bloodthirsty Assyrians. They make for messy Old Testament stories. Sennacherib's chief emissary to beleaguered Hezekiah, King of Judah, crudely threatens that the Jews will "eat their own dung and drink their own urine." Joe C. Churchgoer would rather have violence on television than bathroom talk in the Bible. He wants his God sanitized and his cup running over with ceremonial tea, not sacrificial blood.

The Christian swashbuckler learns to relish the robust flavor of meaty tales that flesh out spiritual principles by translating them into rugged action. In their historical setting he recognizes His timeless, unchanging God. Amidst the plotting and slaughtering of adversaries he traces divine peacemaking. His faith is nerved and steeled as he lives in Hezekiah's skin and tastes the taxing emotions of extreme fear and extreme abandonment on God alone.

When Sennacherib's army is decimated by disease and he meets death at the hands of sons, Christian Swashbuckler is not embarrassed for his God. He remembers the Assyrians' taunt, "Do you think that mere words are strategy and power for war?" And Hezekiah's sorely tested confidence, "The Lord will surely deliver us" becomes his own.

Make no mistake though. Christian "swashbuckling" has nothing to do with eccentric behavior and boastful manner. It is a profoundly centered inner strength. The Carpenter of Nazareth had it. His "daredevil" attitude met its final test on the cross.

Isaiah 36:4 ☐ Isaiah 36 and 37

Most blessed of women be Jael, the wife of Heber the Kenite, of tent-dwelling women most blessed . . . She struck Sisera a blow, she crushed his head, she shattered and pierced his temple . . . Where he sank, there he fell dead.

Will the congregation please stand and sing this verse from Deborah's 12th-Century B.C. hymn of praise. Most likely we would rather choke than oblige the mad clergyman. How could we sing this so-called song with any degree of sincerity? Would it help if we sensed Deborah's tenderness in these poignant words, "Out of the window she peered, the mother of Sisera gazed through the lattice: 'Why is his chariot so long in coming?'"

This awful mingling of blood and tears, triumph and tragedy, is recorded in prose in the fourth chapter of Judges. Deborah — prophetess, judge, militant heroine — together with Barak rallied the Israelites in a decisive attack on Sisera, a Canaanite warrior who with his hordes had raided them for twenty years. Barak wound up in the heroes' gallery of faith in Hebrews 11:32. Perhaps there is a touch of male chauvinism in that. Barak had refused the campaign until Deborah agreed to march with him. "And she said, 'I will surely go with you; nevertheless, the road on which you are going will not lead to your glory, for the Lord will sell Sisera into the hand of a woman.'"

That is the point! Deborah acknowledged the hand of the Lord in the affairs of her day and when He triumphed, she celebrated their deliverance in gloriously graphic song. Listen to the magnificent words of this liberated woman: "From heaven fought the stars, from their courses they fought on against Sisera. The torrent Kishon swept them away . . . March on, my soul, with might!"

Judges 5:24-27 ☐ Judges 5

Through him then let us continually offer up a sacrifice of praise to God, that is, the fruit of lips that acknowledge his name.

If lay ministry is to become more than a fascination for the fortunate few with time and interest to receive training and encouragement, we need to examine the "sacrifice of praise" in the light of the New Testament priesthood.

Peter explodes our parochial notions with this passionate plea to a persecuted and dispersed church that could hardly stage the kind of leadership seminars we take for granted: "But you are a chosen race, a royal priesthood, a holy nation, God's own people, that you may declare the wonderful deeds of him who called you out of darkness into his marvelous light" (1 Peter 2:9). We routinely associate the call of God with going away to seminary or the mission field abroad. Peter emphatically says come. "Come to him . . . to offer spiritual sacrifices acceptable to God through Jesus Christ" (1 Peter 2:4-5).

Perhaps we ought to say "holy priesthood" when we mean lay ministry, and put the fear of God into the silent Sunday morning majority. The priesthood of all believers is awesome precisely because it is a divine gift, not duty instituted by man and marked by rite and rote. Praise flows naturally from a feasted soul and grateful heart. When we begin to express that praise in the flow of ordinary life and conversation, it becomes the spiritual sacrifice pleasing to our Lord.

A priest stands between almighty God and needy fellow man. Spirit-filled, we identify both with God's character and man's condition. We are a visible, organic bridge. We bridge the gap of theological abstractions with the example of our Christ-enabled life. In the process God becomes real to others as well and faith is reproduced naturally. Such is the promise of joyous priesthood.

Hebrews 13:15 ☐ *Hebrews 13:7-16*

Many Samaritans from that city believed in him because of the woman's testimony, "He told me all that I ever did."

Incredible. Here is heart-stopping, dynamite-packed witnessing. It requires reverence because it exposes our Lord's work. The story goes hand-in-hand with His teaching in verse 35, "I tell you, lift up your eyes, and see how the fields are already white for harvest." He speaks of ease and urgency in evangelism.

High noon! Shimmering heat dancing on the roofs of Sychar. The lonely figure of a woman emerges from the gate. Notice the proud tilt of her head. It says she would rather put up with the heat than the scorching looks of gossiping women who draw water in early morning. How graceful this survivor-type walks considering the load she carries. It consists of the water jar; the emotional freight of moral bankruptcy; the stigma of her mongrel race; the heartbreak of a religion small enough for her understanding but not big enough for her need. Let "High Noon" take place between her and the Savior privately.

Now watch this emotional cripple, this social misfit — watch her leave the jar at the well while she goes and jars the people of Sychar, "He told me all that I ever did!" They could have stoned her for confirming such. Instead, they are stirred to life by the wind of the Spirit. They see in the woman a clean earthen vessel filled with inviting water. No wonder they drink — swallow the bait — and go and receive the gift of salvation for themselves.

What then is our most valuable evangelistic tool? Our personal showdown with Christ, no doubt. Convicted, grace becomes convincing. Transformed, we become transformers. In union with Him, barriers vanish. When His work becomes our witness, witnessing is as natural as breathing. Indeed, the very breath of God is in us. Our personal risk? Considerable — and worth it!

John 4:39 □ John 4:1-42

O LORD, thou hast searched me and known me!

O David, you should have dropped the subject right then and there! Or the King could have dropped His subject, David, right into the "Pit" of fatal embarrassments. Who can forget the rape and pregnancy of Bathsheba — an affair so bungled that it culminated in murder? But Psalm 51 is public proof of David's restoration to favor.

Why then is David freshly disturbing us: O Lord, you have prowled and poked around in the hidden recesses of my mind and emotions and discovered the key to the trunk in the attic where I keep my secrets. There are pictures and words and tightly coiled angers, pills and cancers and death never buried. There are costumes to dress my living nightmares, and hidden explosives tied to each piece. O Lord!

"O Lord, thou hast searched me and known me!" Why does it suddenly sound like a sigh of relief? O Lord, I nearly killed myself and others dragging that trunk all over damnation hoping to rid myself of its secrets. You followed me until my strength gave out. Then you put your key to the lock and took everything out. Not one thing shocked you. As I read your thoughts they were precious to me. I saw myself when you first thought of me and formed me in my mother's womb. I discovered hope and wanted to wrest it from you and lock it in my trunk for safekeeping. But you had that removed along with my sorrows and said that my hope was in you — and you would never leave me. O Lord!

Sense the tenderness between God and David in those thankful words. Appropriate the robust energy of the triumphant conclusion, "Search me, O God, and know my heart! Try me and know my thoughts! And see if there be any wicked way in me, and lead me in the way everlasting!"

Psalm 139:1 ☐ *Psalm 139*

The men did so, and took two milch cows and yoked them to the cart, and shut up their calves at home. And they put the ark of the LORD on the cart, and the box with the golden mice and the images of their tumors.

The ancients had ways of exorcising their ills that strike us as humorous. It is permissible to laugh if we give them equal time to scrutinize our customs. The main consideration is that the living God worked out His purpose in concert with the primitive concepts of the day and His lesson endures.

In the days when Samuel was judge, the Philistines did battle with Israel who fared poorly. So they sent for the ark of the covenant at Shiloh and when it arrived in camp, a great roar of approval went up. The Philistines figured that a powerful idol had joined the enemy's rank and in due time they captured it. They brought it as a souvenir to their god Dagon and placed it at his side. To their chagrin Dagon could not take the competition and fell face down before the ark. His unperceiving priests propped him back up — knock on wood — but Dagon defied them and had a terminal fall. From then on the ark wore out its welcome fast.

Bubonic plague afflicted the land and its people suffered emerods, which is King James English for Hebrew hemorrhoids — no laughing matter as any TV commercial will solemnly assure us. A bit of gentle humor applies to the ancient artisan who was commissioned to cast five golden mice and five golden emerods. These were sent as a guilt offering to the powerful God of Israel.

Perhaps the Philistines would chuckle at the money raked in by some of our mental health professionals. Perhaps a golden emerod is akin to a five-thousand-dollar phobia, put on public parade for the purpose of exorcising it. Be it as it may, the ancients do teach us a graphically illustrated truth: We cannot hide what God wants brought out into the open.

1 Samuel 6:10-11 ☐ *1 Samuel 5:1-6:16*

And you, who were dead in trespasses . . . God made alive together with him . . . having canceled the bond which stood against us with its legal demands; this he set aside, nailing it to the cross.

Paul is hammering home a vital distinction that is crucial to our overall health. Grace is mere spiritual luxury if we continue to die inch by inch because of debilitating memories. Grace with shirt sleeves rolled up insists that the past is dead and buried; "we have been born anew to a living hope through the resurrection. . . "

Does a pardoned convict elect to remain behind bars? Many a Christian would rather suffer from an impeded life than consent to the ministrations of a "shrink." When our soul shrinks back from the foremost source of healing, we grieve God more than we do a spurned professional. Why shrink back from the starkly simple truth that Christ paid an awesome price for the sheer privilege of seeing our burdens permanently lifted?

The things that haunt us in the quiet moments of our busy lives are the hidden traitors to the wholeness that constitutes the very heart of salvation. We may have subscribed to the pop psychology of "Forget it! Life is too short!" — but our psyche is not long fooled. All spiritually unredeemed business creates unholy energy that drains and damages us in insidious ways.

We must resolutely confess before God — perhaps in the company of a trusted encourager — the taxing memory, and then declare it dead and paid for in full. In doing so we do not empty ourselves of memories, but are relieved of parasitical energy that saps us of mental, physical and emotional health. The spiritual process becomes ultimately rewarding when grace is finally fleshed out in the person happily at home in our own skin.

Colossians 2:13-14 □ *Colossians 2:8-15*

When you come, bring the cloak that I left with Carpus at Troas, also the books, and above all the parchments. Alexander the coppersmith did me great harm; the Lord will requite him for his deeds.

Last-minute pressures, whether we must conclude a letter or conversation, can play havoc with the mind. The trivial and important race each other in a perplexing free-for-all: In closing, Aunt Helen's cat had kittens and when you are home next time you have to clear out your bureau because Dad wants to put his stamps in there. Did you hear that Harry was killed in a motorcycle accident? Write soon and tell us how you did in the finals. Do they still serve soggy French toast? Love, Mom.

Paul rattles off a whole list of names and things that occupy him at the last minute, not necessarily in order of importance. It is really all parenthetical to the main thrust of the final chapter: "I have fought the good fight" and "the Lord stood by me and gave me strength."

If Paul had had the extra time and paper, that rather casual mention of Alexander could have been presented as red-hot drama. When Alexander the Son of a Gun did Paul great harm, he was taxed to the utmost not by the coppersmith's action, but his own reaction. There is a good reason to believe that the former persecutor's blood boiled violently. The Holy Spirit is not in the milque-toast business. He did not mean for Paul the Fighter to take it lying down. So He slugged it out with Paul on the battleground of his soul until he could honestly say, "The Lord will requite him for his deeds."

If hostile energy had still been part of Paul's chemistry, God would not have allowed His statesman to mention Alexander's name in the letter. The Holy Spirit would have checked him and battled afresh. "The Lord will requite him for his deeds." Only tested grace with guts can say that.

2 Timothy 4:13-14

For, in the first place, when you assemble as a church, I hear that there are divisions among you; and I partly believe it, for there must be factions among you in order that those who are genuine among you may be recognized.

Paul is in good company; we only "partly believe" what he says. We say there must be unity in the church and factions should not be recognized. Gossip, rumors and grumblers — yes. Factions — no! The dignity of the church must be preserved at all cost. It is, after all, not the circus. Wrong, says Paul the spiritual Ringmaster.

In ancient Rome a faction happened to be one of the divisions of charioteers who raced in the circus, distinguishable by the color of their costumes. In turn, the cheering masses took to wearing the color of their favorite team. The modern sports scene did not invent a thing. In applying Roman circus jargon to the church, Paul in effect is saying to us: Think faction and you know who the clowns are. Think faction and you know who runs things well. Think faction and you will recognize if we have our act together. Show your true color!

If dignity is still the name of the game because we have elevated churchmanship to such a high degree, let us redefine the church as the forum where the acts of the Holy Spirit are to take place. The forum is, of course, the marketplace — and the sooner the church moves there the better our public places will become.

Wherever we "assemble as a church" we are the "called out." Called out to a special place and purpose as salt and light to the world, we are to be within reach of those who despair of darkness and despise blandness. The name of the game is contest, not holy huddle. If the church is to become the forum of genuine faith, we had better start recognizing factions and showing true color to Jesus Christ.

1 Corinthians 11:18-19

Therefore, since we are surrounded by so great a cloud of witnesses . . . let us run with perseverance the race that is set before us, looking to Jesus the pioneer and perfecter . . .

The track looks abandoned and the stadium deserted, except for a nondescript group of family and friends eager to watch their pride and joy train. Those in the grandstand do not have hot-dog-and-peanut-flavored names: Abel, Enoch, Sarah, Moses, Rahab the harlot, Samson . . . but they do know every weight and sin the runner must lay aside before he can effectively run. The weight of public opinion. The sin of self-sufficiency. Before the runner is allowed to run laps he must train on that kind of obstacle course, lest he run in circles of frustration. It is punishing warm-up but the audience cheers as if it were the main event.

The main event is perseverance. The Coach embodies and enforces it. Skills and styles and the way they are judged change with the times and their sophistication. Perseverance must excel in and of itself. It is hardly a spectator sport, but rather a discipline aimed at pleasing the Pioneer and Perfecter of our faith alone. It means cramps and nausea and exhaustion — and always the quest for efficient breathing. Pushed to our natural limits and lungs seared with pain, we want to draw the shallow breaths of ordinary life. But Jesus insists that the second wind of the Holy Spirit comes again and again to those who deeply ache for Him.

Of Moses it is said, "He endured as seeing him who is invisible." That is the joyous reward of the runner. Possessed of a faith pioneered and perfected by none other than Jesus, we can endure the temporal and visible as a fleeting scene, while we are anchored to the exceeding reality of eternity. Such is the paradox and assurance of the perseverer.

Hebrews 12:1-2 ☐ *Hebrews 11:1-12:2*

Enoch walked with God; and he was not, for God took him.

"He has showed you, O man, what is good; and what does the Lord require of you but to do justice, and to love kindness, and to walk humbly with your God?" (Micah 6:8). To probe even deeper into the mystery of Enoch's walk, we must consider a few "begats": Adam, Seth, Enosh, Kenan, Mahalalel, Jared, Enoch, Methuselah, Lamech, and Noah.

Adam was created in the image of God. Because of sin, in Noah's day "the Lord saw that the wickedness of man was great in the earth . . ." But when He blessed Noah after the Flood, God reiterated the preciousness of His crowning creation, "Whoever sheds the blood of man, by man shall his blood be shed; for God made man in his own image." At Calvary the blood of the Redeemer would purchase back moral likeness, enabling us to be called holy. The natural likeness of intellectual and emotional capacity continued to exist.

The idea of Genesis genealogy is not to quibble over a thousand or a million years here and there, but to zero in on key truth. Man from the beginning carried with him a sense of his image of God. He instinctively understood the unfolding of redemptive history. The recording of key names and births and spiritual bench marks forged vital links in keeping alive God's yearning for man and man's yearning for God.

Enoch's walk with God — between Eden and the Flood — was so exemplary that he was spared physical death. His walk began after the birth of his first son. Had the walk with the child of his own image stirred the memory of Eden's privilege? Did he so live out his image of God that it enabled the Creator to demonstrate the reward of immortality to Enoch's contemporaries? What if we stirred up our remembered gift of Eden and became a vital link in fleshing out the image of God? That is the purpose of Redemption.

Genesis 5:24 □ *Genesis 5*

For thus says the high and lofty One who inhabits eternity, whose name is Holy: "I dwell in the high and holy place, and also with him who is of a contrite and humble spirit . . .

Why not be as practical as God? We try to measure up to a deity that exists mostly in our imagination; impossibly lofty, at least ten feet tall and incredibly complicated. As a result we deify the clergy because they have domesticated God enough to make Him publicly satisfying.

We need to shake off learned inspiration long enough to develop instinct. If deep within our genetic make-up there is innate knowledge of God, we owe it to ourselves to excavate it to the conscious surface. Eternity is not measured in millennia but in the simple truth that God is the same yesterday, today and tomorrow. So we do not dig a hole into time, but explore the wholeness that exists around us right now.

Follow young parents with their firstborn from hospital to home, both thrilled and scared to death. Indoctrinated by books, classes and experts, they have absorbed all the lofty rhetoric about bonding and impacting. They are in such awe and agreement that by the time they place the embodiment of their learning into a brand-new crib, they have zero confidence. And then the baby cries and the breast promptly leaks milk. From times immemorial babies have cried and nursed and been comforted with the gentle swaying motion that duplicates the mystery of the womb. Instinct develops our own expertise and places the experts' inspiration in proper perspective.

To the brains at Athens who maintained an altar "To an unknown god," the intellectual giant of the church said, "Yet he is not far from each one of us, for 'In him we live and move and have our being'; as even some of your poets have said, 'For we are indeed his offspring'" (Acts 17:27-28). If we act on that powerful instinct, God himself will mightily inspire us.

Isaiah 57:15

I waited patiently for the LORD; *he inclined to me and heard my cry.*

The newborn infant cannot wait and so he wails. As his digestive system matures, he becomes more civilized. Other changes occur. The eyes begin to focus. The shadowy presence hovering over him becomes a smiling face that emits pleasing sounds. The baby smiles back and coos.

Emotional ties are nurtured by the daily ministrations of his parents. The simple rhythm of feeding, burping, diapering, etc. establishes a frame of reference that he can grasp because he derives obvious comfort from it. One day the miracle happens: the baby awakens and does not immediately cry. Freed from the introspection of a tyrannical stomach, he kicks up his legs and studies the acrobatics of tiny fingers released from the clenched fist. A fascinating world is opening to him daily — and it expands in direct proportion to his growing ability to experience it by sight and touch for himself. Yet his central existence revolves around the parent who responds to his cry of need.

If we have never savored our spiritual infancy and because of that are cranky, unfulfilled theologians, we are invited to retrace it. As we parallel our natural and spiritual development, we are struck by the image of God that so clearly complements our femaleness and maleness. Has He not given us spiritual milk from His own breast — the basic nourishment of love thrust at our basic need in the flesh of Jesus Christ? Did He not burp us when He withdrew understanding for truth we could not yet digest? Did He not diaper us when He quietly removed the consequences of our carelessness? The God who fathered us has mothered us well.

"I waited patiently . . ." The next time we feel like crying for God, shall we first gauge our maturity impulse? Perhaps we should check off reasons for basic confidence and then cheer on our growing sense of adventure. God is only a smile away.

Psalm 40:1 ☐ *Psalm 40*

*He drew me up from the desolate pit, out of the miry bog, and
set my feet upon a rock, making my steps secure.*

Ancient youth and modern teenager down in the dumps.
The pitfalls of awful adolescence and the wonderful timeless-
ness of it all! The translators note that in Hebrew the desolate
pit is rendered "pit of tumult." Ah, the pain and promise of our
tumultuous years!

There is little virtue in childlike faith that has never under-
gone the ferment of honest, anguished questioning. The
relative security of childhood faith is valid within the limited
experience that mostly centers on the home turf. But when the
cynical circumstances of life pull the familiar rug from under
our feet, we had better not stand on the untested convictions of
the child. A child in trouble knows that his parents are bound
to deliver him from it. The seasoned saint learns that the
quickest way out of trouble is inevitably through it. In time we
take to problems like a weightlifter takes to his weights — it is
the stuff that builds muscle and makes us spiritually fit.

When childhood fades into oblivion — and indeed we push
it away because new longings are stirred and it no longer
satisfies — we enter the time of the "miry bog" where familiar
footholds are ruthlessly removed. We want to step out on our
own but go under again and again rather than forward. We are
angry that the familiar landscape of faith no longer exists. We
develop crushes on those with charisma and feel let down when
they cannot fill the void of our tormented, expectant heart.
Experiences that we sought eagerly turn sour, and when chron-
ologicially speaking we should be at our peak, we are washed
up on the shores of confusion.

The Rock of Jesus Christ is an optical illusion until we have
found ourselves in the bottomless pit of violently aborted self-
sufficiency. When that Rock becomes real we have a security
that can never be threatened again.

Psalm 40:2 ☐ *Psalm 40*

He put a new song in my mouth, a song of praise to our God.
Many will see and fear, and put their trust in the LORD.

The day we claim our birthright — of Father, Son, Holy
Spirit — we have truly come of age and the new song of praise
in our mouth reverberates through the very heavens. God is
"enthroned on the praises" of His people.

Praise occupies a unique place in the ways we manifest our
spiritual maturity. It can never be counterfeit! Every single
spiritual gift — prophecy, tongues, healing, miracles — can be
faked. From the magicians at Pharaoh's court right down to the
spiritual stuntmen of our age, impressive shows can be had
without the Good Housekeeping Seal of heaven. True to the
warning in Revelation, there are congregations today who
masquerade as "lampstands," but their light has been removed
because they left their first love, Jesus Christ.

Our practice of thanks depends on the benevolent acts and
serendipities of God. Praise is independent of all external
motivation. It flows from the well of salvation at the core of
our being. That well is fed by the streams of the Holy Spirit —
issuing from and addressing the very character of God. Praise
is the exquisite attainment of truth that we were created in His
own image and likeness; it validates His eminent joy over our
creation — "And behold, it was very good."

"Many will see and fear, and put their trust in the Lord."
Praise that flows joyously from the life of a saint becomes
discernible spiritual authority. It is acknowledged with
reverence; God's own greatness is recognized. Praise generates
witnessing power that draws directly to the Person of Jesus
Christ. A person of praise is genuinely humble. There are no
neon signs advertising that he ranks with angels in ministering
to God. But he does.

Psalm 40:3 ☐ *Psalm 40*

Nevertheless, do not rejoice in this, that the spirits are subject to you; but rejoice that your names are written in heaven.

We pray so routinely in Jesus' name, Amen. Is it habit or invitation to power? When we hold healing services and emphasize our prayerful concern for the "whole" person, are we so cognizant of the effect of thoughts and emotions on the body, or are we protecting ourselves against disappointment when no visible healing takes place? What about the disturbed person who is the bane of clergy and worshiper alike? Why are we polite pacifiers but not passionate peacemakers? Where do we need Christ's correction as we go about using His name?

In the latter days of His ministry Jesus appointed seventy others in addition to the twelve disciples. These He sent by twos into every town and place He was about to enter. They were to heal the sick and say to them, "The kingdom of God has come near to you." As a parting shot in the arm of the dazed duos — just put yourself in their shoes! — He assured them, "He who hears you hears me, and he who rejects you rejects me . . ."

They probably took off like men with a dentist's appointment, only to run back like Cub Scouts after a terrific scavenger hunt, "Lord, even the demons are subject to us in your name!" Boy, if they could franchise that name as the McDonald's of Miracles — just imagine — over 1000 healed! But Jesus reduced the sizzle to a sobering statement: Be glad you are rightly related to God. Only that counts for good!

There is no other truth, "no other name under heaven given among men by which we must be saved." If the church is to act decisively on that truth, how do we score our confidence? How many healed of infirmities? How many healed of demons? How many served in Christ's name? If that name is habit, none! If it is our eternal habitation, we count ourselves blessed!

Luke 10:20 ☐ *Luke 10:1-23*

For I have not spoken on my own authority; the Father who sent me has himself given me commandment what to say and what to speak. And I know that his commandment is eternal life.

When the Word incarnate uses such striking language, it merits our attention. There is veiled promise — not redundancy — in the phrase, ". . . what to say and what to speak." Verse forty-four has already revealed the intensely emotional state Jesus was in when He "cried out and said, 'He who believes in me, believes not in me but in him who sent me."

A bit of amateur detective work sheds light on the hunch that this is not run-of-the-mill saying and speaking. It is not speech, not utterance of sound. To "say" means to "bring word" in the form of individual expression, in the sense of "an indivisible entity or totality which cannot be separated into parts without altering the character or significance of these parts." To "speak" means to speak after, proclaim publicly — to praise!

Of course the gospel writer was more succinct than the dictionary writer. "And the Word became flesh" delivers more punch than mere "individual expression." "And the Word was God" is far easier on the eye than "an indivisible entity . . ." But familiarity can breed rote and we lose the power of revelation. If Christians were to be quizzed on the most trenchant saying of Christ, "love" would be the runaway choice. But attached to that oft-expressed love is a ho-hum element that flowers and fades with the Christmas season. We have made it a part-time expression.

"The Father who sent me has himself given me commandment what to say and what to speak." His commandment is eternal life. Whether some will spend it with Him may depend on only one thing: Do we so know and identify with our Lord — not His teachings, but the Teacher — that we know "what to say and what to speak" in His name?

John 12:49-50 ☐ *John 12:44-50*

These things have I spoken to you, that my joy may be in you, and, that your joy may be full.

The doorbell rings; it must be the repairman. For what has He come? So many things are wrong. We have lost track of the many calls we made. No wonder. We are burdened with our neighbor's affairs as well, not to mention the headaches at church. What shall we tell Jesus when He walks in and opens His tool chest to go to work?

The doorbell rings and we fly to the door. There stands Jesus, leaning in the door frame, wearing His biggest smile and holding out the loveliest bunch of flowers. And we? We slam the door in His face! Not once or twice, but perhaps a whole lifetime. Oh yes, we still go to heaven. But we, the good religious, helped fulfill Isaiah's prophecy, "He was despised and rejected by men . . . and we esteemed him not" (53:3).

We little esteem the compliment of a fellow Christian. Perhaps we have made a comment or performed a small deed that elicits a spontaneous affirmation of our standing in Christ. The standard pious reply? "Oh, it was nothing. It certainly wasn't me. Once in a while Christ does come through in me. Praise the Lord." It sounds terribly humble and spiritual — what it exactly is: terrible. If we say that, we have just withered another blossom in the bouquet of joy Christ meant for us to delight in.

Christ did not come from heaven to "come through us once in a while" like a freight train that drops off a package for us if we are lucky. He came to dwell in us fully and to manifest that fulness as joy! When the fulness spills over into the life of another we are to savor the blessing. We say thank you when complimented on a new tie. Shall we not say thank you when praised for the new life in us? Until we make joy our top priority we use God's name in vain and that profanity is greater than the casual "goddamn" of the unsaved.

John 15:11 ☐ John 15:1-11

For this reason I bow my knees before the Father . . .

This is not the prayer posture of penitence or petition. Something threw Paul to his knees! The proper Jewish way of prayer — both for the upright and downcast in Paul's time — was to stand. Jesus' parable of pleasing prayer illustrates this. "The Pharisee stood and prayed thus . . . But the tax collector, standing far off, would not even lift up his eyes to heaven . . ." (Luke 18:11,13).

What was the magnitude of revelation that literally "floored" Paul? This proud Pharisee and chief sinner had received power to comprehend "the breadth and length and height and depth" of Christ's love "which surpasses knowledge." "Filled with all the fulness of God," Paul was felled by joy. This was not sentiment, but the very substance of unconditional surrender. As such it was an act of enormous consecration and consequence on behalf of "all the saints." You and I who run on flashlight batteries are destined for nuclear power as well.

Have we known this rapture to the very heights of powerful paradox: Because of Christ's debasement, God "highly exalted him and bestowed on him the name which is above every name, that at the name of Jesus every knee should bow . . . to the glory of God the Father" (Philippians 2:9-11). Have we been struck by the force of prophecy that elevates the passage far beyond our range of options: "To me every knee shall bow, every tongue shall swear" (Isaiah 45:23). Baal worship in ancient Israel involved kneeling and touching lips to the mouth of idols. If God's joy does not throw us, His jealousy will!

Many Christians employ the posture of bent knees. But does the Body of Christ exhibit the power of the bowed knee? At stake is not the reputation of the local church, but the very glory of God the Father. Perhaps we must start our "descent" to power with penitence and petition.

Ephesians 3:14 □ *Ephesians 3:14-19*

When Daniel knew that the document had been signed, he went to his house where he had windows in his upper chamber open toward Jerusalem; and he got down upon his knees three times a day and prayed and gave thanks before his God, as he had done previously.

The document of infamy would land Daniel in the lions' den. That was child's play compared to the drama lurking behind those cool words, ". . . as he had done previously." Daniel's devotional life is overshadowed by the history at the heart of his routinely powerful prayers.

Stepping back some 300 years into the seven days that marked the dedication of Solomon's temple, we realize the enormity of the event when we gag at the sacrifice of 22,000 oxen and 120,000 sheep. When fire fell from heaven to consume the king's offering, "the priests could not enter the house of the Lord, because the glory of the Lord filled the Lord's house" (2 Chronicles 7:2-5). Holy Smoke, indeed!

Slaughterhouse setting and flawed ruler aside, the true meat of the story is found in Solomon's epic prayer of consecration. This portion of the prayer directly inspired Daniel's prayer life: "If they sin against thee — for there is no man who does not sin — and thou . . . dost give them to an enemy, so that they are carried away captive to the land of the enemy . . . if they repent with all their mind and with all their heart . . . and pray to thee toward their land . . . and the house which I have built for thy name; then hear thou in heaven thy dwelling place their prayer and their supplication, and maintain their cause . . ." (1 Kings 8).

God's covenant plus man's consecration equal magnificent consequences within the timeless community of faith — for His name's sake. Routinely powerful prayers for us? Holy Smoke, glory be — yes!

Daniel 6:10 □ *Daniel 6*

Then King Darius wrote to all the peoples, nations, and languages that dwell in all the earth: "Peace be multiplied to you."

That small, well-worn piece about Daniel in the lions' den is eclipsed by the magnificence of the King's Peace. Not that this was the great Darius who put Persia on the map in the wake of Cyrus' death and the revolts that subsequently shook the empire. That Darius reigned during the post-exilic period. And that Darius was given to violent prose in the cause of our Lord, "Also I make a decree that if any one alters this edict, a beam shall be pulled out of his house, and he shall be pulled out of his house, and he shall be impaled upon it, and his house shall be made a dunghill" (Ezra 6:11).

Our Darius was merely "the Mede" who had captured Babylon and ruled it as governor-type during King Cyrus' absences. Technically speaking, our Darius said quite a mouthful when in the wake of Daniel's deliverance from the lions he addressed his decree "to all the peoples, nations, and languages that dwell in all the earth." In terms of world community his decree had the clout of a poster in a neighborhood supermarket. Or did it? Was government able to pull this one off?

Not surprisingly perhaps, Darius' decree is a remarkable paraphrase of prophecy: "Turn to me and be saved, all the ends of the earth! For I am God, and there is no other. By myself I have sworn, from my mouth has gone forth in righteousness a word that shall not return: 'To me every knee shall bow, every tongue shall swear'" (Isaiah 45:22-23).

It follows then that government did pull it off, "For to us a child is born, to us a son is given; and the government will be upon his shoulder, and his name will be called 'Wonderful Counselor, Mighty God, Everlasting Father, Prince of Peace'" (Isaiah 9:6). May peace be multiplied to you and me as together we discover the true might of His name. In Jesus' name, Amen.

Daniel 6:25 ☐ *Daniel 6*

Because you did not serve the LORD *your God with joyfulness and gladness of heart, by reason of the abundance of all things, therefore you shall serve your enemies . . . and in want of all things . . .*

Commandment turned curse. This is not ecclesiastical mumbo jumbo, but elementary neighborhood gym jargon. Use it or lose it! That goes for muscle, mind, or the love of God. The mystery of the "wrath of God" is ridiculously simple. If our flabby will sees in God too tough a taskmaster, He will in love acquiesce to that will and relinquish us into self-mastery.

Slowly, imperceptibly, His resources dwindle away. In time we are forced to feed on the natural substance of heredity and environment. Soon we reap the whirlwind of the vengefully bred extinction that has haunted the species from the dawn of time. When self-love is extinct and leaves behind the wasteland of our self-despising, we have arrived at the wrath of God. Cut off from the impulse of love, we project on Him all our negations. The wrath of God, then, is inherently in our own condition, not in His character. God is love!

When God's commandment is spurned and natural capacity takes over, the human condition is capable of such curse — literally, excommunication — as this: "The most tender and delicately bred woman among you . . . will grudge to the husband of her bosom . . . her afterbirth that comes out from between her feet and her children whom she bears, because she will eat them secretly . . ."(Deuteronomy 28:56-57). You understand, the lady is sneaking food; she will not share bloody membrane or scrawny newborn with her starving family! Shall we blame this on God who is love?

God in His mercy gave Israel ten commandments to keep them from self-degradation. How quick we are to boast of grace. But grace never rules out exercise of will. If we ignore that, the Mosaic curse of the law is as potent as ever. How much of our civilized world is crumbling from the wrath of God right now?

Deuteronmy 28:47-48 ☐ *Deuteronomy 28*

And Jesus looking upon him loved him, and said to him, "You lack one thing . . ."

If we think for one moment that the wealthy young man's main problem was money, we are conveniently letting ourselves off the hook by sheer virtue of not beng filthy rich. His downfall came from excess flab of will, which explains why his "countenance fell."

Shall we replay the scene in an updated setting? The man is fiddling with the controls of his new TV set when by chance he hits on our church's weekly program. With a flicker of annoyance he means to switch channels, when something grabs his ear. Reluctantly he tunes in the following week, feeling a bit foolish over his perked interest. Before long he is hooked on the message and has his secretary arrange for an appointment with the preacher.

What must I do to join your church? I really admire your style. I have been a model son, an ethical businessman, a devoted husband, a responsible community leader, a positive thinker. But I sense something lacking . . .

Why, thank you, sir, and welcome to the family. There is one thing, of course. You are required to join the five-week New Members Class and at the conclusion share in a brief personal testimony what our Lord means to you.

. . . Oh, I'm afraid that's not possible. I don't have that kind of time. Well, I guess I'll still catch you on TV once in a while . . .

"And Jesus looking upon him loved him . . ." It is the kind of heart-stopping look that follows a highwire walker on his first try without a net. He has one chance. If he hesitates for even one moment he has already blown it. The one courageous act of will is in truth a life-or-death matter. God's love cannot save us the agony of basic decision. His gift of free will mandates that we alone exercise it!

Mark 10:21 ☐ *Mark 10:17-22*

Therefore God gave them up in the lusts of their hearts . . .
because they . . . worshiped and served the creature rather
than the Creator, who is blessed for ever! Amen.

This is not nearly the great sock-it-to-the-perverts harangue
that the "foolish and heartless" — selfsame catalog of "improper
conduct" — would like it to be. Rather, it exposes a cross section
of God's heart that has imbedded in it an angel with a flaming
sword more terrible than that which shut up Eden.

Here God goes walking in the night of His soul when He is
haunted by echoes reverberating through the corridors of time.
"Come now, let us reason together . . . I spread out my hands
all the day to a rebellious people . . . For God so loved the
world!"

The cross won't admit God to the place where His failure
and rejection are eternally stored and sealed with the flame of
pain deep within His heart. Paul's "Amen" signifies solemn
ratification of a death pact that has fatally joined man's willfulness to God's. Having wooed and warned and unleashed all of
Creation's witness to win our free will, He must put the seal of
the solemn, deliberate "So be it!" to our terminal willfulness.
Being inherently moral, He cannot force our love, only His
sovereign purpose in history. There follows in the subsequent
verses not a catalog of vices for the self-righteous to gloat over,
but an obituary of those dead and buried in the great heart of
their rejected God.

If our irrational fear of homosexuals has perverted our
ability to love and forgive — we are never, never to speak the
terrible Amen of abandonment! — we had better consider the
full curse of "giving up" on God. Shall we disfellowship God
while He grieves? Shall we trample on the pain in His heart? Or
shall we draw near and bless Him and all creation with our
compassion!

Romans 1:24 ☐ *Romans 1:18-32*

They have healed the wound of my people lightly, saying "Peace, peace," when there is no peace.

The fiery blast of anger erupts from the embers of anguish in God's heart. We fan them with the breath of our toothy grin to which is stuck the obnoxious platitude: Just give your troubles to the Lord and everything will come up roses!

If we pride ourselves in simplistic faith, we are condemned by its shallowness. No raw knees, no dirty hands, no eyes stung by tears. It is not the sexual pervert who first needs to come out of the closet of his own private hell. The prig in us needs to be dragged into the hot blast of public exposure before the Righteous Judge.

The measure of our own morality — often safely rutted in nothing more than middle-class lack of opportunity — offers not one ounce of hope to those trapped in their moral morass. Of course, we do have our occasional stunning wet dream that makes our morning coffee taste funny from the strange brew of piqued interest in possibilities that we never consciously knew existed. Disconcerted, we slam the lid on such suggestion and with hot little puffs of steamed indignation proceed to blow Satan away. Don't sneak your nasty X-rated movie equipment into my bedroom at night, snorts the prude. But Satan is merely watching our home movies.

Until we apply the blood of Jesus to our own deepest need of exposure for what we really are, we use the "precious blood" formula to bind Satan in vain. On the contrary, he will return to give aid and comfort to the prude in us. With luck he will groom us into the perfect prig. When there is no sense of crying need within ourselves — when we have never looked like a cockroach on its back — we cannot possibly identify with the "walking wounded" of an alienated world. Content with precious religion, we abdicate costly relationship. Such peace breeds rot and stinks to high heaven.

Jeremiah 8:11 □ *Jeremiah 8:8-12*

I came to cast fire upon the earth; and would that it were already kindled. I have a baptism to be baptized with; and how I am constrained until it is accomplished! Do you think that I have come to give peace on earth? No, I tell you, but rather division . . .

Help! Revolution! The age of comfort on a dizzying skid right smack into the age of confrontation! If we are tempted to run for cover, the sword of the Spirit cuts to the quick: This fire will not singe the crown of our hair, but rage and reign in our hearts and there impart purity and righteous passion, consuming the dross of our dim-witted deceptions and forging a crown of eternal glory.

If this revolutionary baptism of the Holy Spirit does not fit our religious norm, we cannot blame Jesus. He never divided people into charismatic and noncharismatic, only self-righteous and unrighteous. His idea of "division" was not to employ tongues to quibble over the merits of individual gifts. The idea of the sword was to slash away at all shallow comforts and convictions until we would prize the Giver above all gifts.

Ministering in the days of His flesh, Jesus was vexed by the frustration of having to impart eternal truth to finite minds. Small children with a fondness for playing house and doctor cannot be lectured on marriage and illicit sex, only loved and steered by example into responsible adulthood. Once they are in their parents' shoes the patient teaching comes full circle.

The baptism of the Holy Spirit is a profound bursting of God's age into ours. It is divine illumination that enables us to reap the harvest of truth — sown like "seed of light" by Jesus, the Truth incarnate. It is our joy-filled initiation into the life-long habit of Christ's more abundant life.

Luke 12:49-51 □ *Luke 12:49-53*

My beloved speaks and says to me: "Arise, my love, my fair one, and come away. . . . The time of singing has come . . ."

The baptism of the Holy Spirit enables the intimacy and immediacy of joyous intercourse with God. It is harmony of communion that crests again and again in mutual delight. When God says, "Arise . . . come away" for an experience of consummate intimacy with me — I rouse myself from the commonplace and join Him, joyously aware of my inherent desirability. Walking into His arms, I come alive in the flowering of my personality and the mingling of mutual esteem. No one loves better than God and no one affirms more radiantly the gift of my sexuality. It is "super" natural self-fulfillment.

Sex means genitalia. Spirit-baptized sexuality is geniality with God. The word *genial* originally related to marriage and procreation. Such geniality generates inner security that makes us attractive to others regardless of sex or marital status. The gift of sexuality does not advertise itself as desirable body, but as serenity of personality. As such it does not stir up lust or jealousy, is not reserved for shapely youth. It requires no spiritual chastity belt, no scholarly footnotes to this Song of Songs that would explain away its vivid earthiness.

"My beloved is mine and I am his." Such communion with the Creator is the baptizing work of the Holy Spirit. If we have never known it, we lack true union with Him. Perhaps we carry on a solemn engagement with the church and are satisfied with our attachment to a place.

"Arise, my love, my fair one . . . the time of singing has come." Shall we tell God we are too busy with the work of the church to take time for intimacy with Him? Shall we then rouse ourselves to the full height of dignity and sing stiffly, "Jesus, Lover of my soul, let me to Thy bosom fly . . .?"

Song of Solomon 2:10-12 □ Song of Solomon 2:8-17

One day, when Moses had grown up, he went out to his people and looked on their burdens . .

And God heard their groaning. . . . And God saw the people of Israel, and God knew their condition.

These two poignantly related statements take on added weight when we realize that forty years lie between them. Over 350,000 hours of incessant pleading that God would relieve His people of their suffering. Moses did not have God's kind of stoicism and slew himself an Egyptian. That one rash act grew into a forty-year lesson that endures to this day: God can only do something if we are willing to be something, namely, God's very own woman or man.

During Moses' nomad days as a shepherd in Midian, God had ample opportunity to hammer out His chosen instrument of deliverance on the anvil of anguish. We may be too quick to dismiss that forty-year period as a mere footnote to a career that eventually spanned nearly every book of the Bible. But if we fit forty years of forced labor and exile into our own life experience, we begin to appreciate the painstaking labor of love that goes into the grooming of a friend of God.

Conditions of "groaning" exist all around us today. God's coolly assessing eye is roaming the land even now. He looks for one thing only. It is the one man, the one woman who resembles Moses' parenthetical description in Numbers 12:3, "Now the man Moses was very meek, more than all men that were on the face of the earth."

Meek meant "much enduring," even "disinterested." From inept involvement with his people Moses had progressed to intimate identification with his Lord's interest alone. Out of God's character flowed the might that affected the conditions of all subsequent generations — to this very day.

Exodus 2:11;2:24-25 □ Exodus 2

*They angered him at the waters of Meribah, and it went ill with
Moses on their account . . .*

Blessed be the LORD. *. . . And let all the people say, "Amen."*

Moses' anger cost him entry to the Promised Land. Is this
how God treats a friend? One brief moment of exasperation
eclipsed by the habitual obstinacy of a people so great that in
time God Himself "abhorred his heritage." No wonder they
made Moses' "spirit bitter, and he spoke words that were rash."
Let that sink in as exclamation point to forty years of incredibly hard labor. "Nevertheless he regarded their distress, when
he heard their cry." God's faithfulness to His "abhorred
heritage" enables us to go back to the waters of Meribah and
heal our own disappointment.

Same old story: No water, no confidence in Moses. That
was rubbed in so viciously that he fell on his face before God.
His instructions, "Take the rod . . . assemble the congregation
. . . and *tell* the rock before their eyes to yield its water."
Confidence restored, Moses' blood rushed to his head and by
God — he was going to show them! With a taunting cry to the
"rebels" he struck the rock viciously twice. Water came rushing
forth and Moses was washed up. He had not believed God's
word and had not sanctified Him in the eyes of Israel. The
plain lesson: God cannot tolerate disobedience that leads to
self-glorification.

The hidden lesson: The purpose of His friendship with
Moses was to weave redemptive analogy into the fabric of
Israel's history, by which all nations would come to trace the
steadfast love of their Redeemer. Moses, the beloved friend,
understood that sacred, sovereign purpose.

The rock was Christ, struck for our offense. So, we can
freely drink from His living water. That is what our long-
suffering Lord needed to teach at Meribah. Let all the people
say, "Amen!"

Psalm 106:32, 48

The LORD will fulfill his purpose for me; thy steadfast love, O LORD, endures for ever. Do not forsake the work of thy hands.

We prize usefulness to the Lord and abhor personal failure. But faith and failure mesh nicely. Failure knocks the wobbly legs off posturing faith and makes it crash — and come to rest — in the hardening concrete of grace reality.

"The Lord will fulfill his purpose for me." The objective standard of the Word assigns failure to enlarged promise. David speaks time-tested reassurance. He speaks for Moses and for you and me today. Murderer, adulterer, anonymous sinner — all enter into abiding fruitfulness not because of fitness, but because of friendship with God. The Old Testament comes alive with God's personal pleasure in Moses and David. Lest we miss the personal implication, the New Testament irrevocably weds friendship to usefulness: "I have called you friends . . . I chose you and appointed you . . . that your fruit should abide."

"Thy steadfast love, O Lord, endures for ever." In every age the gracious nature of God has been fleshed out in common life to point to Christ, Word and Grace incarnate. For Moses it rained manna ("What is it?") from heaven. It was the Bread of Life, a stubborn sweetness that no desert bitterness could cancel. In the lean days of flight from vengeful Saul, David helped himself to the "Showbread of the Presence" in the temple. Forerunner of the messianic King, David overruled the law and was nourished by grace. We partake of the sacrament — the pledge — of the Lord's Supper, "Take, eat; this is my body." With Christ so obviously for us, can failure undo us?

"Do not forsake the work of thy hands." He won't. Moses could not inherit Canaan. David was forced to inherit a sword of strife. He who appoints is qualified to dis-appoint us as well. But to God's friend comes deeper truth. We are the work of His nail-scarred hands. In Jesus Christ we are destined for an inheritance "which is imperishable, undefiled, and unfading, kept in heaven" for us.

Psalm 138:8

But we impart a secret and hidden wisdom of God, which God decreed before the ages for our glorification.

The sovereign purpose of God transcends every age, every work, every individual. Taking root in human situations, it is never of obvious epic proportions or we would be overwhelmed. This is good reason why Paul received from the Lord and also delivered to us, "that our Lord Jesus . . . took bread, and when he had given thanks, he broke it, and said, 'This is my body which is broken for you.'" The purpose of God focused in the person of Jesus Christ — and broken down into manageable daily bread — makes sense.

The rub comes when the bread of heaven is broken down into a grain of wheat that must fall into the ground and die. The grain-of-wheat principle taking root in our life is not of epic proportions. We do not die heroes' deaths on spiritual battlefields of Yorktown or Gettysburg. We die in daily, tiny, strategic obediences that no one cares about. Sometimes our darkness is so dense and heavy that we doubt if God cares. Then we cry out with Moses' abject longing, "Show me thy glory."

He really meant his glory — his justification which God had decreed before the ages. As Moses saw his, so we can see ours. Why puzzle over the mystery when the majesty of God's caring is so obvious, "I will make all my goodness pass before you, and will proclaim before you my name 'The LORD . . . (Exodus 33:19).

Our personal vision of "glorification" is in God's "I"! "I will make *all* my goodness pass before you." Suddenly long-scuttled, haphazard memories of painful drudgery and discipline come alive in the unifying awareness of God's sovereign purpose in them. "The Lord" says that He is fully in charge and right on target with us. The "back" side of God's glory is our new perspective luminous with praise!

1 Corinthians 2:7 ☐ *1 Corinthians 2:6-14*

*Now when they saw the boldness of Peter and John, and
perceived that they were uneducated, common men, they
wondered; and they recognized that they had been with Jesus.*

"They" were nothing to sneeze at, whether known as the
great council of the Sanhedrin, the high priest's clique, or
Jerusalem's bluebloods and ivy leaguers. Picture a joint session
of House and Senate — not to confer accolades on a returned
space hero but to rake two nondescript missionaries over the
coals.

The disciples' sect did not even have an official name. That
came after Paul's first public ministry in Antioch, where he
taught the doctrine of Christ with such singular clarity that for
the first time His followers were called Christians. But already
their "sect" had attracted enough notoriety to harmonize with
the tenor of descriptions recorded in the "Acts" of the Holy
Spirit elsewhere: "For we have found this man a pestilent
fellow, an agitator among all the Jews . . . and a ringleader of
the sect of the Nazarenes" (Acts 24:5). "For with regard to this
sect we know that everywhere it is spoken against" (28:22).

So why the fury and fascination of gathered clergy and
aristocracy? They saw the boldness of Peter and John. There
was clear visual impact. By contrast, they had to employ the
reasoning power of "perceiving" to peg their commonplace
background. So what did they see?

Peter and John were outspoken. Their word was out. Their
speech exhibited such excellence of mind and authoritative
grasp of truth that only one conclusion could be reached — the
Word was out. "They" saw the conquering hero of death!
Where are the accolades of the close-mouthed church member?
The bold Christ longs to escape the dull decorum of our private
piety. He is lusting for a good show and the world is game.

Acts 4:13 ☐ *Acts 4:1-22*

They all gave heed to him, from the least to the greatest, saying, "This man is that power of God which is called Great." And they gave heed to him, because for a long time he had amazed them with his magic.

The world begs for a good show and is willing to credit God even if the performer is Simon of Samaria, erstwhile fraud. The supernatural begs to be harnessed and paraded before men who groan in the bonds of natural limitation. If the church fails to get the Show of the Incarnation on the road, then the show of impostors will continue to fill the world's aching void. Witness the phenomenon of the widely circulated "psychic garbage" — swallowed by the gullible public who makes the supermarket tabloid its spiritual guide. Picture in contrast the closed-circuit "elitism" of the church and its spiritual projection in the market place.

If we are fuzzy about the role of the supernatural in today's church, we must urgently rediscover this: The church is inherently supernatural as the superlative expression of divine intervention in human affairs. As a mystical body, our premier call is to continual supernatural endowment by the same Spirit who spun earth into orbit and sprang Christ from the tomb. Amazing grace, not ho-hum grace! As long as the church exhibits the superficial at the expense of the "super" natural, those dealing in frauds and the occult continue to have a field day.

Jesus urged prayer to the Lord of the harvest to send laborers out into His field. God does not want us to recruit more programs and candidates that fit our own bias of winning souls. Christ won all souls 2000 years ago! Our job is to deliver as many as possible. For that we need to recruit the Person of the Holy Spirit. He will deliver us from our impotent performance of The Incarnation. He gets the show on the road! Will we pray?

Acts 8:10 ☐ *Acts 8:9-25*

I have filled him with the Spirit of God, with ability and intelligence, with knowledge and all craftsmanship . . .

If we worry about the "spooky" aspects of the Holy Ghost, here is God's smile poured into our soul. If cultural conditioning or irrational fear of the unknown have deprived us of the riches of God, He means now to rouse the bugaboos of our reservations and put them to eternal rest.

The Holy Spirit does not violate personality, but enhances it with God's inherent excellence — evidenced in ability, intelligence, knowledge and all craftsmanship. His joyous affirmation strikes down the fetish of anti-intellectualism rampant in some circles. Intellect, like sun and rain, is God's common grace to all men. Only intelligent faith can be "wise as serpents and innocent as doves."

How satisfying to know that the boy Jesus was apprenticed to Joseph, the carpenter. How lovingly He must have fingered the satiny contours of finely planed wood and felt the keen joy of the craftsman who respects his work. Solomon echoes that appreciation, "The Preacher sought to find pleasing words . . ." for "a word fitly spoken is like apples of gold in a setting of silver."

Perhaps the church survived the Dark Age of repression and manipulation by an elitist hierarchy precisely because soaring cathedrals and great works of art authenticated the Holy Spirit's work of elevating God's character in man beyond his own base instinct. If ever in doubt, we have this sure word also; "Now we have received . . . the Spirit which is from God, that we might understand the gifts bestowed on us by God. . . . 'For who has known the mind of the Lord so as to instruct him?' But we have the mind of Christ" (1 Corinthians 2:12,16). Allow the Holy Spirit free rein in your life and God's riches become focused in you!

Exodus 31:3 ☐ *Exodus 31:1-11*

Go and tell John . . . the blind receive their sight and the lame walk . . . and the poor have good news preached to them. And blessed is he who takes no offense at me.

Touche! We want more for the poor. Can Jesus not formulate a foolproof social Gospel? But Christ does not preach "sermonizing." He talks "lifestyle" as public proclamation.

Our Spirit-emboldened life is to praise the riches of Christ in the public places. Then the poor won't have to give their last dollar to prospering pseudosaviors and their sorry marketplace religion that sells conditional hope. If we preach our Gospel right we release into the lives of the poor "ability and intelligence, with knowledge and all craftsmanship."

This workmanship of the Holy Spirit was first proclaimed to those chosen to make the "tent of the meeting," which symbolically housed the presence of God. When a pup tent and orange crate would have been more practical in terms of wear and tear, God inspired artistic endeavor to spell out in precious materials a truth whose meaning fairly exploded with the Resurrection. The tent is the transitory "house of life" with which both rich and poor can identify. Because of the splendor of Christ's redemptive work, we go from tent to temple. As the eternal God inhabits our house of life He creates from within "ability and intelligence . . ." Personify this liberating truth to the poor!

They need divinely ordained self-esteem more than our seasonal turkeys. Why do we not trust them with money? Might they spend some on nonessentials because they have hungers other than food? God honored the need for visible dignity in His ancient people. We should hold the turkey once in awhile and give cash. The poor need to have the good news proclaimed to their sense of dignity!

Matthew 11:4-6 □ *Matthew 11:2-6*

I will extol thee. . . . Every day I will bless thee. . . . Great is the LORD, *and greatly to be praised . . .*

Christ's "more abundant life" is not the number of blessings He owes us according to our calculations ranging from basics to luxuries. Christ's more abundant life is inherently rooted in His first beatitude, "Blessed are the poor in spirit, for theirs *is* the kingdom of heaven."

In matters of the "kingdom" of our nation, our satisfaction with a particular president is not ultimately calculated along party lines, but on how well he discharges his office for the benefit of the whole nation. In judging, do we employ the long or the short view? To the Confederate widow Lincoln might have been a good man, but was a disastrous president. The historian extols his unqualified greatness.

"Great is the Lord, and greatly to be praised." History has already judged divine government. The choice on how satisfyingly we taste our own personal slice of that greatness narrows down to this: Are we willing to serve within the government process — or are we content to be the constituent in Hot Spot, Arizona, who waits for an ocean of blessings to swamp his desert abode?

David exhorts us to become God's press secretary. As such it is our job to take mental notes of every move He makes. We observe Him in the minute details of administrating domestic and global matters. His exhausting schedule is taxing to us, but in the process our respect and admiration for His wisdom and perseverance grows steadily. When we meet with the press we have no trouble extolling His greatness! Will we bless God daily with our adoration? Will we daily acknowledge that He is "faithful in all his words, and gracious in all his deeds"? If we do, we exercise our poverty of spirit into His more abundant life.

Psalm 145:1-3 □ *Psalm 145*

I give your priesthood as a gift. . . . I am your portion and your inheritance . . .

Aaron's Promised Land did not flow with the milk and honey of his own land grant, hacienda and siestas. He was the grubby padre of unglamorous Early California who blazed trails for his Sovereign by trudging through deserts and hilly coast land and suffered from rattlesnakes, earthquakes and un-cooperative Indians. But when he put on Spain's finest embroidered linen and lace and celebrated Sunday Mass, he proclaimed the gift of his priesthood!

Big Deal! we say — and until we say it with the right into-nation and intent of heart, we must go right back to the sewing room where Aaron's parish ladies sat and executed God's com-mandment, "And you shall make holy garments for Aaron your brother, for glory and beauty." God endowed with an "able mind" those chosen to invest with excellence of sym-bolism Aaron's outwardly discerned consecration, right down to the bells on his robe. (Exodus 28) As Christ's holy catholic church we are to wear the gift of our priesthood with dignity and celebration.

Many Protestant laymen and women aspire to the office of elder or deacon, but relatively few get stuck with the identify-ing carnation and — shhh — some dull meetings. In exuberant contrast, every single lay-priest wears the mantle of God's personal witness, and tied to his heart is the name of every single person destined to come into the glorious inheritance of his Lord's promises.

If occasionally we do chafe at the discipline of making all of our life the Lord's meeting place, shall we not joyfully call to mind this astounding fact: Christ, the High Priest, has clothed Himself with the seamless garment of our own flesh — and so affirms in our very body the beauty and glory of God's own holiness. Shall we not say Amen and Yes, Lord—with bells on!

Numbers 18:7,20 ☐ *Numbers 18:1-20*

You did not choose me, but I chose you. . . .

That explains the shock we get when we hand Jesus our resignation and He pulls out the contract with our name penned in red. Titled *Emancipation Proclamation*, it reads: "But thanks be to God, that you . . . have become obedient from the heart . . . and having been set free from sin, have become slaves of righteousness" (Romans 6:17-18). Did we ever consciously sign on for that?

His "Follow me" is never command, but always invitation, for "many are called, but few are chosen." Once He gives the nod we march off to postgraduate studies at the University of Obedience. Nothing corny about our alma mater: "Enter by the narrow gate; for the gate is wide and the way is easy, that leads to destruction, and those who enter by it are many. For the gate is narrow and the way is hard, that leads to life, and those who find it are few" (Matthew 7:13-14).

We quickly unlearn a few things. Few follow our Lord. We follow a talent or inclination that we want to develop along spiritual lines suited to our temperament. We want to write and perform and give Jesus ten percent. With a good waiter making at least fifteen, Jesus waits. In fact, Jesus continues to coolly decline all our abilities and accomplishments until we begin to lose faith in ourselves. When we are worn down sufficiently to cry out, "Take my life!" — He gently tells us that He has indeed taken it already. Then He grinds us into the exceedingly fine stuff of perfect submission. It takes long years of narrowing us down to the point where God is "pleased to reveal his Son to me" — for what purpose?

"I chose you and appointed you that you should go and bear fruit and that your fruit should *abide*; so that whatever you ask the Father in my name, he may give it to you." Then we ask — and then we write and sing and perform around the eternal theme of our *Emancipation Proclamation!*

John 15:16 ☐ *John 15:12-17*

But if he says to you, "I will not go out from you," because he loves you and your household . . . then you shall take an awl, and thrust it through his ear into the door, and he shall be your bondman for ever. And to your bondwoman you shall do likewise.

Is there a woman aching to live out her life fully in submission to Christ? Is she so dominated by His love that she will forsake her bondage of unequality for the bond of the ear-pierced slave with the pierced Servant of man alone? Then the Head of the church has "opened her ear" and in the "roll of the book" it is written of her, "I delight to do thy will, O my God" (Psalm 40:6-8).

To the slave woman of old the Promised Land spelled freedom after six years of service. Upon her release the master furnished her liberally with supplies to launch her on her own career. It was an act of commemorating his own departure from Egypt.

Those Israelites had fast misused their freedom by usurping Moses' leadership and talking Aaron into the Golden Calf disaster that cost the lives of 3000 men. "And Moses said, 'Today you have ordained yourselves for the service of the LORD, each one at the cost of his son and of his brother . . .'" (Exodus 32:29). On that sorry day much painful truth was rammed into the ears of the house of Israel. When Aaron assumed the gift of his true priesthood, Moses killed a "ram of ordination" and "took some of its blood and put it on the tip of Aaron's right ear . . ." (Leviticus 8:22-23).

Shall the liberated woman deliver herself into worship of some glittering self-made symbol of authority and pay a price — or shall she wear the sign of her redeemed womanhood in the tip of her ear in honored identification with the pierced Bondman of eternity?

Deuteronomy 15:16-17 ☐ Deuteronomy 15:12-18

What shall I render to the LORD for all his bounty to me? I will lift up the cup of salvation and call on the name of the Lord.

How often we have pressed Christ into the role of Kentucky Chicken Colonel and demanded a lot of "cluck for a buck" when the storms of life raged and unplugged our appliances! Inevitably He did it with the grace of the servant who habitually goes the second mile. How often have we savored the sweet dessert of the Shepherd Psalm on our lips, "Thou preparest a table before me in the presence of my enemies . . . Surely goodness and mercy shall follow me all the days of my life . . ."

The Hebrew meaning of "follow" has also the connotation of "pursue," so that goodness and mercy do "sheep dog" duty. The idea is to herd us into the gladness of God where our feasted soul is enthroned forever. From this position of ultimate security and satisfaction has the time not come for us to give a banquet of life in honor of our King? Shall we not compel those from the highways and hedges of our own life to join in a festive toast to the Pioneer and Perfecter of our joy?

What in a nutshell is salvation? The essence of it must be in that cup lest we resort to boring oratory or awkward hemming and hawing. Salvation means deliverance, wholeness, ease. We shall put the ease of our supernatural comfort in the salutary cup and simply say, "O Lord, I am thy servant. Thou hast loosed my bonds. Praise the Lord." The cheer will bring down the rafters of heaven.

When have we last raised a "toast" that was not cut and dried in the banquet hall of our sanctuary? "Worthy is the Lamb who was slain, to receive power and wealth and wisdom and might and honor and glory and blessing." Let that punctuate our order of worship and we shall stagger out of church filled with the glad "wine of astonishment."

Psalm 116:12-13 □ *Psalm 116*

But about midnight Paul and Silas were praying and singing hymns to God, and the prisoners were listening to them, and suddenly there was a great earthquake . . .

Faith does not exclude fear and it is permissible to whistle in the dark. But Paul and Silas were not whistling. They were having a picnic in their box seat at the Hollywood Bowl. They were living it up with silver and cloth napkins, candles and Beef Wellington — all in anticipation of the Beethoven Spectacular with fireworks and cannon fusillade.

If there is the timid soul who would rather take a proper course than poetic license, let him narrate properly: Paul and Silas, hassled and beaten with rods, were suffering from insomnia in prison and whistled in the dark. It summoned a tremor that shocked the stocks off them. They said "Praise the Lord!" and hightailed it out of there. The jailer had a small funeral and no donations were made to the Center for Suicide Prevention. The authorities were mad. Amen.

"So be it" nothing! When God writes the script, it pulsates with His wonderful imagination — and downright delicious things happen to the bullies. When our heroes' worthwhile sideshow was canceled by the big event, the fireworks of God's faithfulness erupted all around. Paul assured the jailer that all his unfettered charges were safely gathered in the bosom of God. With the Gospel amply illustrated, Paul delivered the charge of salvation to the jailer. The sacraments of baptism and compassionate first aid were exchanged.

Meanwhile, the magistrates suffered the aftershocks of having verified our heroes' Roman citizenship. Police were dispatched to discreetly escort them out of prison. But Paul leaned back into the comfort of his stocks and said expansively, "Let those gentlemen come and apologize in person. Then we shall leave peaceably." God authors no dull scripts.

Acts 16:25-26 □ *Acts 16:16-40*

*By day the LORD commands his steadfast love; and at night his
song is with me . . .*

There is no pussyfooting around when Hollywood royalty
goes to London to visit the Queen. They pack their bag with
every trick inside. Once on the spot, there must be no blemish;
a command performance demands professionalism. The artist's
"song in the night" comes when Her Majesty appears backstage
to amiably chat with her peers of a lesser realm. Such basking
in reflected glory!

The Christian on the spot has run out of tricks. His solil-
oquy is not polished performance, but faltering faith, "Why are
you cast down, O my soul . . .? Hope in God; for I shall again
praise him . . . My soul is cast down." When faith is in that
spotlight, the curtain of grace rises on the command
performance of God's steadfast love. When tears have been our
food day and night, while men say to us continually, "Where is
your God?" — then He Himself is on the spot.

How does the song in the night appear? When we gorge on
food at dinner, we wind up lying in bed uncomfortably sleep-
less, serenaded by a cacophony of stomach noises. We can
now choose to reflect on the miserable performance of our
overindulgence, or on the marvelous performance of body
chemistry that cleans up our act. Being consummately professional in our stubborn humanity, we will rather chew on guilt
and antacid than applaud our gallant gastric secretions.

At night we can really lower ourselves into the echo
chambers of despair. But God won't yield His spot to a dirge.
He commands a song. If we have rehearsed His praise in the
days of our sunlight, that echo will float down into the night of
our soul and we will bask in the reflected glory of His steadfast
love. God performs His professed faithfulness the moment we
choose to command it!

Psalm 42:8 □ *Psalm 42*

Because of the multitude of oppressions people cry out . . . But none says, "Where is God my Maker, who gives songs in the night, who teaches us more than the beasts of the earth . . .?

We would rather choke on our pride than admit to the possibility that we have God's faithfulness by the collar. Our pet theory of the largely ceremonial Master is hard to shake; the Protestant work ethic wants to save God from getting His hands dirty if we can help it. Oh, how we help it!

God has His own pet theories about spiritual ignorance bred from arrogance. May His displeasure be less biting than the prophet's prose, "His watchmen are blind, they are all without knowledge; they are all dumb dogs, they cannot bark; dreaming, lying down, loving to slumber. The dogs have a mighty appeitite; they never have enough" (Isaiah 56:10-11).

Our pets' antics invite us to become appreciative observers. On the surface our animals entertain, but in reality they shrewdly train us. One soulful gaze and a few wags of the tail, and the dog has his master by the leash and out on a walk. He all but talks, says his adoring master. Why should I, chuckles the "dumb" dog to himself, when a silly wag of the tail earns me my whole livelihood and admiration to boot!

Now just wait a minute, interrupts the cat lover, and tells her tale of feline brilliance. The cat can induce insanity with her insistent meowing for the one specific food she craves at a given moment. Yet the owner will meekly oblige the beast and fall all over it when it gives off pleasant vibrations once in awhile. Elihu marvels with God. If "dumb" animals can so eloquently teach us, how much more shall God teach us about His longing to care for us in our low estate! Has God ever given you songs in the night? Why not?

Job 35:9-10

If you then, who are evil, know how to give good gifts to your children, how much more will the heavenly Father give the Holy Spirit to those who ask him!

"Praise the Lord" in casual conversation should be retired to give "How much more!" a chance. Every good thing that comes to mind should be pushed aggressively into the "How much more!" range of God's creative newness. That would give faith the razor's edge to cut us loose from wanting to be good when we must be great.

A minor swimming pool accident illustrates our problem. A drowning insect attracts pity because of its heroic struggle. We gently cradle it in our hand and move it to a safe spot on the sun-splashed decking. There we watch it slowly come around until it suddenly takes flight in a burst of exuberance. What if this tiny bug went home and told its kin it had met the savior. What if it described the flesh-and-blood hand and the mysterious lifting power independent of wings. Would the insects be justified in praying to this benevolent force and expect good things in the future? Of course, but they could never pray big enough! How could they perceive the enormous range of human potential?

Can we now understand God's frustration that we ask and seek so little and knock so rarely? What grieves Him is that we do not have the insect's excuse. Still, we scurry through life like worker ants in our frantic little patterns of effort and dedication, when just for the sheer pleasure of a holiday outing God would want us to be soaring, gliding eagles — released from our narrow visions.

Called to be God's great people, we are promised wings for our imagination and weights for anchoring bold claims to reality. That "how much more" gift is the Holy Spirit. How much more there is to our life *for* Christ, when that Christ *is* our life. Please, He says, no more pint-size prayers to empty the oceans of His Father's resources!

Luke 11:13 □ *Luke 11:1-13*

I will not leave you desolate . . .

What does "desolate" taste like? Take a gulp of imagination and swallow hard. Live abandoned in a dilapidated desert shack. Suck poisonous irony into your lungs as you lean bloodied against the rock of your silver mine, an ice cream scoop dangling from your betrayed hands. Let burning sand trickle through your fingers as you try to cover the open mass grave where the bleached bones and rotting flesh of your dead hopes mock your desire to forget them.

Watch Jesus pack His bags as He leaves for home. Watch Him strip off the priceless rugs and wall hangings and hear the unmuffled cries of the sick and demented. Watch His luggage swell with angels and shepherds and wise men, and when the manger is tucked in at last, watch Him slap on the seal of the star. And when His glory has left and the keys of the kingdom have turned for the last time, find yourself shut up in an orphanage that becomes a hospice for the dying.

Read the Sermon on the Mount and understand for the first time that Jesus meant every word of it. Try to love your enemy and know instead such hatred that you are eaten alive by the acid churning in you. Experience persecution without blessing and shrink in vain from the hammering sound of the gallows outside. Taste the despair of having to be perfect as your heavenly Father is perfect and then start plucking out your eye and chopping off your limbs.

Famished for Christ, be plunged into a famine not of bread and of water, but of "hearing the words of the Lord." And when God has given you "cleanness of teeth" because there is nothing whatsoever left to taste — then wake up from your nightmare and hear the Lord's promise, "I will not leave you desolate; I will come to you."

John 14:18 □ *John 14*

If a man loves me, he will keep my word, and my Father will love him, and we will come to him and make our home with him.

The Galilean walks the Milky Way and peers out through the galaxies. "The heavens are telling the glory of God; and the firmament proclaims his handiwork. The sun comes forth like a bridegroom leaving his chamber, and like a strong man runs its course with joy." The Galilean likewise must return to the Visited Planet.

He strides back across heaven's glory to His Father's throne and heart and speaks to Him about the harvest festival of Pentecost. In baring His highpriestly heart, He displays Calvary's wounding. He must go back and complete His earthly ministry. But the Father cannot bear to be separated again.

As Father and Son return to the house of our life that is to be their permanent home, Jesus revels in the freshly stirred memories of campfires on the beach, children in His arms, Martha making knishes, the wine steward at Cana all in a tizzy . . . The Father, not at all immune to His Son's infectious mood, is rather pensive, nonetheless, as He takes it all in. Compared to home this is a slum tenement and the cheers cannot hide the hideous effects of habitual neglect. There is no heat, no running water . . .

The Father knows His Son's obedience merits better than this. He is well-justified in commandeering all of eternity's resources to bring this place up to certain standards. Because of His love for the Son — and His Son's love for His friends — a piece of heaven shall now be created on earth. Is such imagining sacrilegious? Only to the extent that we have not even begun to scratch the surface of God's revelation to those who "keep my word!"

John 14:23 □ *John 14*

These men who have turned the world upside down have come here also . . .

Catch the unrest of the wildfire sparked by Pentecost! The church is no longer an inflated body of light ceremoniously suspended above common life like a Goodyear blimp, advertising an air of self-importance.

On Pentecost God set fire to our couch of comfort on which we grandly reclined and popped platitudes into our mouth, spitting tiny seeds of truth to the random world at our window. The Holy Spirit galvanizes intellect into action and fires the will of the weak-but-willing to move as one formidable Christ into those very places where we step on toes and topple our image as a gleaming monument to the past.

Because Pentecost ignites a movement to the future, it explodes with amazement and perplexity. Wind and fire highlight chaff we never knew existed. The flames of faith are fanned in every direction, unloosing praise and persecution of unparalleled proportions. When God's majesty rides herd on His people, myths must flee and misconceptions be vacated. There is one Head to the Body and Christ will scatter us to the four winds if we do not heed His gospel alone.

Our inner life is regenerated along the God-size outward challenge. Fellowship among believers becomes a survival matter. The Holy Spirit showcases individuals like Peter and John to teach confrontation — the art of "facing together." He highlights a Barnabas as a model encourager. He pops the anonymous "three thousand" (Acts 2:41-42) into our New Members Class to force us into drastically revised "body language." Together we forego blandly polite community affairs in favor of intimacy with a previously ignored Simon the tanner or Cornelius of the Italian cohort. In radical realignments rooted in allegiance to Jesus Christ alone we become those equipped to turn His world right-side-up.

Acts 17:6

When we cry, "Abba! Father!" it is the Spirit himself bearing witness . . . that we are children of God, and if children, then heirs . . . provided we suffer with him . . .

"Abba! Father!" Hear the mother tongue of Jesus Christ that becomes the prayer language of the believer at Pentecost! It is not Aramaic or the optional gift of tongues. It is not language but relationship; unspeakable love expressed in a heart cry of recognition. It ultimately translates into action: "Abba, Father, all things are possible to thee; remove this cup from me; yet not what I will, but what thou wilt."

Some committed to the cause of Christ conceive of the church as an organization conformed to ideals we can reasonably deal with. The believer who cries, "Abba! Father!" has his lungs seared by the agonizing breath of Christ that ruthlessly draws the impossible into our own range of possibilities. He achingly knows the difference between naturally endowed commitment to a cause and supernatural transformation into the very identity of the suffering Servant.

Collective commitment to any worthy cause is short-lived because conformity centers on temporal leadership amidst changing circumstances. Our commitment to the person of Jesus Christ imparts eternity's own perspective and resiliency. The Father's spirit of adoption translates our union with Christ into unity with fellow heirs spanning the ages. It is organic family unity vital to the claiming of our family inheritance of divine power invested in service.

"Abba! Father!" Hear the mother tongue of Christ's abject loneliness at Gethsemane which healed us of ours. Speak the mother tongue of intimate identification with the Father's interests at all cost. Let our "Abba! Father!" become the birth cry of a church freed from the womb of our own limited nurture. Pushed out into a world of no limits, we — Christ's bonded blood kin — become the incarnation of His last will and testament.

Romans 8:15-17 □ Romans 8:1-17

Since you are eager for manifestations of the Spirit, strive to excel in building up the church.

We would just as soon settle for a honeymoon cottage and permanently engage in the private fireworks of our initial experience with the Holy Spirit. In our intensely personal moments with God we can fit His whole kingdom into our enraptured soul and become convinced that such highs are normative for the spirit-filled Christian. Well, how mature an assessment of marriage would we expect from honeymooning newlyweds?

Manifestations of the Spirit are to be sought for ministry, not magic moments. They are not bubbly stuff to raise up a champagne edition of Christianity; the raw needs of the world cry out for fresh living water. Manifestations of the Spirit harmonize the sacred with the ordinary, dull and commonplace. They do not validate our standing before God. Our worth was established once and for all when Jesus shed His blood as ransom for our life.

Spiritual manifestations must not be divorced from the person of Jesus Christ. The person of the Holy Spirit complements that of the Savior. "And I will pray the Father, and he will give you another Counselor, to be with you for ever . . ." (John 14:16-17). His function is to be rejected by the natural world, yet to redeem it supernaturally from the power of death and hell.

We cannot build the church from private experience. The Cornerstone must prevail. We must single-mindedly join the gift of our being "chosen and precious" to that of our fellow heirs in Christ. Then diversity and unity will not be mutually exclusive, nor the church a strange colony of "honeymoon cottages" to amuse a disbelieving world. The church of Jesus Christ is the most excellent of spiritual manifestations. She is the gift that keeps on giving when our ecstasies have been tempered by spiritual dish pan hands.

1 Corinthians 14:12 □ *1 Corinthians 14:1-12*

And they were bringing children to him that he might touch them. . . . And he took them in his arms and blessed them . . .

Do we sneer at the politician who kisses babies in the course of vote-hustling? What if we followed their mothers to the poll? Do they remember the candidate for his platform or that brief personal touch? Does it matter if the baby smiled or screamed? For one brief moment the stranger affirmed an element of common humanity and most likely gained himself a friend. If only the church were so in touch with reality.

Would Sunday schools suffer their present decline — would sex sin be as rampant in society today if the church had taught its truths more by touch and less by terminology? We are born to touch and be touched — to be linked to our fellow human beings in this most elemental form. It is a need we never outgrow.

How interesting that the Apostle Paul, patron saint of aloof bachelors, would adjure the saints at Corinth to "greet one another with a holy kiss." Were these not the saints tarnished by sex scandal? Stern, no-nonsense Paul did not soberly warn hands off, but warmly encouraged his struggling charges to demonstrate affection and affirmation for one another. The holy kiss and the "laying on of hugs" need to become part of the church's blessings again. Perhaps for some a dreary massage parlor is the only answer to their hunger for touch.

If politicians can learn to touch strangers, so can we. Jesus set the example. He bitingly ignored the lofty theologians in His crowd and responded generously to the need expressed by women; as wives and mothers they knew the joy and power of touch. By intuition they warmed up to a greatness of love that Paul restated as doctrine in Romans 5:6, "While we were still weak, at the right time Christ died for the ungodly." Now is the right time to demonstrate His godly love by literally opening our arms to a love-starved world.

Mark 10:13,16 □ Mark 10:13-16.

Jesus looked up and said to her, "Woman, where are they? Has no one condemned you?" She said, "No one, Lord." And Jesus said, "Neither do I condemn you; go, and do not sin again."

"If God be for us, who can be against us?" Are we so caught up in the act of Redemption — Christ joining His sinless body to our sullied life — that our body language becomes as convincing as our Lord's? Watch Him!

Jesus sits in the temple teaching. He speaks *ex cathedra* — "from the chair" — symbolizing authority. A sudden commotion sends a tingle through the crowd. A hapless woman has been hauled out of bed by the temple's vice squad and is pushed in front of Jesus. The crime is adultery, but the accusation is aimed at Him. Can this itinerant preacher and crowd-pleaser really buck the establishment when it comes to basics? How will He judge? Watch Him relax! Watch Jesus doodle in the dust on the ground, His thoughts turned inward — the calm in the eye of the storm.

What if the woman were brought to our church to test our spiritual reflexes? We would press a styrofoam cup in her hands and wish she were not smoking nervously while we make futile calls to welfare bureaucracies. A brave soul would finally offer to take her home and timid smiles would be exchanged. After several days of strained effort to draw the woman out and have her like our middle-class ways, she would quietly slip away. Relief would overcome regret and after awhile our prayers for her would fade into oblivion as well, having done — sigh — all we could.

Jesus did not say to the woman, "Come! Come enter into my reform program." He said, "Go . . ." It was the Redeemer's benediction of freedom. He came not to judge, but to set free. If we open our arms to the world as God's appointed reformers, the embrace will be tainted and rejected. If we offer the Redeemer's love, our touch will reflect His authority. Expansive gestures mean little. Experienced grace says it all: God is for us!

John 8:10-11 ☐ *John 8:1-11*

All day long I have held out my hands to a disobedient and contrary people.

If we are to be lovers with God's own disposition, we had better let the weight of these words sink in. The temptation for the church is to pile on program upon program to attract attention in response to the world's condition, when in fact we must respond to God's character. His inherent patience may not change our world, but it will change us. Is that not where real hope is shaped?

Who of us has not at one time extended a spontaneous hand in greeting, only to find signals crossed and our gesture ignored? Nothing more than a bit of social blundering and already there is a taste of rejection, a resolve to be more cautious.

What about God standing there all day with hands outstretched imploringly? Lift up your arms and feel the lead seep in almost immediately. Read the quote from Isaiah in its entirety and let the weight sink in through your excruciatingly painful limbs. "I was ready to be sought by those who did not ask for me; I was ready to be found by those who did not seek me. I said, 'Here am I, here am I,' to a nation that did not call on my name. I spread out my hands all the day to a rebellious people, who walk in a way that is not good, following their own devices; a people who provoke me to my face continually . .. " (Isaiah 65:1-3). By now you have to drop your arms or die. Let the executioner nail your hands to the cross and vividly imagine the agonizing, all-encompassing length of God's "all day long"!

This we must clearly understand: we do not offer our embrace to the world because it is eager for our mediating love. We stretch out our hands because we honor our patient, passionate God. When disappointment and rejection are our lot, a surge of gratitude shall propel our tired arms into His steadfast embrace. In His compassion we will find our patience strengthened again.

Romans 10:21

*I am speaking the truth in Christ, I am not lying . . . that I have
great sorrow and unceasing anguish in my heart.*

Paul, God's chosen apostle to the Gentiles, suffers from
chronic depression because his fellow Jews disavow the
Messiah. Go ahead, someone . . . Someone tell Paul that his
pessimism is an affront to faith. Someone quote him Scripture
on unceasing joy and peace that passes all understanding.
Someone introduce him to a Christian psychologist to discuss
preacher burnout. Someone suggest golf. Someone slip him
money so he can splurge on books and rediscover how good
self-love can feel. Someone, for heaven's sake, remind Paul of
his phenomenal successes!

Someone might as well slip a knife to the passionate lover
of God and ask him to cut out the heart of flesh and sew the old
stone in its place. But it will do no good. Those who possess the
mind of Christ to this day inherit God's emotions as well. His
own great sorrows will always find a heart of flesh and inconvenience those of a shallower faith by mere association.

God's incomparable patience that spanned the "all day
long" of Israel's ancient history to Calvary was never one of
cool detachment. His very emotions were expressed through
the lives of those who suffered vicariously, albeit realistically.
"Some were tortured. . . . Others suffered mocking and
scourging, and even chains and imprisonment. They were
stoned, they were sawn in two . . . they went about in skins of
sheep and goats, destitute, afflicted, ill-treated . . ." (Hebrews
11:35-37).

Not everyone beloved of God is called to feel so deeply,
cling so stubbornly. But all share responsibility to keep God's
covenant visions from becoming more easily managed theological abstractions. Paul's kind of honesty must be encouraged
and empathy offered in quiet, loving, undemanding ways.
Because he bared his heart and risked his reputation, we can
acknowledge the paradox of faith that is both tear-soaked and
joyous at once.

Romans 9:1-2 □ *Romans 9:1-5*

In the world you have tribulation; but be of good cheer, I have overcome the world.

One of Christendom's great classic lines and we hesitate to swallow it! The thought of tribulation fails to bring out the cheerleader in us. Are the shadows of persecution darkening our land? Is a cataclysmic time clock ticking away ominously? Our good cheer sits like a pound of glued confetti in our stomach, hoping to be traded for the bliss of ignorance.

What if Christ employed today's vernacular to make this all less Greek to us? What if He explained: As you walk the path of obedience where I have walked, be prepared to step from one wad of chewing gum into another. But learn to laugh it off — a sharp stick will help — and keep remembering that I have arrived at our destination and reserved your place already!

Of course the Greek *thlipsis* does not refer to chewing gum, but a lenient linguist might allow for sticky situations. Tribulation is that which makes us chafe, feel pressured and burdened. It is what we long to throw off, escape from, kiss goodbye once and for all — even if it is only drudgery of work or the sheer cussedness of mechanical marvels that keep breaking down. Tribulation is the swamp we want to cross in a hurry to get to the field we hope to leisurely cultivate for a luxuriant growth of faith. But Jesus cautions that we will always be swamped with trials large and small and that our investment of faith begins and ends precisely there.

"For whatever is born of God overcomes the world; and this is the victory that overcomes the world, our faith. Who is it that overcomes the world but he who believes that Jesus is the Son of God?" (1 John 5:4-5). If in God's economy we pay a price for sharing His visions, we also win the prize of tasting His victories. We take courage — are of good cheer — because Christ validated His claim as Son of God by His death and resurrection.

John 16:33 ☐ *John 16:16-33*

When they came to Capernaum, the collectors of the half-shekel tax went up to Peter and said, "Does not your teacher pay the tax?" He said, "Yes." And when he came home, Jesus spoke to him first, saying, "What do you think, Simon?"

For a change Simon thinks right on the money and a fish puts its money where his mouth is. Read this granddaddy of all fish stories that tax our credulity! When the moral comes home, we find Jesus speaking to us as well, saying, "What do you think?"

The history of the half-shekel tax dates back to Exodus when a census was ordered and each person numbered paid a ransom for himself to the Lord. The original "atonement money" became the silver sockets, hooks and rods of Israel's amazing portable house of worship. (Exodus 30:11-16; 38:25-38)

When the collectors baited Peter with the question of the temple tax, they were casting for confrontation with the teacher who taught, "Before Abraham was, I am." Peter, sensing a trap, hastily enrolled Jesus in the program. He would explain his dilemma to Him later, knowing deep within how ludicrous it was for the Lord to be thus obligated. Amazingly, Jesus beat him to the punch and made him fully rationalize his sentiment. Then, not wishing to offend the authorities, He sent Peter fishing. The first fish coming up had a shekel hidden in its mouth, which paid the tax for both men. "What do you think?"

We must either be delighted or disturbed. Like children we delight in a cartoon-like hero who employs mental telepathy and X-ray vision to run the show and outwit friend and foe alike. But children learn that cartoon heroes and their feats are not for real. Is the Jesus of this story for real? Does our faith swallow the fish story? Will our next tax return reflect it? Do the fishy establishments of our day allow us to be off the hook as the true sons of God? How does Christ perceive His absolute lordship in our heart at this very moment?

Matthew 17:24-25 ☐ *Matthew 17:24-27*

Jesus said to them, "Children, have you any fish?" They answered him, "No." He said to them, "Cast the net on the right side of the boat, and you will find some."

There is no escaping it: Jesus has a way with fish! But are we catching the lesson? Where is the net profit of instruction for a meat-and-potatoes generation? Right off, Jesus meets us exactly where we are physically and at our point of need spiritually.

The emotional trauma of the Crucifixion, the mystery of the Resurrection — now you see me now you don't — had taken their toll on the disciples. Trapped by a sense of failure in a limbo of dubiosity, Peter roused himself to retreat into a safer past. "I am going fishing." He and his buddies promptly spent a dismal night catching absolutely nothing.

At daybreak on the deserted beach a seeming stranger calls them children. Little ones in faith. He could have easily said, "Hey, dummies!" Children — I will multiply your faith. Catch His tenderness. As the loaded net comes up, a light goes on in the disciple whom Jesus loved especially because he was so needy: "It is the Lord!" Peter, stripped for work, now puts on his clothes and dives into the water on his hasty way to meet Him — diving right into his future as the fisher of men. A breakfast of fish and bread is awaiting him, but Jesus invites Peter to add some of his own fresh catch to the feast. That way he has to count them — 153 large specimens — and marvel how the net held. This is one fish story he has to buy hook, line and sinker!

Peter the crude fisherman became a statesman for Jesus Christ. Our Lord trained him in his natural element with its built-in positive and negative learning situations. Jesus loved him through his childhood of faith and failure into his maturity as faithful follower. Have we caught the encouragement? Jesus trains and loves us where we are — right here and now!

John 21:5-6 ☐ *John 21:1-14*

Lifting up his eyes, then, and seeing that a multitude was coming to him, Jesus said to Philip, "How are we to buy bread . . ." This he said to test him . . .

Five small loaves and two fish fed five thousand hungry men. To guard against sceptics, Jesus ordered the leftovers gathered up. There were twelve baskets — filled "with fragments from the five barley loaves." How do we react to these larger-than-life stories the Gospels dish up to feed our faith?

"Examine yourselves, to see whether you are holding to your faith. Test yourselves. Do you not realize that Jesus Christ is in you?" (2 Corinthians 13:5). Somewhere along the line we shall have to go from reaction to transaction on the basis of this very miracle that had the ancients exclaim, "This is indeed the prophet who is to come into the world!" In us, Christ's own, the revelation of His truth and power must keep coming into the world. That is our sole purpose.

We all possess right now the lad's five barley loaves and two fish — the essence of individual insignificance when measured against the large pressing needs of any given moment. We can hoard our insignificance as sinfully as an eccentric miser hoards his wealth! We can hold Christ and the hungry at bay until doomsday if we insist on managing and multiplying our modest resources alone. We really watch jealously over them because we lust for that glut of satisfaction that the five thousand experienced. We shall never taste it unless we empty ourselves of such faithless greed.

Jesus took the lad's offering, lifted His eyes to heaven, gave thanks and broke it into "fragments," continually distributing these. There is our pattern for the miracle of multiplication. Will we surrender our hoarded insignificance to the lordship of Jesus Christ? Dare we become His broken bread that goes on satisfying all concerned?

John 6:5-6 □ *John 6:1-14*

Well done, good and faithful servant; you have been faithful over a little . . . enter into the joy of your master.

Did you hear the one about the not-too-bright kid who left home to join the circus? Surprisingly, he was hired on the spot and his occasional letters glowed with pleasure over his show business career. He was with the elephant act and could not praise the gentle creatures' cleverness enough. When the circus came to town his kin flocked to the opening performance. Imagine their chagrin when their late bloomer turned out to be in charge of elephant droppings. "Isn't show biz wonderful?" he enthused when he came around to greet them afterwards.

God would be tickled pink if the Great Ecclesiastical Talent Hunt would produce a rash of such enthusiasts. Marvelous if someone would love hauling raw meat for the great cats and bananas for the monkeys. Splendid if tent rips were stitched and clowns' pants patched with panache. Too bad we all want to be shot out of the cannon or rest our head between the polar bear's molars.

Of course this is absurd. The church is filled with people who itch for the big time and watch the stars — speakers, singers, artists — with undisguised envy. If only they had been given a deeper voice or higher education . . . If only God did not have chronically understaffed Sunday schools! If only He had regular rides for senior citizens and hot meals for shut-ins! If only God had men there with laps and hugs for little ones! If only God had a whole lot more of the "faithful over a little" people!

The parables of talents and pounds alike make it painfully clear that God has entrusted to all some kind of stewardship. Why look for the exotic goose that lays the golden egg when we practically trip over the elephant in our path? Of course "show biz" *is* wonderful when our small faithfulness lights up God's face!

Matthew 25:21 □ *Matthew 25:14-30*

For as his share is who goes down into the battle, so shall his share be who stays by the baggage; they shall share alike.

"Then David came to the two hundred men, who had been too exhausted to follow . . . and . . . he saluted them. Then all the wicked and base fellows . . . said, 'Because they did not go with us, we will not give them any of the spoil . . .' But David said, 'You shall not do so, my brothers . . .'" (1 Samuel 30:21-23).

What made David affirm the dropouts and address the disgruntled as brothers? Extenuating circumstances? All six hundred warriors shared the strain of his Philistine exile. All had just geared up for war in the ranks of their hosts, only to be dismissed as untrustworthy. Returning to their temporary home they found the town looted and burned, their families carried off by the raiders. The men had wept to the point of exhaustion and threatened to stone David. "But David strengthened himself in the Lord his God." His own profound experience of grace made him profoundly gracious!

The proof of experienced grace is not how it bears on circumstances, but how it affects the heart and reflects into the lives of others. To take this matter of applied grace further, a quick word survey of Scripture gives us an idea of what David had and what we have to work with in terms of grace doctrine.

The King James Version employs *grace* 38 times in the Old Testament. Nine references express hope to "find" it; 18 affirm they "found" it in the sight of God. The word *gracious* appears 28 times, mostly as an appeal to Him. In contrast, the New Testament uses *gracious* twice and *grace* 128 times. Paul, "chiefest" of sinners, refers to it 89 times; the gospel writers only 4 times. Christ's death and resurrection obviously brought the theme out in the open as the Holy Spirit expounded it. Have we become a proportionately more gracious people because of it?

1 Samuel 30:24 □ *1 Samuel 29 and 30*

Now to him who is able to strengthen you according to my gospel. . . . to the only wise God be glory . . .

My gospel! Does that smack of an inflated ego? Or does it suggest that you and I must have a gospel so personal, so convincing, so ascribing glory to the only wise God — that with Paul we cry out, "Woe to me if I do not preach my gospel!"

My gospel, boasts Paul, will *strengthen* you; a term meaning to establish, "to turn resolutely in a certain direction." The great Light that struck down Saul made an ash heap of his life built on the prestige and passion of his natural heritage. Intercepted by grace, blinded, Paul then experienced being launched "resolutely in a certain direction." To arrive at his gospel he rocked the infant church with dissent, weaning her from the pabulum of cultural conditioning and forcing the meat of eternal truth into her.

How do we impart bite to our personal gospel? There is a spiritual, intellectual, emotional and practical pattern traced from Paul's life, eclipsed by his focus on the crucified and risen Lord alone. First, Paul did not initially "confer with flesh and blood." Separating himself unto God in Arabia, he received from Him spiritual instruction and discipline. Secondly, he spent ten years back in Tarsus weaving goat hair into tents while exercising his intellect along with his faith. He tenaciously thought through the gospel truth until it was nothing but the truth, so help me God. Thirdly, he accepted the price — "fighting without and fear within" — of going public with his gospel. Fourthly, he joined himself to people in love, whether in person or by letter.

"My" gospel is grace personified. It is not sweet syrup gluing us into a perpetual state of bliss but muriatic acid that keeps foaming up and eating away at everything that does not make its boast in the cross of Christ alone.

Romans 16:25-27

Fear not, you worm Jacob, you men of Israel. . . . Behold, I will make of you a threshing sledge, new, sharp, and having teeth . . .

"Jacob" has grown old before his time. For too long he has eaten the soft bread of sin. Now his jaws hang slack and the toothless gums give him the feeble appearance of a useless old man who commands no honor, inspires no affection. What of the virile, venerated patriarch whose limp had blessed Israel?

All night long Jacob had wrestled with God even when his thigh was put out of joint and God asked him to call it off. "But Jacob said, 'I will not let you go, unless you bless me.' And he said to him, 'What is your name?' And he said, 'Jacob.' Then he said, 'Your name shall no more be called Jacob, but Israel, for you have striven with God and with man, and have prevailed.' (Genesis 32:26-28).

The name Jacob meant "heel-catcher" because at his birth he was found to hold on to the heel of his twin brother Esau. When God renamed him Israel, He testified as much to Himself as to His wrestling partner. The *el* in Israel means "god." In bestowing the name that came to identify and bless his nation, he called Jacob "God's fighter," or "having power with God."

Ironically, as zealous ritualists the Jews avoided eating the sinew of an animal's hind quarters, perpetually honoring Jacob's limp by this tradition. Tragically, neither did they feed on the strength of Jacob's God. Wooed by the pagan cultures in their midst, they soon ate their bread of hospitality and drank their milk of human kindness. Slowly, imperceptibly, "Jacob" lost his bite. In the end Israel cried to God from a shriveled, toothless mouth. Does our gospel still have Paul's kind of teeth in it? Or has it become worm-like, soft, safely burrowed underground where no one takes offense at it? Do we cry to God as fighters or the badly fear-ridden?

Redemptoristine Nuns
Monastery of St. Alphonsus
Liguori, Missouri 63057

Isaiah 41:14-15

Great is Artemis of the Ephesians!

Just how great was the lady better known to some as Diana? Would you believe as great as motherhood and apple pie, judging from the many breasts on her effigy and the fact that almighty Jupiter (Zeus) supposedly dropped her sacred image from heaven into the lap of luxury at Ephesus. She reposed in a magnificent temple that was one of the Seven Wonders of the ancient world and the apple of the eye to those who milked her image for all it was worth in silver. Ephesus was a major trading and political center, the capital of the Roman province called Asia, which is western Turkey today.

Unfortunately for the silversmiths and souvenir hawkers Paul had not yet developed the technique of the modern-day evangelist who campaigns in Idol City for only a few days and later sends a helpful book if so desired.

Paul set up shop in the synagogue and "for three months spoke boldly, arguing and pleading about the kingdom of God." When the local parish was fed up with this firebrand who ruined bingo and potlucks, he moved his act to the academy of Tyrannus, a sympathetic philosopher-teacher. There he argued daily for another two years, God backing him up with extraordinary miracles and a spectacular book-burning party by converts from magic arts, who let "fifty thousand pieces of silver" go up in smoke. No wonder Demetrius and the Chamber of Commerce had their nose full. And so a great shout went up, "Great is Artemis of the Ephesians!" and quite a hullabaloo was had. Paul did pack up after that, but by then the word of God had grown "and prevailed mightily."

Great is the Age of our Civilized Enlightening! Idol City is flourishing, providing employment, cultural enrichment, and community pride. Who would want to argue and plead — tenaciously, personally — about the kingdom of God in such a setting? By Jupiter, times have changed! (Have they?)

Acts 19:28 ☐ *Acts 19:23-41*

But recall the former days when, after you were enlightened, you endured a hard struggle with sufferings. . . . and joyfully accepted the plundering of your property . . .

First century Christianity, we gather, was no picnic. A public confession of Christ risked immediate public reprisals. These ran the gamut from economic sanctions to bodily harm. The practice of having "all things in common" was not early communist ideology, but quick necessity. As converts lost jobs and homes and family support, it was essential for a community of faith to spring up and stand in the breach.

In theory we applaud God's wisdom in allowing persecution. It made for lay evangelists so effective that in comparison today's doctor-of-divinity candidate is a mere babe in the woods. In practice we say thanks, but no thanks. Do we applaud the writer of Hebrews for chiding these seasoned saints for catching a breather from the rigors of faith? "It is a fearful thing," he exclaims, "to fall into the hands of the living God" and so presses them to think and act in keen anticipation of the Day when God will judge his people.

We live so dully on the edge of judgment. It is simply not relevant to our present experience and practice of faith. Our twentieth century Christianity has become a picnic! In fact, our "public confession" of Christ, the degree of our enlightening, can be somewhat assessed by observing the community of faith at a potluck supper in fellowship hall.

The main dish is prepared in the church kitchen. Some volunteers are asked to contribute cash, some a salad or dessert. Would you care to hear the grumbling, see the greed attending the love feast? The humor stops abruptly when we give this human zoo a name — Christ's own! — and remember the horror of those who "joyfully accepted the plundering of their property." Must we not burst into tears? As we measure our former days against the Day of Revelation, had we not better endure a hard struggle of re-evaluating our present degree of enlightening?

Hebrews 10:32-34 □ *Hebrews 10:19-39*

But I have this against you, that you have abandoned the love you had at first.

The theme is familiar to the newspaper advice columnist who presides over the ills of the Average Wife. Her letter reads perennially the same: My husband is a decent, hard-working man. We have a nice home and financial security. He is good to the kids and treats me well. My friends think I'm so lucky. So what's my gripe? I'm not sure, but lately all I want to do is cry. I want to be touched and held without having sex. I want my mate to share his thoughts with me, go for a walk with me, read a book or gaze at the stars with me. Isn't that what we used to do when we were young and poor and happy?

Grow up, lady, snaps back the columnist — just bristling with common sense! Wake up and thank your lucky stars. Kisses and fancy words are cheap. Learn to appreciate your decent, hard-working man who brings home the bread and bacon. Join a ladies' reading circle. Write poetry. Volunteer time in a nursing home and put your empty arms around the needy elderly. Get a new hairdo. Have you had a medical checkup lately?

Among those who rain down the blistering comments on complaint or columnist are never the mates of the mournful wives. Looking up from the sports page they would be dumbfounded to find themselves the object of public scorn and scrutiny. Being average red-blooded men they would think the world had gone crazy if all of a sudden it expected them to read poetry or hold hands with the woman they have lived and slept with all these years. High time for grandchildren, so the lady can get busy again. Jeez!

Jesus, make no mistake, is the "wife" who wrote the original letter of complaint and warning to the church at Ephesus. "He who has an ear, let him hear what the Spirit says to the churches."

Revelation 2:4 □ Revelation 2:1-7

Now if any one builds on the foundation with gold, silver . . . hay, straw — each man's work will become manifest; for the Day will disclose it, because it will be revealed with fire . . .

To many a marriage comes the day of reckoning when a dumbfounded mate finds himself groping in the rubble of the predictable life that just crashed in on him. To the husband served with walking papers by his high school sweetheart it comes as a shock that she would jeopardize the fruit of long years of labor — children, assets, reputation — just because he failed to satisfy her emotional and spiritual needs. Did he not attend church and buy candy on their anniversary? "I thought we had a good thing going," he confesses, genuinely perplexed. "You never asked — you never listened!" sobs the mate who has become a disturbing stranger overnight.

The idea here is not to digress into soap opera plots, but to initiate dialogue with the true love of our life, Jesus Christ. "For no other foundation can any one lay than that which is laid, which is Jesus Christ." Our spiritual destiny must be built on His Person. If marriage requires constant nurture and a sacred commitment to keep communication alive and growing, how much more shall we invest these safeguards in our love relationship with Him.

We must put down our busy agenda long enough — no, push it away resolutely — to look Jesus in the eye. His look points to Scripture — His neglected love letters. Jesus Christ yearns to be cherished for who He is intrinsically — not an institution — but a Person synonymous with love, possessed of spiritual and emotional needs that you and I are privileged to satisfy!

Church work can never take the place of conversational prayer and meditation on His Word. Jesus Christ deserves to be so cherished. When will we look up from the sports page of our undiscerning life and come alive to the gathering storm on the face so dear, so disturbed?

1 Corinthians 3:12-13 □ *1 Corinthians 3:10-13*

If the work which any man has built on the foundation survives, he will receive a reward. If any man's work is burned up, he will suffer loss, though he himself will be saved, but only as through fire.

The hell of fiery regret? Ask the fellow whose life went up in smoke through unexpected divorce. One day he was Joe Cool with a home and all creature comforts. The next he was a statistic in a motel room — so broken he wanted to sob on his dog's neck, only the pet went with the house. He can laugh about it now, having picked up the pieces and appreciating the more perceptive person living in his skin. Outwardly the wound has healed where the amputation of the past took place, but the burning phantom pain of regret will create its own haunting reality nevertheless.

Salvation and hell fire do not mix. Paul cannot mean that on the Day of Jesus Christ He will take us out to the woodshed to administer a lasting burning sensation to our "behind." Our past is free of all condemnation because of His perfect Atonement.

Paul does state — unequivocally so — that if we are careless in our personal relationship to Christ it will indelibly stamp as worthless, from eternity's viewpoint, our life's labor! On that momentous Day when we must appear before Him to acknowledge His mercy, we will not mourn the loss of reward for our own sake. The hot flame of regret will singe our delivered soul when we recognize the conspicuous worth of our Savior — and we do not have a crown of reward to cast at His feet in humble adoration! "Worthy is the Lamb who was slain, to receive power and wealth . . ."

God implores us to live on the edge of judgment not as those who shiver on the edge of fear, but as those who realistically make it the growing edge of their faith. Every day merits our focus on the grand and glorious Day of Jesus Christ as an opportunity to bless Him. "Worthy is the Lamb who was slain, to receive . . . wisdom and might and honor and glory and blessing!"

1 Corinthians 3:14-15 □ 1 Corinthians 3:10-15

Blessed are the pure in heart, for they shall see God.

If this means what we think it means, count us out! We are like the housewife who puts forth heroic effort to give sparkle to her home. The moment the wax hits the floor the cat comes swaggering in with a flapping bird in her mouth. The minute the bathroom is antiseptically clean the family's basketball star gets "aimlessly" sick to his stomach.

Why do we have this curious notion that if only we could somehow beat ourselves into show condition, a curtain would rise somewhere on a showpiece God? With such mentality we deserve to stare at the layered belly of a monumental Buddha. "Have I been with you so long, and yet you do not know me, Philip? He who has seen me has seen the Father; how can you say, 'Show us the Father'?"

If Jesus is to be the foundation of our being and doing in such a way that it will connect with our worth to Him revealed on Judgment Day, then every day has to be a day in which we can see forever. That is clearly a tall order. We know what it takes to put a man on the moon. It was a calculated move of such enormity it had the whole world crane its neck and scratch its head in wonderment. Who will calculate our trajectory so we will not miss the mark so infinitely higher and more mysterious than our luminous neighbor in space?

Happy are we because Jesus Christ is our Lodestar! If we filter our daily vision through His atoning work, our works cannot miss the mark. In Him the mark is personified and at "see level." But what of impure thoughts? They will always swarm up like gnats from somewhere. Unlike the moon traveler who begins his journey in a sterile environment, we stay exposed to a dirty world. In Christ's name we tell those gnats to buzz off and we swat them with His forgiveness. Mostly we rejoice in the Lodestar who illuminates heart and mind daily so darkness cannot take root and breed evil. Happy days are here — forever.

Matthew 5:8

Beloved, we are God's children now; it does not yet appear what we shall be, but we know that when he appears we shall be like him, for we shall see him as he is. And every one who thus hopes in him purifies himself as he is pure.

If we suffered from an alcoholic father, we are careful with drink. If our mother and grandmother died of cancer, we have that pap smear regularly. If talents run in our genes, we proudly express them through the generations. If ugly noses and early baldness mark the clan — tough! We can only "purify" so much. Still, there is a choice. We can exercise our godly heritage or be victimized by our natural one.

Take a critical look at the elderly. If they magnified the Lord Jesus in the days of their natural vigor, their youngness of heart and freshness of faith continually delight us. If they never rose beyond the elevated culture of formal religion, their rigidity overwhelms us. Every quirk has been frozen into place. Like stoics they sit in the church pew, impeccably masked. They are the petulant fogies who whine and criticize instead of cheering and praying for the new crop of saints. How sad when infirmities take their toll — when the farewells come hard and fast — and the rigor mortis of the dead relationship with Christ comes to light in their comfortless condition.

When we say "carnal Christian" we think sex maniac instead of benign little old lady or gent. The carnal Christian is none other than one who foolishly refuses to go into his Father's family business after having come of age.

"Beloved," cries the beloved disciple once known as son of thunder, "leave behind the crippling limitations of your natural heredity and welcome the transformation that comes to the expectant child of God!"

1 John 3:2-3 ☐ 1 John 3:1-10

No man has ever seen God; if we love one another, God abides in us and his love is perfected in us.

No man has ever seen God? Lovers of mystery, arise. This calls for the skill of the consummate sleuth. Let us assemble in the library and hear the witnesses.

Moses: "But," God said, "You cannot see my face; for man shall not see me and live."

John: No one has ever seen God; the only Son, who is in the bosom of the Father, he has made him known.

Jesus: If you had known me, you would have known my Father also; henceforth you know him and have seen him.

Jesus: See my hands and my feet, that it is I myself; handle me, and see; for a spirit has not flesh and bones . . .

Jesus: God is spirit, and those who worship him must worship in spirit and truth.

Face it, sleuths, this mystery cannot be neatly tied up with the classic line, "The butler did it." At best we can love the butler! Why do we allow ourselves to be tantalized by such inherent tension in Scripture? Are we the child who must know about Santa Claus? Are we the child of our age who thinks of the brain as a computer — the heart as such no longer the composite of will, intellect and emotions? If we could say, "Will the real God please stand up," would we hold our breath because His superior computer could blow our circuits — or because He might be so old-fashioned as to give us goosebumps of recognition?

The mother of identical twins orients herself by each child's distinct, essential character. "God is love." We must take our clue from His essential character. What does love look like? Perfected in us it looks like Jesus Christ. Does He look like His Father? What if God turns out to look like you and me because of Christ in us, "the hope of glory"? Lovers of mystery, the meeting is adjourned. Go love that butler!

1 John 4:12

Let brotherly love continue.

The noble sentiment does not fool us for a minute. "Brothers" is what one gets stuck with! Falling in love with kindred spirits is much more fun; loving strangers more glamorous. "Let brotherly love continue." The line smacks of a boring childhood refrain we had hoped to escape forever. Remember the squabbling of siblings — the litany of complaints recited to the parental arbiter in hopes of obtaining dramatic relief? Remember the sentence we were slapped with, the crisply voiced condemnation that brought crocodile tears to our eyes, "You are older, you should know better!"

In Jesus Christ, our Elder Brother, we are charged with being "older" for the rest of our lives. If tears help, let them come from the commendation of our Lord's humiliation: "Now before the feast of the Passover, when Jesus knew that his hour had come to depart out of this world to the Father, having loved his own who were in the world, he loved them to the end." How? By laying aside His garments, girding Himself with a towel, and washing the disciples' feet. "A new commandment I give to you, that you love one another, even as I have loved you . . ."

We want to give brothers our time and attention as a drill sergeant — long enough to whip them into shape — and when we turn them loose on the parade grounds we mean to bask in our own spit and polish. In reality the brothers constantly parade their warts and weaknesses and no amount of indignation will change that. If we do not want hypocrites in church, we must see that in the context of brotherly love as well.

If such "pedestrian" love is to continue, we must fall in love afresh with our Lord again and again. How? By laying aside our pride, girding ourselves with productive intent, and practicing service to the sons and daughters of the King.

Hebrews 13:1

How beautiful upon the mountains are the feet of him who brings good tidings . . . who publishes salvation, who says to Zion, "Your God reigns."

If our feet connect us to the ground and gas pedal more than to spiritual truth, it is because we have not appreciated them lately. The only ones to get excited about feet these days are antique hounds who adore claw and ball, ogee bracket, snake and French scroll. Then there is the podiatrist who sadly cradles in his gentle hands the torture victims of civilization and marvels at the feet of old: "Forty years didst thou sustain them in the wilderness, and . . . their feet did not swell."

Detroit decidedly did not influence Scripture; feet are mentioned over 260 times. How can we do proper justice to the beautiful feet of the messenger on the mountain, if the only graceful image that comes to our mind is that of a mountain goat? Do not picture him a mountaineer swathed in Sir Edmund Hillary attire. We are not after Mount Everest, but a pinnacle of truth that applies to us here and now.

Could we not say that the graceful messenger is one who goes out of his way — one who rises fresh to every occasion to proclaim the integrity of the gospel? Wherever we so step out in risky trust we have our Lord's assurance that He will give us "hind's feet," which is the surefootedness of faith. The precipitous places then become the testing grounds of which we later jubilantly say, "Thou didst give a wide place for my steps under me, and my feet did not slip."

Again, do not think feat, but feet; Mount Zion, not Mount Everest. Zion was the height in the northeastern part of Jerusalem where once stood Solomon's temple; it was the ancient seat of government of the kingdom of Judah. "Zion" symbolizes the earthly abode of God, it is the church. The graceful messenger elevates his gospel beyond ordinary churchmanship. He does the extraordinary. He washes feet with aplomb!

Isaiah 52:7 □ Isaiah 52:7-10

For God is not so unjust as to overlook your work and the love which you showed for his sake in serving the saints, as you still do.

Beware of spiritual overkill. It does not honor the God who rendered us "approved as is" in Jesus Christ. Have we ever laughed and loafed with Him? Have we ever walked off the job and kept on walking, snapping off a fragrant blade of grass here and there? Jesus did — and He taught us to walk without being leashed to that pet monster *Guilt*.

We recall Him strolling through the grainfields on the Sabbath, catching heat from the Pharisees for allowing His disciples to pluck ears of grain. Bask in the sunshine of His authority, "The sabbath was made for man, not man for the sabbath." Watch the Bread of Life and His companions "loaf" through the fields. Hear them tell their corny jokes and catch their belly laughs. Take to heart this essential nourishment from the Father — the experience of the feasted soul — the times when He uniquely sees to our need and we reap benefits we did not sow.

We are not heaven's robots oiled by the Holy Spirit to run relentlessly until metal fatigue puts us out to pasture. We are God's beloved people anointed with His oil of gladness. Dare to be the plucky disciple who joins Jesus joyously as He walks us through His harvest of holy hilarity.

We need not schedule our "times of wonderful refreshment from the presence of the Lord." Most often they are the serendipities appointed by His generous and watchful heart. If our service to the saints becomes so absorbing that we run the danger of becoming "amateur providences" — instead of priests pointing people to their growing edge of faith through pain and pressure — we need to be led into the rest of our own feasted soul. This soul is loyal to God alone; the laughing saint cannot be leashed by guilt to a lesser, more exacting master!

Hebrews 6:10 □ *Hebrews 6:9-12*

The Lord God has given me the tongue of those who are taught, that I may know how to sustain with a word him that is weary. Morning by morning he wakens, he wakens my ear, to hear as those who are taught.

We learn the hard way. In our zeal to be Father's little helper we bite off more than we can chew. We become "amateur providences" to the people we love and serve. Instead of speaking encouragement and guidance, we interpose *ourselves* as way, truth, and life. In time we feel exhausted, resentful, used. Guilt makes us redouble our efforts and people marvel at our long-suffering. They call us wonderful counselor, mighty doer of good, everlasting Father-substitute — while we go to pieces.

If we allow God to waken — really waken — our ear first thing in the morning, it will save us from screaming at the top of our spiritual lungs in the heat of the day. Think back to the last time you threw off troubled sleep at dawn — a bundle of nerves flailing against a mountain of "musts."

Friend A is depressed. Friend B is ill. Friend C has spiritual doubts. The kids need underwear and the dog shots. The lawn has cutworms, relatives are coming, and we must prepare for a Bible study on the great tribulation. No saint should be so flattened at five in the morning.

When God descends into our "netherlands," He does not bring boots to assault our mountain. He gently retrieves our sore thumb from the hole in the dike and emphatically says, "Be still, and know that I am God! If you believe in me, out of your heart shall flow rivers of living water." Until you rest on that peace, stop piecing together the world. You cannot be utterly selfless until experiential salvation has knit your innermost self into wholeness. Own yourself, as it were, before giving yourself away. Only then can you really do good and escape the fate of the "no good" do-gooder.

Isaiah 50:4

With joy you will draw water from the wells of salvation. And you will say in that day: "Give thanks to the LORD, call upon his name . . ."

Our natural juices go only so far. Then it is curtains on our moving performance of being poured out for the needs of the world. Our swan song? Well, we tried. Well, so long. How little we know about wells! The importance of digging deeper into the subject is illustrated by Jesus, "And whoever gives to one of these little ones even a cup of cold water because he is a disciple, truly, I say to you, he shall not lose his reward." That cold water could only come through effort from the deep of a well. Palestine has heavy rainfall during its wet season, but the land is mostly porous limestone. Water runs off rapidly or collects in stagnant pools and marshes. That explains the biblical delight and necessity of "living water" derived from running stream or fountain. Wells were hewn from solid rock and covered with a large stone to keep sun and soil out. A chief attraction of the Promised Land was its existing wells.

The well of salvation is excavated from heaven's bedrock. Jesus Christ was the workman who constructed for us the luxury model with broad steps leading right down to the spring. The water surface lends itself to reflection. We can touch our face to its coolness and dip in our hand for an immediate thirst-quencher. We need not grapple with rope and bucket. Our living water comes literally with no strings attached.

Let us never merely sympathize with people's ills — nor overstep our authority in bringing relief to troubled lives. Our loving labor is to lead them down those steps to the wellspring of Christ for genuine reflection, refreshment and regeneration. When we part company at the Fountain of Mercy we do it with a mutual reminder, "Give thanks to the LORD, call upon his name . . ."

Isaiah 12:3-4 ☐ *Isaiah 12*

Hearken to me, you who pursue deliverance, you who seek the
LORD; look to the rock from which you were hewn, and to the
quarry from which you were digged.

What about pressures brought on by external forces
beyond our control? What if the backbone of a nation disinte-
grates from moral laxity? What if the sagging bulk of a weakly
governed body attaches itself to our frail constitution and we
cannot afford the luxury of scorn along political party lines,
because rising costs, crime and joblessness hurt us personally?

Everybody adores a soft baby. Softness in later years elicits
groans. Sagging flesh insults soaring spirits. Overnight we
become the exercise freak who huffs and puffs in an orgy of
self-punishment. How a cartoonist's pen would drip with glee
when flabby will abruptly calls a halt to pain and its absence
leaves us so ecstatic we promptly go on a calorie binge.

No such luck with our exercise of larger responsibilities. We
can escape politics, but not God's pinch test. If He detects
excess apathy on our spiritual frame, He will make us into His
hard pressed people. Internal force must exceed external pressure if His will is to become fleshed out. Can our resolute
exercise of faith bear directly on a nation's fiber? Consider
Isaiah's theology of geology.

Limestone is rock evolved mostly from organic matter. The
altered constitution is effected by pressure, heat and water.
Such metamorphism results in marble. Michelangelo had some
of this "wasted away" (from a Greek root for marble) stuff
brought to his studio. The continued process of applied pressure revealed the towering truth of his David. In contrast,
Isaiah would have us admire a different male body. His rock is
Abraham — in view of his wasted flesh "as good as dead." The
quarry is derisive Sarah — still childless at eighty-nine. Their
compressed witness: "Is anything too hard for the Lord?" As
heirs of the Promise let our inherited pressures go to work for
Him!

Isaiah 51:1

So Isaac dwelt in Gerar. When the men of the place asked him about his wife, he said, "She is my sister". . . .

As Abraham lied about his wife to save his skin, so did Isaac. As in his father's day a fair woman might end up in some crowned bully's harem, so in the son's she might be coveted by a potent peeping tom. ("Abimelech king of the Philistines looked out of a window and saw Isaac fondling Rebekah his wife.") If the patriarchs loved their women, they treasured their own flesh more demonstratively still.

Because history does repeat itself, God must write His Story creatively. Abraham's tedious linear trek from Haran to Canaan lasted a hundred years, the times he was forced to go in circles before God, an eternity. Toss a pebble into a pond and watch the ripple as it travels in ever widening circles to the distant shore. In his humanity the patriarch was more pebble than rock, but look who is still making waves!

God pressed four great faith trials on Abraham. 1. Go from your country and relatives to an unknown future of prosperity and posterity. 2. Separate yourself from Lot, fellow believer, beloved nephew and possible heir. With Lot went the fruitful Jordan valley. 3. Abandon your ambitious plans for Ishmael. He was his cherished firstborn at age eighty-six. 4. Offer up Isaac! He was the trusting son of promise, for whose birth he had patiently waited twenty-five years.

How did Abraham's seed of faith multiply into a stand of oaks, the planting of God's righteousness among nations, instead of him turning into a nut? Why patriarch and not paranoid? For every season of vigorous pruning God gave him a vigorous season of bloom. He died a satisfied old man. Will we invite God's rigorous pruning — spiritual circumcision of the highest order — on a personal and national level? The God of patriarchs is not after petunias, but oaks of righteousness. Is that not the timber from which are built great men and nations?

Genesis 26:6-7 ☐ *Genesis 26:1-11*

He said, "Take your son, your only son Isaac, whom you love, and go to the land of Moriah, and offer him there as a burnt offering . . ."

How can we tell if God's creative design is not cut from the cloth of our imagination? Would we not suspect Satan of subjecting God's friend to the ordeal of human sacrifice, a practice expressly forbidden elsewhere in Scripture?

The narrative of the ordeal is unemotional. Abraham apparently did not rend his garments, rack his brain, or rally spiritual advisers. There was no all-night jam session harping on the pros and cons. He rose early in the morning and went. What went on between him and God we do not know. To his traveling companions he said, ". . . I and the lad will go yonder and worship, and come again to you." To Isaac's puzzled question about the burnt offering he evenly replied, "God will provide himself the lamb . . . my son." And so He did. On Moriah and Calvary!

The faith chapter in Hebrews attests to Abraham's strong belief in resurrection. "Is anything too hard for the Lord?" Therefore he "put forth his hand, and took the knife to slay his son." Notice how the author of Genesis employs verbs to explicitly affirm Abraham's faith as active obedience. Why the test? God clearly did not wish to consummate the act of sacrifice, only the sacrificial attitude. In putting Abraham through the actual motions, he exposed his motives for worship as nothing else could. Abraham now knew for sure himself that the Giver, not the gift, merits supreme loyalty. God requires and rewards "worthship" in spirit and in truth. After Mount Moriah, Abraham was the most delivered of all men. Never once would he have to fear for Isaac and his progeny again, having calmly stood the test of absolute trust and surrender.

Why dismiss as impossible the unthinkable tests of our faith? Why imagine the worst when God invites us to imagine the highest? Who or what is the snare in our expression of "worthship"?

Genesis 22:2 □ *Genesis 22:1-19*

Satan stood up against Israel, and incited David to number Israel.

The devil made me do it! It is a primitive line, yet in subtle disguises not infrequently used by the Christian. How much is Satan really worth as scapegoat? To get an estimate, we return to Mount Moriah where the deep things of God — not of Satan — fell into place for David. In his day it was known as the threshing floor of Ornan the Jebusite. It became the site of Solomon's temple at David's bidding.

In his heyday as warrior-king success went literally to his head. His loyal commander-in-chief Joab secured for him the Ammonite crown. Another nephew slew a giant with extra fingers and toes on his extremities. Monstrous pride caused David to order a census.

Joab smelled trouble immediately and told David so. In all of Israel there was not enough room for both God and David's swelled head. Nevertheless, to keep his own, Joab completed the task in nine months and twenty days. It was a proper gestation period to bring forth the monstrous consequence — 70,000 innocent men dead and Jerusalem on the verge of catastrophic judgment. "It is I who have sinned," a horror-struck David cried out and built an altar on the threshing floor of Ornan, because there he was fully convicted and utterly pardoned. The official place of worship was at Gibeon, but his sin had so alienated him from God that in fear he had avoided it.

The devil made me do it? "It is I who have sinned!" Satan's role as scapegoat is not worth beans if a ruffian like Joab can plainly see what is cooking. There is one good thing to be said for Satan, however. His sudden interest in us can tip us off to spiritual danger just around the corner. Wherever we itch and he scratches, with that uncertainty we must appear at once before God at Gibeon. Or else we too report to Ornan's place for a thrashing!

1 Chronicles 21:1 ☐ *1 Chronicles 21:1-17*

The Lord said to Satan, "Whence have you come?" Satan answered the Lord, "From going to and fro on the earth, and from walking up and down on it."

There he is, the original busybody who minds other people's business and his own store all at once. We marvel at the easy conversational tone of God's fearsome exchange with Satan, which was a mutually hatched plot against God's faithful friend Job. It did illuminate grace — the hard way!

It comes as an added revelation that in the Bible Satan makes his official debut in the Book of Job, and that other Old Testament passages mention him hardly at all. From his proper introduction in Job we know that he is not some imaginary mafia-type with a pitchfork in his violin case. Satan is not merely a symbol for evil influence, but an actual created being with intellect, emotions and will. God's dialogue with him establishes these facts fully.

Why did the Old Testament believers not say Satan-this and Satan-that as does the modern day Christian? Could it be that the very advent of grace has subtly perverted our preconceptions and we are God's primitive people?

In ancient times base instincts were met by basic justice. Wrongs were righted by drastic physical measures. Today, life and limbs are preserved, but the soul takes a beating. Long after the false angel of light has been expelled from heaven, we allow him to "illuminate" our humanity and dominate too many Christian conversations. Satan creates doubt and despair. Job's Redeemer speaks peace and instills this primary instinct: Satan and grace have nothing left to say to each other. Calvary terminated the dialogue! To be sure, the Adversary in his silent fury makes for grief a while longer. Let the Suffering Servant handle it for us. Let our conversations acknowledge His might and mercy. No more limelight for Satan, please.

Job 1:7 □ Job 1:6-12

An evil and adulterous generation seeks for a sign; but no sign shall be given to it except the sign of the prophet Jonah.

In the tough decisions of our life we are not adverse to signs either. We want simplistic traffic signals that speed us through the cloverleaf and redeposit us on the highway leading to the familiar, flourishing faith. Such outward signs would handily detour us around the dusty pioneer settlement in our heart. The name — King's Place. Population: 1. The unmistakable message of the battered traffic sign: YIELD.

Paradoxically, we fuss most where God has already given direction. It is not as if he blindfolded and spun us around. We squirm precisely because instinct of faith tells us that a fresh season of yielding has come upon us. In pondering the new obedience we pace back and forth mentally, debating our innate strength. Convinced of its inadequacy, we then seek to convince ourselves that we misunderstood God. Now we clamor for the clear sign that will merge us once again with the normal flow of faith and relieve us from the disquiet of disobedience.

When pointed toward Nineveh, Jonah pondered the human impossibility of his God-size task. His crash course in yielding cost him dearly. It was marked by signs so vivid, so simplistic, that our own sophisticated faith is tempted to question this whale of a story. As we flail around in the dark, slimy cavity of our own gutless trust we gasp for true light and breath. When we have exhausted our store of human reasoning, we are flung at the feet of our Lord where we become strangely content to lay hold of His mercy alone. Miraculously, His might becomes real from then on.

"For as Jonah was . . . in the belly of the whale, so will the Son of man be . . . in the heart of the earth." In yielding to His death we receive His resurrection. This power signals persistently the ONE WAY of fruitful obedience. It marks us as God's credible prophet.

Matthew 12:39 □ *Matthew 12:38-42*

Thus says the king, "Put this fellow in prison and feed him scant fare . . . until I come in peace."

When Syria attacked Israel twice and at last the Syrian king was captured, Ahab signed a trade agreement instead of a death warrant. Three years later the Syrians still occupied Ramoth-gilead, which vexed wishy-washy Ahab. When Jehoshaphat, king of Judah, came for a friendly visit, guess who offered to take him sightseeing in Ramoth-gilead. War being the good clean fun of ancient kings, Jehoshaphat was game as long as some prophets were consulted first.

Four hundred yes men came forth to bow and ballyhoo before Ahab and his frowning guest. When Micaiah — summoned at Jehoshaphat's insistence — joined the impressively choreographed bobbing babblers of lies, their leader was waving horns of iron to symbolize Ahab's prowess in battle. Warned to be bullish in his prediciton in order to present closed ranks for the king's pleasure, Micaiah nevertheless had to unceremoniously say "bull."

Ahab had warned against this professional killjoy and promptly sulked when Micaiah sarcastically wished him luck. He seethed with rage when the prophet told of the superior council in heaven at which a spirit stood up with a scheme so Ahab would not have a leg to stand on. "I will go forth, and will be a lying spirit in the mouth of all his prophets." Ahab's death warrant was signed. The horn waver slapped Micaiah, the king ordered scant bread and water for him, and that is the last we hear of his fate. Ahab departed this life at Ramoth-gilead.

What is the sign of a true prophet? According to Micaiah, he "who is like Jehovah" must like his own company best because he will have plenty of it. "As the Lord lives, what my God says, that I will speak." Have we faced the loneliness that comes with such keen perception and iron-horned faith?

1 Kings 22:27 ☐ *1 Kings 22:1-40*

And why is this granted me, that the mother of my Lord should come to me?

"I have come to take lessons in how to be lonely, Elizabeth. You were lonely when your friends long ago took their babies to the playground. You were lonely when they joined Girl Scouts and PTA. You went to their bake sales and smiled at their excited chatter, but their language was foreign to you. Inside you cried and kept wondering why God had singled you out for such pain. Even now you are lonely. People whisper behind your back. Your husband is locked inside his own secret world.

"I am lonely, Elizabeth, and scared. They have been so good to me at home, but an invisible wall has come up between us. They look at me quizzically but keep their conversation purposely light, as if I were sick or too young to understand some family matter. I feel shut out. Joseph is so kind, too polite almost. Everytime I look at him I feel guilty, as if I had somehow ruined his life. Sometimes I fear for my mind, but my body is changing and I cannot walk away from the mystery. Elizabeth, what will my future be like?"

At age twelve Mary's son acted as if she did not exist. At the wedding at Cana when she appealed to his special nature, He verbally brushed her off, "O woman, what have you to do with me?" Later, when she had her fill of His public notoriety and wanted him home for His protection as well as hers, Jesus calmly announced to His disciples, "Who are my mother and my brothers? Here are my mother and my brothers! Whoever does the will of God is my brother, and sister, and mother."

Only at the foot of the cross did Jesus pay homage to Mary's lonely ordeal. "When Jesus saw his mother, and the disciple whom he loved standing near, he said to his mother, 'Woman, behold, your son!'" If we remember Mary for her Magnificat, let us also remember her loneliness as an undeniable element of our own faith.

Luke 1:43 □ *Luke 1:39-45*

Go out quickly to the streets and lanes of the city, and bring in
the poor and maimed and blind and lame. . . . Go out . . . and
compel people to come in . . .

The victims are still straggling in, each bringing a corner of
his own lonely world into the church. The lonely, sad to say,
can also be the selfish and hard to please. They carry their hurt
as a badge of distinction, entitling them to ride on the minister-
ial staff's shirttails as the sole demonstration of their own
higher worth. They follow the leaders from group to group,
never staying behind to develop ties and a ministry of their own.

In contrast, the saint who permits God to remove the
conscious experience of blessing and abandon him to barren
places for a deeper, surer faith in Him alone, never exhibits
such pathological loneliness. He consistently practices the art
of initiative love, a sure sign of spiritual maturity. It permits
him not only to cry out, "Help me!" when needed but more
pointedly still to quietly step into silent places of need with the
loving assurance, "I will befriend you because I do know how
you feel!"

The lonely often change churches as one changes clothes.
They go from one "unfriendly people" to another without
facing the simple truth that they could have stayed on as the
new trend-setter. Shy and tongue-tied? If we pattern ourselves
after our Lord, we let our actions divulge our attitudes. The
moment we opt for service, no matter how modest in scope,
we nudge open the door to healing fellowship.

Deep at the heart of chronic loneliness is self-despising. We
resent being poor, maimed, blind or lame. We are dishonest
about our reasons for coming into the Father's House. The
purpose of the banquet is to celebrate His all-sufficiency, not
ours. If pride isolates us, no one can help. As God's glad guests,
let us continue to compel people to come in — into a deeper
realization of grace and a more honest expression of truth.

Luke 14:21-23 □ *Luke 14:15-24*

There he found a man named Aeneas, who had been bedridden for eight years and was paralyzed. And Peter said to him, "Aeneas, Jesus Christ heals you; rise and make your bed."

Compare the compelling directness of Peter to our own complex dealings. At the healing service singing creates mood. Fervent prayer is offered for the pre-screened paralytic. If he gets to his feet, great. If not, he will testify to inner glow.

Or consider the Board of Deacons alerted to the man's pitiable condition. A delegation visits, offers prayers of general comfort, and assists materially. His recurring depressions eventually mark him for professional evaluation. Institutional care seems inevitable. Unfair generalizations? Then we must either ignore such compelling Scripture or seek to apply its truth realistically to contemporary situations. If "realistic" means anything less than the supernatural Jesus mediated through faith, we had better look the other way entirely.

"Aeneas, Jesus Christ heals you; rise and make your bed." The compelling directness is fourfold. 1. Aeneas! Peter connects to the essential character, not the incidental condition. The man was "Aeneas" long before he was conscious sinner, sufferer or seeker. 2. Jesus Christ heals you! Peter quickly focuses on the Person and power of our Lord, not on his credentials as representative. 3. Rise! He immediately presses for a practical response, before subversive mental processes sabotage the man's will. 4. Make your bed! Peter forces the man to prove to himself that faith is not religious thinking, but productive living.

Modern Peter, Jesus Christ charges you; rise to your calling and find your paralytic. He might be the long-term unemployed in your neighborhood who has lost hope and nerve. Friend, Jesus Christ qualifies you; leave the house and go find your opportunity to serve.

Acts 9:33-34 □ *Acts 9:32-35*

Peter put them all outside and knelt down and prayed; then turning to the body he said, "Tabitha, rise." And she opened her eyes . . .

Quite an eye-opener to have inept Peter get even with us for laughing at him. Who of us will blunder into a "slumber room" to bring cheer to mourners and consternation to the mortician? "And he gave her his hand and lifted her up." Bravo!

Peter clearly had his prestige as apostle and Tabitha's (Aramaic for "gazelle"; Dorcas in Greek) popularity as exemplary saint going for him. She died surrounded by friends and he was quickly summoned to Joppa from nearby Lydda where he had just healed the paralytic. Beseeching women showed him garments her loving hands had made.

Kneeling and praying, Peter was resolutely turned away from the body. His thoughts were turned back to the resurrection of Jairus' daughter at which he had been a privileged witness. On the way to his house they were delayed by a woman who touched the hem of Jesus' garment, creating quite an emotional stir. "Do not fear, only believe," Jesus reassured the parents of the sick child by now dead. Once in the room with her, He took the little girl's hand and said, *"Talitha cumi"* and immediately she got up and walked around. Talitha — Tabitha? Gazelle — quick on the feet? Surely it was at this point that Peter took his leap of faith, turned to the body and said, "Tabitha cumi!" She responded and Peter took her by the hand to present her alive.

Women touching garments, the selective use of Aramaic, the accent on lightfootedness — were these amazing common denominators merely coincidental? Of course not. Jesus prepared Peter for Joppa at the house of Jairus. He will not bring us cold to our zenith of faith either. The secret is to turn away from the "body" in quiet trust and concentrated reflection, until Jesus is able to trigger the eye-opener! Then, one quick leap of faith and the rest will take care of itself.

Acts 9:40 □ Acts 9:36-43

For you shall go out in joy, and be led forth in peace; the mountains and hills before you shall break forth into singing, and all the trees . . . shall clap their hands.

The awakened eye of the heart smiles. When we first gave God a hand we had no songs. Now the winter of our grim faith is past; His season of yielding is upon us. Exuberant mountains and trees proclaim the miracle of secret hopes becoming sacred happenings. Nature's paean of praise ushers us into God's momentous *now* where faith and future stand poised for revelation.

Sense the lightheartedness of Isaiah's rewarded faith by contrasting his singing mountains with our sighing ones. We speak figuratively of mountains of work and bemoan what happens to molehills. Real mountains make for fine background, but for puffing and panting up close. The grimly religious make a career of stern ascent as if heaven were a mute monolith to be conquered.

There does come a zenith of faith to the saint whose season of "trying hard" has stretched into long years of hard trial. The furnace of affliction consumes the dross of self-sufficiency. On the anvil of anguish we receive the blows that prove divine gold to be the most malleable of all metals. When endurance has produced character and with it uncrushable hope, we are so schooled in experiential grace that all that life sends is received as coming from the benevolent hand of our Savior alone.

When our consecration is so finely wrought that we catch a breathtaking glimmer of God's abiding satisfaction, eternal things fall into temporal place. The process of painful discipline is transformed into the joyously sung processional of those who actively enter into fulfilled promise. We celebrate not the satisfaction of personal vindication, but the sanctity of entering into God's widening purpose. When nature itself echoes the rhythm of quickened revelation, the stage is set for the greater things of our great God.

Isaiah 55:12

. . . Joseph, who was sold as a slave. His feet were hurt with fetters, his neck was put in a collar of iron . . .

Dreams turned nightmares — how we strain at our own fetters to escape circumstances that seemingly betray our Christian witness and personal reputation! We long to record the story of our faith from the perspective of what is commonly considered as right and proper.

Drawing us into the grand sweep of this poetically compressed history lesson regarding God's covenant people, the psalmist pricks our bubble of awe with a discomforting close-up of Joseph. It is a literary device to remove us abruptly from the spectators' stand and thrust us feelingly into the grinding minuteness of the mills of eternal purpose. We too are Joseph, uniquely beloved and singled out to bless our Father — yet mysteriously lowered into a witches' caldron from which bitter memories are stirred if we take circumstances too personally.

Joseph, the cynic would say, deserved painful disillusionment, having been his father's self-righteous pet and a pest to his brothers. The chronicler of God's higher intent gladly thickens the plot to contrast our inherent frailty with His intrinsic faithfulness.

What Christian does not reel from repeated blows below the belt and pin his hope on some perspective that leaves at least his reputation intact? Pinned down by defeat, we declare Satan our powerful jailer. The psalmist invites us to take our collars of iron not personally, but purposefully. Joseph's fetters forged the vital link between Abraham's Canaan and Israel's destiny of promise. From this perspective of perfected praise we understand that our own brief story of faith is destined to become a stanza in eternity's ongoing hymn of praise. With God ultimately responsible for His own reputation, why worry unduly about our own?

Psalm 105:17-18 □ *Psalm 105*

*What is this dream that you have dreamed? Shall I and your
mother and your brothers indeed come to bow . . . before you?*

We distrust the outspoken dreamer in God's family to this
day. Joseph's youthful innocence coupled with the natural
brashness of one distinctly favored made him oblivious to the
dangers ahead. What does his basic confidence teach us about
meeting God-sized family conflict head-on?

Joseph's early display of self-confidence was the result of
being the cherished son of Jacob's old age. His early experience
of lavish love made him risk-prone, but conditioned him to
embrace the greater risks of God. His sensitivity that made him
an unwelcome dreamer at home in time elevated him to the
rank of chief administrator in Egypt. It bore directly on the
welfare of his family as well as on God's enlarged purpose for
the generations to come.

In personifying God's purpose, Joseph became separated
from the love that had launched his destiny. Separated unto
God, his self-confidence was subjected to conflict until it re-
emerged purified as an expression of God's own love for His
family. When famine ended Israel's early fortunes in Canaan,
Joseph instigated a royal welcome for Jacob's family into
Egypt's land of Goshen. Here the dreamer's dreams achieved
the climactic triumph of ultimate separation unto God's
purpose for all time and eternity.

Shepherds were loathsome to the sophisticated, agricultural
Egyptian. Goshen, too far removed from the Nile irrigation
canals, was ideal grazing country for the Hebrews and their
flocks. Thus protected from cultural assimilation, Israel was
preserved as God's chosen people. Sensing the end of his time,
Jacob blessed Joseph and the God of risky dreams, calling Him
"my shepherd" for the first time in Scripture. This Shepherd
still gives dreams and we must live them out no matter what
the cost of separation. His lavish love binds up the wounds of
costly purpose wrought from chosen people.

Genesis 37:10 □ *Genesis 37:1-11*

We put no obstacle in any one's way, so that no fault may be found with our ministry, but as servants of God we commend ourselves . . . in honor and dishonor, in ill repute and good repute.

Paul has just axed our simplistic notion that all is automatically kosher from the moment we embrace God's ministry as our own. Quite the contrary, he implies. Our own clear delineations of faith become amazingly blurred when superimposed on the maze of life's complexities that swirl up all around us. If through it all we concentrate on our personal image, we become the spiritual hypochondriac who takes his pulse every five minutes and squanders energy on one imagined crisis after another.

At the heart of an authentic God-given ministry is the very pulse beat of His steadfast love. If we keenly stay atuned to it we realize the great abandonment to Jesus Christ that shields us from the need to curry public favor or engage in morbid self-examination. Paul sums up such grace under pressure: "I am not aware of anything against myself, but I am not thereby acquitted. It is the Lord who judges me. Therefore do not pronounce judgment before the time, before the Lord comes, who will bring to light the things now hidden in darkness and will disclose the purposes of the heart" (1 Corinthians 4:4-5).

That is fine for the long run, but how do we handle an immediate crisis of threatened credibility? We are hypersensitive to criticism and want to invoke the kosher label for all we do and are — once and for all.

Perhaps our cautious faith, so image-prone, needs to recover the rugged individualism of the early saints who patterned their ministries not after public opinion polls, but on the person of the slandered, spat-upon Savior. "When reviled, we bless; when persecuted, we endure; when slandered, we try to conciliate; we have become, and are now, as the refuse of the world . . ." Is that not a breath of fresh air in our stifled thinking about the risks and rewards of personal ministry?

2 Corinthians 6:3,8 ☐ *2 Corinthians 6:1-10*

*I have become all things to all men, that I might by all means
save some. I do it all for the sake of the gospel, that I may share
in its blessing.*

In graduation exercises across the land one piece of advice
is repeatedly given to our eager young, "This above all: to
thine own self be true . . ." That explains in part perhaps the
ranks of academia's finest who have dropped out of ordinary
life to religiously "find themselves." True education, a wag has
ventured, is the ability to distinguish between Shakespeare and
Scripture. "Eat, drink, and be merry" happens to be straight
out of Luke's gospel. The famous quote to the young is not.

If Paul remained true to himself, he would still be the
product of his heredity and environment. Brilliant, articulate,
dedicated — yes. Foolish for the sake of the gospel — no! Intellectually perhaps we understand why he became as a Jew to the
Jews; as one outside the law to those outside the law . . . But
have we appropriated this gospel truth existentially?

What if by tradition and personal temperament we take
pride in being known as Mrs. John Doe. Have we freely
become Ms. Jane Doe to the struggling feminist? Or take the
Latin American in our society. Shall we forever insist that he
become a red-blooded American first before we declare him
eligible for participation in the fulness of God's blessings?

Women's libbers, illegal aliens, childless-by-choice couples,
bleeding-heart liberals . . . Who or what makes us see red?
Paul begs us to apply Christ's shed blood to our belligerent
heart. If we take pride in the product of who we are and then
try to sell our gospel as one sells a self-improvement course, we
sow deceit and sorrow. If existential gospel truth is the sales-
man and we are the product tailored to the personal need that
feminist, Latino, or Vietnam veteran all share alike, we shall
together incorporate the blessings of the timeless Good News.

1 Corinthians 9:22-23 ☐ *1 Corinthians 9:19-23*

For whoever would save his life will lose it; and whoever loses his life for my sake and the gospel's will save it.

Does the prospect of martyrdom jolt us? Or have we become so jaded in our uneventful eight-to-five faith that the idea never even enters our head? Few of us find ourselves in Christ's shock troops braving jungles and political powder kegs where kidnappings and stray bullets become a way of life.

Jesus attaches only one condition to our qualification for martyrdom, "If any man would come after me, let him deny himself and take up his cross and follow me." We commonly associate martyrdom with spectacular death and gory suffering. A far more subtle truth is at stake. "Martyr" means nothing more than "witness." Beware of subtly corrupting the word with the idea of "victim." Jesus Christ was not victimized by the crucifixion. Nailed to the cross He was supremely victorious in His faithful witness to the Father!

Our own martyrdom is not a question of life or death. Our eventual physical demise by cancer or coronary disease might be more unpleasant than the swift death knell by a hostile bullet. Death as such has been dealt the death knell at Calvary. Because of it Christ wants us to think *life* always. But we must rethink in terms of losing it, that He might gain His advantage through it. He invites our witness not of occasional works and words, but of unconditional oneness with Him. He literally means to help Himself to your life and mine so that He can continue the absolute oneness He had with the Father, which makes for His own unsurpassable witness.

How do we lose our life? By acting the careless child. In daily, deliberate acts of will we so care for our relationship with Christ alone that in time we lose all self-consciousness about secondary considerations. Enjoying oneness with the father, does a child weep for the trinkets lost along the way, or rejoice in the promise of all the new and better that in due time will surely be given?

Mark 8:35 ☐ *Mark 8:34-38*

*And when the burnt offering began, the song to the LORD
began also, and the trumpets . . .*

Some of us never sing the song to the Lord and hear the
trumpets because of one tiny omission. We fail to strike the
match and set it to our offering. The friction between our
natural and spiritual life generates such heat that we regard
that as superfluous. Or we naively wait for friction to give way
to otherworldly harmony, so mood can do the work of the
match. In short, we would rather bask in the warm glow of
domesticated faith than stand the intense heat of sacrifice.

Some go about the "burnt offering" as some go about losing
weight. We recognize the need and will *definitely* go on a diet.
The resolution feels so good that we can afford to delay the
discipline. Then sheer guilt starts us on that blasted diet. Eventually we look around to discover overall serene and attractive
people in many shapes and sizes. So we backslide, expecting to
get tough if our tolerance changes.

Some never sing that one crucial song to the Lord because
they are too busy adjusting tolerance levels. Do I really have to
cure that habit? Is that hobby really too hard on my resources?
Is there any harm if I use up the remaining few tranquilizers?
Why attach undue significance to that harmless flirtation? Are
not all things lawful to the responsible Christian, even though
some things may not be helpful? Arrogantly, stupidly, we
decline God's help and engage in our religious science of
measuring tolerance.

Sin is not that one habit or hobby or hidden iffy thing. Sin
is separation from God. Sin is worshiping at the stony effigy of
our own rigid moral judgment. The song and the trumpets
come when we strike the match of volitional surrender and say
"to hell" with holding back from God any longer. Martyrs sing
when the flames leap up to consume the sorry chaff of horded
self-righteousness!

2 Chronicles 29:27

But the high places were not taken away. Nevertheless the heart of Asa was wholly true to the Lord . . .

The world we live in demands compromise. Shall we vote Asa the patron saint of all successful compromisers? King of Judah around 900 B.C., Asa instituted social and religious reforms that ushered in a welcome period of peaceful prosperity. Shall we thus conclude that we can leave our own "high places" intact as long as our heart is in the right place?

Asa rehabilitated Judah with a covenant to make the only true God their "Most High." But the high places were not taken away! Asa incidentally, in his old age broke faith with God and bought protection from Syria. Hotly chided by the prophet Hanani, he jailed him. Other acts of oppression followed. Asa also became "diseased in his feet." In the end might he have stooped to the high places if his feet had carried him there? What in truth happens in high places?

"And the people of Israel did secretly against the Lord their God things that were not right. . . . They burned incense on all the high places, as the nations did whom the LORD carried away before them. . . . They went after false idols, and became false. . . . So these nations feared the LORD, and also served their graven images; their children likewise, and their children's children as the fathers did, so they do to this day" (2 Kings 17).

So we have declared our security in the Most High and our modern fertility gods have lost their former appeal. Therefore we leave them in place. So we have joined Weight Watchers and leave the freezer stocked with candy bars. We have joined Alcoholics Anonymous and leave in plain sight the elegant bottle gleaming with liquid amber. So we have made Asa our patron saint. Where and when will the secret oppression and falsehood begin?

1 Kings 15:14 □ *1 Kings 15:9-15*

Indeed I count everything as loss because of the surpassing worth of knowing Christ Jesus my Lord. For his sake I have suffered the loss of all things, and count them as refuse . . .

Two distinctions need to be made immediately. First, Paul refers to Jesus not as His Savior or Friend, but Lord. The relationship clearly implies the preeminence of the One with authority to extract obedience from the other. Secondly, Paul had not given up garbage. He had not thrown away his baseball cards and girlie magazines, but all rights to himself.

We are willing to render sacrifice for the sake of love. There is emotional satisfaction in the bargain. As the people who say "the Lord" this and "the Lord" that with astonishing familiarity, how do we feel about costly sacrifice that prizes the Lordship of Christ not in feeling but fact?

The Book of Acts illuminates this lordship that comes to satisfy unlike any other relationship. After Peter and John were arrested for healing the man lame from birth, they were charged by the Sanhedrin not to speak or teach "at all" in the name of Jesus. They were released under threats so grave that they promptly sought out their friends to discuss their predicament. "And when they heard it, they lifted their voices together to God and said, 'Sovereign Lord' . . ." This was not an exercise of respect, but resignation — an abdication of all individual rights to personal liberty and the pursuit of happiness. The word used literally meant "despot"!

This Despot, this sovereign Lord was the Christ who so revealed Himself *in* Paul that he could plainly recognize His supreme worth through the resulting ministry. If we wait for the Lord to reveal Himself *to* us in order to motivate a sacrificial life, we shall wait forever. When the Most High creates His heaven in us, it is not for the prestige of our piety, but for the power of His resurrection.

Philippians 3:8 □ Philippians 3:1-11

Truly, I say to you, there is no man who has left house or wife or brothers or parents or children, for the sake of the kingdom of God, who will not receive manifold more in this time, and in the age to come eternal life.

What is bothersome about those picture-perfect, wholesome family reruns on television? Devoid of sex and violence, they teach sportsmanship, loyalty, and admirable communication skills. If the characters said grace at meals they could pass for the picture-perfect Christian family. Or could they?

Why are the parents never shown haggard, the children never downright impossible? Why are there no lingering tensions, no long silences, no deep lonelinesses? Where are the ugly times, the broken things that defy mending?

A glance through Christian periodicals reveals a similar simplistic approach. The ideal family in advertisements is portrayed by handsome, smiling parents with 2.3 adorable children already saved, praise the Lord. One can just smell the niceness of their life in suburbia, enhanced of course by mother's weekly home Bible study and father's model eldership at church.

We need to be jolted by the rugged reality of this aching gospel truth: The "despot" Jesus Christ — the meaning could apply to an autocratic Old-World husband — can raise havoc with today's family whether it be that of the clergy or layperson. Either mate can be impelled "to leave" and follow Him without ever leaving the comforts of home. The resulting stresses and scars make a laughing stock of the picture-perfect Christian family. Lest we rush in with pious counsel or condemnation, we best remember that to such chosen ones Christ has already extended His commendation and comfort. His reality is not lived at the picture-window level, but in the gut region. Providential grace, not glossy ideal, steers the stormy course.

Luke 18:29-30

But Hannah answered, "No, my lord, I am a woman sorely troubled; I have drunk neither wine nor strong drink, but I have been pouring out my soul before the LORD.

To Eli the priest she looked like a common drunk. To Elkanah her husband she was a puzzlement. Although childless, Hannah nevertheless had everything a wife could ask for. In an age when woman's worth was often measured by her ability to breed, she enjoyed the distinction of being cherished for herself. Peninnah who bore Elkanah's children did not know the passionate embrace that was Hannah's. This sensitive, loving husband plaintively asked, "Am I not more to you than ten sons?"

For a seemingly religious woman Hannah appeared plenty petty. Each year when the family traveled to Shilo for their religious holiday, she managed to ruin it for Elkanah. True, her rival used the occasion to brag about her children and to taunt her. But did Hannah have to swallow the bait? Could she not have swallowed her pride and countered the attacks with gentle love? Could she not have soothed Peninnah's jealousy and won her heart by taking pride and delight in her children?

"Do not regard your maidservant as a base woman, for all along I have been speaking out of my great anxiety and vexation." Hannah so craved a son that she vowed to dedicate him wholly to the Lord. So Samuel indeed was born and turned over to incompetent Eli at the tender age of three. Why? Because Hannah needed to know the thrill of pregnancy and birth — the sweet taste of revenge? Or was it because "the word of the Lord was rare in those days; there was no frequent vision"? History bears out that Samuel was the passionate prophet and patriot God needed for Israel precisely at that point. Was Hannah's puzzling passion merely accidental?

Her Magnificat is telling: "Talk no more so very proudly, let not arrogance come from your mouth; for the Lord is a God of knowledge, and by him actions are weighed."

1 Samuel 1:15 □ *1 Samuel 1:1-20*

*If he rescued righteous Lot . . . (for by what that righteous
man saw and heard as he lived among them, he was vexed in
his righteous soul day after day . . .), then the Lord knows
how to rescue the godly from trial . . .*

Caution: Looking back to Sodom and Gomorrah may be
hazardous to our health. Still, we must look back if we are to
find out by what stretch of imagination Peter is coming to all
these protestations of Lot's righteousness.

Greed had landed Lot in Sodom. Because of quarreling
between their herdsmen, Abraham had suggested they part
company and generously offered Lot first choice. Lot went
whole hog after the more fertile Jordan valley.

Sitting in the city gate one fateful evening Lot met the two
angels who planned to spend the night in the street and urged
them to accept his hospitality. Even so the Sodomites nearly
got to them. Lot, fine host but faltering father, offered his two
unmarried daughters to the mob, but they were spared the
ordeal. The next morning the angels had to drag Lot from the
place about to go down in infamy. Mrs. Lot looked back and
suffered uncommon cardiac arrest. Her darling virgin daughters, raised in the faithless Sodom of Lot's unceasing vexation,
took turns getting their father drunk and in a cave seduced him
in order to be with child. So much for righteous Lot.

Peter is admittedly not writing tongue-in-cheek. "First of all
you must understand this, that no prophecy of scripture is a
matter of one's own interpretation . . . men moved by the
Holy Spirit spoke from God." Peter had an insider's perspective. He had betrayed and fled the Word Incarnate despite his
earnest protestations of loyalty unto death. Jesus had explained
the mystery, "You will all fall away . . . for it is written, 'I will
strike the shepherd, and the sheep of the flock will be
scattered.'" What then is our caution? Judging is hazardous to
our health. Relying on the righteousness we have in Christ is
our only sure deliverance.

2 Peter 2:7-9 ☐ *2 Peter 2:1-10*

See my hands and my feet, that it is I myself; handle me, and see . . .

How can we let people know that we are for real? Don't be afraid to show them your scars, Jesus suggests. As the resurrected Lord He had any number of supernatural options to reveal Himself in convincing ways. How touching that He would first identify Himself by the breaking of bread, giving thanks as had been His custom, and then by the displaying of His nail-scarred hands and feet. The Easter miracle had not come replete with plastic surgery. Christ wore no gloves to mask the painful past. He ascended into heaven bearing His scars, true to His revealed identity as our eternal Burden Bearer.

When some years ago a president of the United States showed off his scar from a gallbladder operation to a whooping press, the nation on the whole reacted indignantly. Only children are allowed their vivid interest in scars as their badges of courage.

We can play cosmetic games of hide-and-seek spiritually. We can pretend that all is smooth in our life. We then make contact like polished marbles — a quick flash of brilliance, a hard fast click — and people are pushed back into pockets of quiet despair. On the surface the well-put-together attract. But to project an image requires energy and vigilance. Because of it no real giving and receiving can take place.

We need not brandish our healing wounds or invite morbid curiosity into the suffering behind our scars. The victim in the burn ward may need nothing more than a reassuring touch from the visitor who has returned to the hospital for another round of skin grafts. No human being is spared pain and disfigurement. The nail-scarred Galilean would not have us pretend otherwise. If we emulate His gentle gallantry, the shared bond of shame and suffering will lead to the breaking of bread and giving thanks together.

Luke 24:39 ☐ *Luke 24:13-43*

*And he took a cup, and when he had given thanks he said,
"Take this, and divide it among yourselves; for I tell you that
from now on I shall not drink of the fruit of the vine until the
kingdom of God comes."*

How many of us participate in the Eucharist — the giving
of thanks — with faithless familiarity that denies the heart of
Holy Communion? What actually are we supposed to feel with
that sliver of bread on our tongue? Why is that which is so
private carried out in public?

The Lord's Supper is traditionally sacred and there is irritation in a nit-picking discussion that chips away at its mystique.
The religious are satisfied with symbolism for its own sake.
Those concerned with spiritual truth need to get at the heart of
the matter.

Jesus came as Emmanuel — God with us — in the garment
and makeup of our common humanity. He joined Himself to
us absolutely, irrevocably. We gladly buy the personal implications of this uncommon bargain. But we stubbornly resist
the public responsibilities of reproducing that bond so crucial
to the larger objectives of the kingdom. "Take this, and divide
it among yourselves!" Our spiritual and practical emphasis
during communion — joint ownership of God's unmerited
favor — must be on the act of passing bread and wine from one
fellow heir to another. It is an amazingly quick cure for the silly
quandary of when to swallow and what to feel. When we
consistently act out our sacred trust of intimate fellowship
among Christ's own, the rewarding emotions and insights will
spring up left and right.

Being the "heart of the matter," Christ passed up the
symbol of the wine at the passover. As the true vine He is
helping Himself to fruit right now. You and I are the grapes He
is squeezing to obtain the new wine of the kingdom. Destined
for the King's common cup, shall not our hearts and lives flow
together now?

Luke 22:17-18 □ *Luke 22:7-23*

But the new wine must be put into fresh wineskins. And no one after drinking old wine desires new; for he says, "The old is good."

New wine sits unpretentiously in squat jugs on supermarket shelves. Old wine reclines in solitary splendor in dark secret places where the genteel dust of time leaves its singular caress. New wine boasts of pleasingly fruity flavor and exuberant character. The bouquet of old wine is rhapsodized in pseudo-spiritual language bordering on reverence.

As the contemporary people of God in an age of unprecedented innovation, we have great affinity for the new. We buy every gadget that tickles our fancy and try every new product that promises the sky. With space exploration and solar energy just getting off the ground, advertisers are licking their chops and projecting the new baby boom of a "sucker born every minute."

As the contemporary people of God in an age of unprecedented opportunity, we are bent old fogies huddled by a coal stove nursing our precious port. We religiously attend church once a week. But we refuse to make faithful commitments to grow in the more intimate settings of adult education classes, conferences and retreats. Pastors and layleaders pray and plan and facilitate programs that expand intellect and the frontiers of faith. Needs are faithfully assessed and support groups formed to extend the comfort and nurture of fellow strugglers. Beyond a small core of faithful enthusiasts and a smattering of the curious, most programs go shamefully begging. Christian periodicals are struggling to survive. How many households of the churched avail themselves of their broad and pertinent information?

Have we ever considered the cost of disappointment and growing discouragement to our fellow Christians? Have we of late examined the label on our grievously gathered complacency? "Unfit for the King!"

Luke 5:38-39 □ *Luke 5*

"Every man serves the good wine first; and when men have drunk freely, then the poor wine; but you have kept the good wine until now." This, the first of his signs, Jesus did at Cana in Galilee, and manifested his glory . . .

Let the teetotaler munch on raisins while we boldly sample this rare vintage wine. Let no one clean up the act by arguing minimal alcohol content. If our Lord could take "glutton and drunkard" in stride, why downgrade His wine that the steward of the feast judged excellent?

Our problem with the wine is symptomatic of our problem with the church. Well-meaning people forever go around turning the heady stuff of the kingdom back into colorless tap water. They wield their magic wand — the yardstick of rigid religiosity — for the sole purpose of casting a decorous pall on all that is fresh and new. Instead of wine stewards they act as embalmers of joy, drawing out the exuberant juices and blowing the dry dust of deadly dullness.

Could it be that many worshipers have never discovered the all-encompassing role of the church in the totality of their life, because spiritual "teetotalers" have taught them to abstain? One can be emphatically forgiven for abstaining from deadly dullness. If that is what we offer, by all means let people only come once a week to pay their respects — and then allow a kinder world to resuscitate them with its pleasures. But if we are true stewards of the feast, we shall close down the mock funeral parlor where glorified dryness lies in state. Does the Bride of Christ not merit a glorious wedding?

A wedding symbolizes holy communion and the start of a brand-new life. It draws into common celebration a wide diversity of people. Christ's heady wine lights up faces, loosens tongues, invites all to linger in the glow of making new friends. When, for God's sake, will we take the hint and drink freely from it?

John 2:10-11 □ John 2:1-11

*But to what shall I compare this generation? It is like children
. . . calling to their playmates, "We piped to you, and you did
not dance; we wailed, and you did not mourn."*

"We played wedding and you did not act happy. We
played funeral and you did not cry. If you are going to be in
our games you have to play fair. It spoils our fun when some
just sit or sulk." These children of long ago were natural
leaders, creating mood, motivating participants, giving marching papers to spoilsports. Jesus must have loved their verve and
directness as He watched them at play in the market places.

We can imagine His rueful smile as well. Ascetic John the
Baptist who made the wilderness his home and ate off the land,
was accused of having a demon. Jesus who met and partied
with people wherever they happened to be was branded a
glutton and tippler, the friend of society's scum.

The kingdom of heaven can be likened to a party, but our
flawed adult games cannot be permitted. The theme of this
celebration evolves around the Host's preferences always. We
cannot introduce rules that fit our personal bias, or insist on
liberties odious to our fellow guests. In the public domain we
remember that both John and Jesus had their lifestyle validated
by the Spirit. Our practice of courteous, sensitive love will
strike the healthy balance between extreme adherents. In the
private sphere we please ourselves as free men and women in
Christ, taking to heart Pauls' enlightenment, "For the kingdom
of God does not mean food and drink but righteousness and
peace and joy in the Holy Spirit."

The "soul food" to be offered to the people of God by the
nurturing Body, the church, needs to meet two essential
criteria. Does it glorify our Lord? Does it promote the fruitfulness of His people? If we decline such fare and refuse to
dance where He joyfully pipes, we shall in time hear His dirge
and mourn!

Matthew 11:16-17 □ *Matthew 11:7-19*

To another he said, "Follow me." But he said, "Lord, let me first go and bury my father." But he said to him, "Leave the dead to bury their own dead . . ."

Jesus did not say, "Son, skip the funeral!" Some of us would jump at the chance. Funerals unleash emotional processes tinged with regret and guilt. We may sense nothing more than relief or discover greed that lusts for the loved one's possessions. Skip the funeral? Gladly, if you insist.

Jesus, however, is saying something far more radical. Get a whiff — a really good whiff — of living death! It is far more offensive and taxing than burials which in truth — by their very customs — impart a measure of strength in a time of stress. When people are so pulled together the inherent comforts of community are ours. Here is precisely where Jesus violates our human conscience. Deliberately — coolly — pull back from conventional needs and obligations. Put your hands to the plow and never look back — or you will not be fit for the kingdom of God!

Why? Because wounding cries of moral outrage will burst in on us and from every silently grieving face a flaming accusation will fly and singe our innermost self. Instead of doing things that used to make us and others feel good, we are pressed into the paramount claims of the kingdom. True to its norms, we shall appear "abnormal" again and again. Our own heart will repeatedly seek to condemn us. If we look back instead of forward, costly emotional cave-ins will delay our usefulness to Christ.

Be productive for me, says Jesus, and stick the spiritually comatose with the maintenance chores. Sternly ignore what people say or think when you stop caring for your senile parent or retarded youngster. Sternly forget man's moral tenets and his capacity for compassion. Let the paramount claims of the kingdom violate your human conscience if need be. Die deliberately to conventional norms. Live for me — resolutely!

Luke 9:59-60

And he left the oxen, and ran after Elijah, and said, "Let me kiss my father and my mother, and then I will follow you . . " And he . . . took the yoke of oxen, and slew them . . .

The great prophet Elijah, wearied from being God's conscience to his vacillating nation, had been authorized to cast his mantle of witness on young Elisha. After a six-year apprenticeship, Elisha witnessed Elijah's miraculous departure by flaming chariot and horses. Inheriting a double share of his prophetic spirit, he then served God's highest interests for fifty-five years. No Old Testament prophet worked more miracles and counseled more kings than Elisha. This dynamo had sought to debut on the strength of his parents' permission!

Scripture is silent on their disposition, but draws a telling picture of Elisha's position when he was tapped for higher duty. He was plowing, "with twelve yoke of oxen before him, and he was the twelfth." There is an impression of perfect fit; he was precisely where the team needed him. No wonder mom and dad merited an explanation. "Elijah passed by him and cast his mantle upon him." Prevenient grace enabled Elisha to grasp the implications, but he had to consider his parents' feelings. So he ran after Elijah to get permission to get permission.

The prophet's cryptic counter question, "Go back again; for what have I done to you?" may leave us puzzled, but Elisha understood. No older man (not even his father) had any say in the matter. God needed him; God would not wait. Now the fledgling follower pulled the shocker. He killed his oxen on the spot, burned the yokes, and gave the resulting meal to his plowing companions. "Then he arose and went after Elijah . . ."

This sobering story must now be translated into our own conflicting loyalties and emotions. Where in our life must God insist on instant, dramatic obedience? Where must we give our puzzled people their first taste of our abnormal behavior? What might has God in store for our ministry?

1 Kings 19:20-21 ☐ *1 Kings 19:19-21*

The kingdom of heaven is like treasure hidden in a field, which a man found and covered up; then in his joy he goes and sells all that he has and buys that field.

Parables reveal, conceal and perpetuate truth. "He who has ears to hear, let him hear." They effectively separated the sheep from the goats. "To you it has been given to know the secrets of the kingdom of heaven, but to them it has not been given." If Jesus now graciously lumps us in with His dense disciples and with a twinkle asks, "Have you understood all this?" we quickly answer yes as well.

What perpetual truth does the parable of the concealed treasure reveal? To our chagrin we discover that playing eager beaver backfires. We start to say that for the sake of the gospel we give up everything to make it our own. Then we stumble over the concealed treasure. Why would the serious believer want to be secretive about living out his commitment? It does not add up.

Next we stumble over the revelation. How many people do we personally know who are passionately devoted to the gospel? Stymied, we look to Scripture for a frame of reference. Beads of holy sweat gather on our brow when we begin to glimpse the one Man that qualifies. If we pursue this logic, the treasure is . . .

Every parable in this chapter identifies "the man" as the Son of man, and the field as the world. When He comes across the rare soul with the firm will to be made His unique possession, Jesus starts paying the price. When in line with His still hidden purpose we begin to reveal peculiar attitudes, His reputation is at stake more than ours. If you and I vicariously, albeit realistically, suffer the pangs of such "life hid with Christ," we shall in time come to light as His treasure. The parable is astounding. It is such joy for Jesus to become strapped on our behalf that the raised eyebrows of the curious and suspicious mean nothing. Let the treasure match the Owner's joy!

Matthew 13:44

Having the eyes of your hearts enlightened, that you may know . . . what are the riches of his glorious inheritance in the saints . . .

How do we popularly perceive abnormality? Why is no one breaking down doors to get into a nursing home? Does it contain the abnormal? As seen from aesthetics and functionality — yes. Bald wrinkled heads, toothless gums, helpless limbs, diapered bodies, dim minds — when gathered into one public display of revealing smells and paraphernalia, these make us cringe with secret horror.

How do we popularly perceive normality? Why is everybody crowding around the nursery? Does it harbor the normal? As seen from aesthetics and functionality — not especially. Bald wrinkled heads, toothless gums, helpless limbs, diapered bodies . . . Why do we crane our necks with obvious delight?

Does locality determine normality or abnormality — treasure or tragedy? It is normal for a newborn to be utterly helpless, but abnormal for the grownup to fall into such a state. Yet in this fallen world a predictable course of aberration from God's norm of constancy and wholeness is traceable from cradle to grave. Into this helpless world precisely has been transplanted the locality of the kingdom of heaven. In Jesus Christ we are the kingdom!

Each saint redeemed from earth's decaying power is cradled in the Father's arms as the precious gift of His crucified Son. Through each such saint the glorious "infancy" of eternity with its unsearchable riches is to be manifested to a woeful world. We are the brand-new breed of humanity in whom the creative force of the eternal finds fresh expression in the dead ends of the world. We go joyously into nursing homes to be the aroma of Christ to urine-soaked shells of forgotten humanity. We are those indwelled by the Father to zestfully love the unwanted. Our glorious inheritance of the same Spirit that hung the stars in their heavens, enables us to impart eternity's pulsebeat to the world's erratic heart!

Ephesians 1:18 □ *Ephesians 1:3-23*

How precious to me are thy thoughts, O God!

There is no sadder monument to man's short-range thinking than the tombstone sentiment, "In our hearts and minds forever!" If the dead were to live by our power of remembrance they would be stone-dead in no time flat. If we really mean "forever" instead of "so long," we have to copy the smart ancients. They built pyramids and stocked burial chambers with symbolic survival matter to guard against lapses of conscious thought.

Hold a good thought for me! People braving a challenge often appeal to our gallant instincts. We often hold that good thought with all the might of a sieve. But let a siren wail at night when our teenager is out and we strain to think the worst at great length. We think brilliantly one hour after a disappointing conversation. We study many weeks for a test and then cannot give our telephone number. What is God to think of such a mixed lot?

"Think magnificently of God," exclaims a joyous psalmist. God has the one-track mind for good we sorely lack. With it He does not just chart plans, but cherishes people. He thinks of you and me delightedly — energetically — both day and night. Happily, His thought life is centered on our very real life, but is not based on it. We derive our thoughts from various internal and external stimuli. Atmospheric conditions as well as biochemical processes can make us see things dark or light. God's thoughts toward us are drawn from one light source only, namely Jesus Christ. Because of Him God thinks magnificently of us!

The very fact that we can reach into the heart of God in our fleeting thoughts, proves the real life of Christ in us which He is constantly seeking to enrich. The dreams we hold for our young the Father holds for us, only His love and great future exceeds ours by far. To God it is no chore to think deeply — and highly — of us. In Jesus Christ we are a fresh wonder to Him every day!

Psalm 139:17 ☐ *Psalm 139*

I came that they may have life, and have it abundantly.

We cannot possibly figure out this more abundant life. It is to be discovered in the process. It is impossible to amass it. We can only acclaim it by living it one day at a time. It does not consist in the measure of gifts, but in the completeness of the Giver.

If we faithlessly lump it in with other theological generalizations, we live as eccentric misers who leave heaven's wealth untapped. Eternal life is not merely the mystery at death's door, but the existential witness of God in the daily life of the Spirit-filled believer. The abundant life is the "Daily Astonisher" at our doorstep, more lovingly placed there than the world's "Daily Deflator" of hope flung in the gutter.

If with our impoverished minds we seek to define the abundant life, we can only operate from the basis of our known lack. Beset by financial problems, we make it a haven of material plenty. Lonely, we picture it as friendship. Sick, we covet through it physical immunity from life's ills. There is danger in such claims. Although God invites our honesty and feels for our pains, He will not be manipulated. In this specific matter of the more abundant life, He owes us exactly one thing and that cannot be dictated, only humbly acknowledged. It is Jesus Christ as indwelling Spirit. Material wealth, mass popularity or robust health may never be ours, but the fruit of the Spirit is guaranteed.

"But the fruit of the Spirit is love, joy, peace, patience, kindness, goodness, faithfulness, gentleness, self-control." To the debilitating conditions of our life, we bring the character of the Deliverer. It is never in the outward circumstances of existence that we feel most severely cramped, but in the fears and frustrations that well up inside and crowd us. If we make the crucified Lord our Tree of Life and feast from His fruit, we take our capacious Eden of rest and re-creation with us wherever life might take us.

John 10:10 ☐ *John 10:7-18*

But when I thought how to understand this, it seemed to me a wearisome task, until I went into the sanctuary of God; then I perceived their end.

If we adhere to a gospel of success we are skating on thin ice. The chilling truth might come crashing in on us suddenly: the ungodly have an abundant life that speaks volumes also, and people are listening and buying into it successfully. Compared to some we appear as paupers and naive peddlers of religious lore.

This persisting dilemma is superbly summed up by Asaph, "But as for me, my feet had almost stumbled. . . . For I was envious of the arrogant, when I saw the prosperity of the wicked. For they have no pangs; their bodies are sound. . . . All in vain have I kept my heart clean. . . . For all the day long I have been stricken, and chastened every morning."

Here the psalmist catches himself. "If I had said, 'I will speak thus', I would have been untrue to the generation of thy children." There exists an undeniable witness that "truly God is good to the upright." As people of faith it is our sacred duty to protect and propagate it. No sour grapes for the new wine of the kingdom, please!

If we are unduly fascinated by case histories of the alternate abundant life, we head into deeper turbulence still. Not all members of that brotherhood are crooks. The legendary self-made man who hit the jackpot through hard work and good luck is very much with us as well. Unless we remove ourselves from such disquiet into the quiet of God's healing presence, we shall waste precious energy maintaining a precarious balancing act on slippery ground. We must resolutely focus on the truth that only Christ's abundant life offers "love, joy, peace, patience, kindness, goodness, faithfulness, gentleness, self-control." If we stick to the fruit of the Spirit, our satisfaction will become fleshed out in the "How much more . . ." of His eternal provision.

Psalm 73:16-17 □ *Psalm 73*

"And I will say to my soul, Soul, you have ample goods laid up . . ." But God said to him, "Fool! This night your soul is required of you . . ."

A shroud has no pockets, a cemetery no space to lay up barns and grain and ample goods. But the chilling aspect concerns not the obvious folly of the fool. The parable solemnly warns that the exact measure we use to breathe life into our present existence bears irrevocably on the quality of life we shall realize in our eternal habitation. We become what we are!

Our word "soul" is derived from the Greek word *psyche*. The noun denotes spirit, life, personality, self — but evolves from a verb meaning to breathe, blow, make cold. To get to the essential nature of the "chilling aspect," we have to take that "cold" one step further. It indicates reduction of temperature by evaporation and means "to chill, to wax cold."

When we apply this precise language to the parable, we perceive quickly that if we warm to the world, we grow cold toward God. If we warm to God, the cold world does not matter. More specifically still, the soul we nurture, now, becomes the soul that will nurture us then. If we depart this life in a condition of self-management, we shall be doomed to self-satisfaction against the backdrop of eternity's measureless wealth. If death surprises us on the vital growing edge toward God, we shall know the delight of continued discovery and true self-realization.

If we breathe life into selfish temporal pursuits, the distilled sum total of their value awaits us as immortality's welcoming embrace when our flesh waxes cold. How chilling to fall into the clutches of fatal shortsightedness! When Jesus urges us to grow rich toward God and lay up treasure in heaven exclusively, He literally invites us to furnish our own eternal mansion. As we enter into dialogue with our own soul, shall we persist with the pleasant conditions of an easier life, or shall we invest it with the matchless character of our Lord?

Luke 12:19-20 ☐ *Luke 12:13-21*

He said to him, "If they do not hear Moses and the prophets, neither will they be convinced if some one should rise from the dead."

What are the hard facts of cold death? Never mind the death-warmed-over tales of Life After Clinical Death that continue to make the rounds of a faddish public. If old truth or fresh truth needs to be nailed into place to stem the tide of Alice-in-Wonderland fantasizing, what better authority than that Veteran of death's coldest embrace, Jesus of Nazareth.

The selfish rich man of His illustration finds himself aflame with regret in a clearly defined place of eternal separation. The sight of poor Lazarus fills him with torment. In life a wretched beggar at his door, in death he is carried by angels into Abraham's bosom. This Hebraism stems from ancient custom that had those at table recline, so that in close conversation the one person's head would practically rest on the bosom of the one sitting next above him. The expression symbolized paradise, God's abode, the blissful proximity to Him.

The dialogue between the trapped rich man and Abraham narrows down to one thing. Forever caught in the self-confinement he had selfishly honed to a fine art in life, he realizes he cannot go back to warn his brothers. Only Lazarus is fit for such a selfless mission. But he, caught up in the bliss of God's presence, is unfit to sojourn again among those who live by snobbery. The chasm of our own immortality is fixed in the here and now.

Moses and the prophets stood for God's inviolable laws. Let their final word on death and dying stand, Jesus cautioned, and declined an amateur mopping-up expedition even coming straight from Abraham's bosom. It is the devil's lie that light and life spring up at death. It is the Spirit's loving mission to so illuminate our daily life that we taste our immortality free from drugs or traumas that may distort the image during clinical death!

Luke 16:31 ☐ *Luke 16:19-31*

And when they say to you, "Consult the mediums and wizards who chirp and mutter," should not a people consult their God? Should they consult the dead on behalf of the living?

We consult them avidly. We are the charmed audience at talk shows who allow doctor and dabbler in the otherwordly to pontificate on the grave issue of life after death. Only it is not grave. When Joe's heart stopped he saw his aunt and her poodle, Fifi. When Jane's vital signs registered zero she meandered through a luscious meadow. The general consensus seems to be that there is both good news and bad news. Yes, Virginia, there is a Santa Claus for all in heaven. But it is one heck of a climb to get up to his lap.

Why do Christians swoop down on the latest printed word on every out-of-body experience with a new twist? The bright light, the feeling of love, the waving relatives reappear in 1001 forms while doctors jab needles into pummeled and electrically charged bodies. Their owners invariably hover above the commotion.

Why did Paul who was caught up into paradise sum up his tremendous spiritual authority in this manner: "But far be it from me to glory except in the cross of our Lord Jesus Christ, by which the world has been crucified to me, and I to the world." Should that not be the firm stance for the responsible Christian to adopt and adhere to right now? What right have we to dabble in emotionalism and sensationalism when we have Jesus Christ's own promise, "I am the resurrection and the life."

Without faith it is impossible to please God. Dare we pull the plug on the pop gospel of undiscerning talk shows? Dare we single-mindedly focus faith on "our Savior Jesus Christ, who abolished death and brought life and immortality to light through the gospel"? If we take our light from dim TV screens and other popularly acclaimed sources, we must be jabbed with this sobering warning, "And no wonder, for even Satan disguises himself as an angel of light."

Isaiah 8:19 □ *Isaiah 8*

And just as it is appointed for men to die once . . .

Hard on the heel of man's fascination with the hereafter follows the toying with reincarnation. Surprisingly, a number of Christians are taken in by that futile quest. Eastern thought and Western metaphysics, combined with our own tantalizing moments of deja vu, allow for speculation. Charlatans and reputable proponents have drawn up some impressive case histories.

Perhaps some Christians compromise their spiritual integrity because religious intolerance spawned the Spanish Inquisition. Embarrassments still happen in that same vein. Past abuses notwithstanding, the Christian's first duty is not to open-mindedness when in the process of independent search *modern* enlightenment is claimed. Our basic provision is the mind of Christ revealed through the Holy Spirit. "I am the light of the world; he who follows me will not walk in darkness . . ."

The concept of reincarnation is based on the fuzzy thesis that a proper state of enlightenment and purification must be achieved before we can dwell with the Essence of pure light. Successive embodiments with their chastenings are to strain the darkness from the soul.

The Book of Revelation pinpoints *God's* provision for pure light in this magnificent description of our future habitation: "And I saw no temple in the city, for its temple is the Lord God Almighty and the Lamb. And the city has no need of sun or moon to shine upon it, for the glory of God is its light, and its lamp is the Lamb" (Revelation 21:22-23).

Our crucified Lord's resurrection refutes every argument for reincarnation. His Word is clear: "The sons of this age marry and are given in marriage; but those who are accounted worthy to attain to that age and to the resurrection from the dead neither marry nor are given in marriage, for they cannot die any more, because they are equal to angels and are sons of God, being sons of the resurrection" (Luke 20:34-36).

Hebrews 9:27

For those who sat in the region and shadow of death light has dawned.

Dawn highlights the night and accents the day. The shadowy night was awash in somber hues. Jesus had just suffered the ordeal of His wilderness fast that was to prove the meat of His ministry, "My food is to do the will of him who sent me . . ." His bruising showdown with Satan had ended in a tie; he would be back at Gethsemane going for the jugular.

Now, John was arrested. His cousin had paid the price of fearlessly censuring Herod Antipas' scandalous elopement with his half-brother's wife. We have an inkling of our Savior's emotions in His reaction to John's execution, "Now when Jesus heard this, he withdrew . . . to a lonely place apart."

After John's arrest, Jesus left Judea for Galilee. In Judea He had been baptized, which established our Redeemer's identification with sinful man in need of regeneration. In Judea also He had been tempted by Satan, verifying His identity as sinless Son of God. Leaving Nazareth Jesus went "and dwelt in Capernaum by the sea, in the territory of Zebulun and Naphtali, that what was spoken by the prophet Isaiah might be fulfilled: 'The land of Zebulun and the land of Naphtali, toward the sea, across the Jordan, Galilee of the Gentiles — the people who sat in darkness have seen a great light . . .'"

"From that time Jesus began to preach, saying, 'Repent, for the kingdom of heaven is at hand.'" At the daybreak of this kingdom age of unprecedented revelation, the Galilean accented man's inherent darkness. We dare not misunderstand the deeds that underlined His peculiar Galilean speech. When He went about "healing every disease and every infirmity," He did not primarily demonstrate compassion, but His capacity as sinless Son of God to forgive sin and illuminate resulting wholeness. This Galilean was executed for blasphemy by religionists. When God's truth dawns on us, do we execute — accomplish its works?

Matthew 4:16 □ Matthew 4:12-17

In the former time he brought into contempt the land of Zebulun and . . . Naphtali, but in the latter time he will make glorious . . . Galilee of the nations.

This land of Zebulun and Naphtali which became the Galilee of the Gentiles (meaning foreigner or fellow countryman), was named after Jacob's sons. Their families were among the twelve tribes that constituted Israel's early lifeblood. One of Isaiah's early laments pinpoints the nature of their darkness: "O house of Jacob, come, let us walk in the light of the Lord. . . . thy people . . . are full of diviners from the east and of soothsayers like the Philistines, and they strike hands with foreigners" (2:5-6).

The glorious irony of God's solution to this persistent problem is striking. To heal Israel's vulnerability to damaging intermingling with foreigners, He blessed the very heel that had been lifted against Him. As Moses lifted up the serpent to heal his snake-bitten people, so God's Galilean was raised up in the Galilee of the Gentiles. So clearly would He accentuate God's light, so distinctly articulate His inclusive love, that no foreign language or custom need ever darken knowledge of Him again. In the Galilee of the nations God concentrated eternity's singular illumination in the lamp of the Lamb (Revelation 21:23).

Galileans were easily spotted by their dialect and enunciation, a fact which cost Peter dearly. They were held in contempt for faulty grammar and malpronunciations. When a Galilean spoke one could not help but notice what he said!

What truth is He accenting to us this day? Where have we failed to walk in His enlightenment? How have we sought to divine direction from sources foreign to the Lamb of God? Are we soothing our conscience with strange sayings that do not honor the straightforward Galilean?

Isaiah 9:1 □ *Isaiah 9:1-7*

You are the light of the world. A city set on a hill cannot be hid.

Ah, God's cliff-hanger! Jesus states a stunning fait accompli about the kind of exposure we are headed for. Are we to stick out like a sore thumb? While we frantically hail Him to hitch a ride to new enlightenment, He is way ahead, thinking not "light" but weighty matter — a city set on a hill!

By nature we are flatlanders with two-dimensional designs that lack spiritual depth. Give us a babbling brook, a clump of trees, and we build our lean-to and indulge in make-do as lovers of romantic lore. Then comes the hefty storm that cuts like a scythe across our little idyll and in the drenching rains that follow we drink bitterly from the lightweight stuff of our pleasantly haphazard life.

The city built on a hill demands forethought and sustained joint effort. Put there for defense, it requires knowledge of enemy locations and possible troop movements. The stones wrenched from the hillside must become the sturdy cisterns and strong outer wall of the settlement. Those in the outlying areas tilling the ground and growing the food for the city will repair to its shelter in times of danger.

How many "light years" passed from the dawn of history until the Light of the world was slowed down to reveal the Son of God? We only know that as the Galilean He was confined in our humanity long enough to illuminate the house of Jacob. To that house yours and mine must be joined. The city of God is to be entered into by all peoples. His light is not given for brilliant flashes of haphazard moments of private bliss. Our inner light must become calculated, concrete expression of outward strength and inward sufficiency — derived from deliberate joint effort with those belonging to the lasting family of the household of God. How many "light years" are left for us to settle into our eternal design?

Matthew 5:14 □ Matthew 5:14-16

*Pray at all times in the Spirit, with all . . . supplication . . .
keep alert with all perseverance, making supplication for all the
saints, and also for me . . .*

The stronghold of God is not the sprawling megalopolis
tied loosely together by freeways that disgorge the speeder into
his particular pocket of anonymity. The city of old hummed
with the sound of animation as interdependence was practiced
at every level of mutual need and common celebration.
Loyalty was not dissipated along individual cultural or political
interests, but invested in the unified desire for self-preservation
against common ills. Military intruders and natural disasters
were met in the strength of joint resistance and endurance.

Paul's prison epistle written from Rome to the "Ephesians"
was in all likelihood a circular letter to the churches in Asia
Minor. Instead of addressing local conflicts, he expands on one
grand central theme: "For he has made known to us in all
wisdom and insight the mystery of his will, according to his
purpose which he set forth in Christ as a plan for the fulness of
time, to unite all things in him, things in heaven and things on
earth."

Out of Jew and Gentile, Paul says, Christ made "one new
man in place of the two, so making peace." Out of the sinner he
made a saint. Out of His empty tomb He raised up the Body of
the church. "So then you are . . . members of the household of
God, built upon the foundation of the apostles and prophets,
Christ Jesus himself being the cornerstone . . ."

This sanctified, set-apart stronghold of God is now
enjoined by Paul to enter into intercessory prayer as if the life-
blood of all saints depended on it! His strength of passion is
poured into this plea for unceasing supplication "for all the
saints, and also for me . . ." Christ's ambassador in chains has
a sense of his life ebbing away. He wants it contained in the
ocean of God's mercy — crashing ashore again in a fresh surge
of power embodied in the witness of those taking his place.

Ephesians 6:18 ☐ *Ephesians 6:18-20*

There is a river whose streams make glad the city of God . . .

If we are to "pray at all times in the Spirit," these healing streams become indispensable. The danger in intercession is to pray in the spirit of human sympathy. It honors neither God nor helps His people.

The intercessor after God's own heart immerses himself — and keeps doing so — in the refreshing streams that flow out of His guidance. God's glad river is His Holy Spirit. Instead of bringing to our intercession the paralyzing effects of our focus on problems, we release into it the power of the Almighty. If we pray from personal bias for quick solutions, we pray from a narrowing-down point of view bound to dead-end. If we draw our perspective from God's flow of wisdom, our spiritual vistas constantly expand and we receive hope and faith in like measure.

Authentic intercession is costly. But lest we secretly bemoan the toll it takes on our time and energy, we must remember who paid the real price. John, writer of Revelation, takes us to the source of the river, "Then he showed me the river of the water of life, bright as crystal, flowing from the throne of God and of the Lamb . . ." His sacrifice enables the invitation given by the Spirit and His church, "Let him who is thirsty come, let him who desires take the water of life without price" (22:1-2;17).

David rounds out the theme of gladness in Psalm 36: "How precious is thy steadfast love, O God! The children of men take refuge in the shadow of thy wings. They feast on the abundance of thy house, and thou givest them drink from the river of thy delights. For with thee is the fountain of life . . ." In the trials of life that draw on the very life-blood of the watchful, persevering saints, shall we pray in grimness or gladness? The authentic intercessor is delighted with God regardless of outcome. And that becomes the prevailing witness blessing all, that the God of sacred purpose is the Provider of our ultimate satisfaction.

Psalm 46:4 □ *Psalm 46*

Blessed are the men whose strength is in thee, in whose heart are the highways to Zion. As they go through the valley of Baca they make it a place of springs . . .

The experience of the valley of Baca is a time of thirsting for God and drinking of tears. *Baca* in Hebrew is the singular of *balsam trees* which grow in parched and barren places; the word also contains the root meaning *to weep.* From the Psalmist's play on words we shall take our own poetic license and declare with the audacity of experienced faith that there is sure balm for the pilgrimage through lonely pain.

Our stronghold of God cannot rest in any one place or person or group of people, but only in Him. But the lifeline of intercession becomes the highway system to God's heart through human hearts.

The intercessor who prays immersed in the glad streams of God's guidance is not afraid of tears for himself or the suffering saint whose heartbeat has become his own through caring. When he prays God's miracles into the barren places of the pilgrimage through pain, he does not specify cheery Astro turf or beach umbrella to create an illusion of rest. It may simply be that two linked by pain weep together and from such tenderness the cross springs to the conscious surface. The tree of life is rooted in the living waters of God. There is no sweeter shade and rest, no truer companionship than that of the cross in the valley of Baca.

Is our valley of Baca a barren time or place or relationship? It does not matter. Tethered by grace to the heart of God through loving intercession, we shall go from strength to strength. Christ came in the fulness of time, in the fulness of God, in the fulness of joy. "And from his fulness we have all received grace upon grace." Both weary intercessor and pilgrim will know the fulness of His promise.

Psalm 84:5-6 □ *Psalm 84*

So, could you not watch with me one hour?

Why do we close our eyes to the hour of crisis? Do spilled guts offend us? Do we suspect that such agony might be ours and so we practice denial? Why did Jesus allow the humiliation of that hour of shared naked weakness?

The watchful love of His dearest friends would have been comfort. But more than a singular act of friendship Jesus had hoped to secure their continued attention as observers of the consummate Teacher. The sight of sleeping Peter did not trigger the wail of a betrayed friend, "Look what I'm going through!" Not the most keenly attuned intimate could have fathomed the abyss of despair through which Christ plunged to hit rock bottom. The Teacher merely commented, "Watch and pray that you may not enter into temptation . . ." If we evade crisis, compromise becomes lifestyle and leads to corruption.

Peter, James and John had been singled out to witness the transfiguration and the resurrection of Jairus' daughter. "No good thing does the Lord withhold from those who walk uprightly." Crisis is beneficial, our Lord needed to teach His disciples and us. What if He had taken the malaise of inner uncertainties into His crucial confrontations with accusers and excecutioners? Christ would have publicly burned in hell! His final utterance from the cross would have lingered in witnesses' ears as, "I am finished!" Thanks to the fierce hour of agony in Gethsemane the fixed agony of the cross was anti-climactic. "It is finished!" declared the triumph of the crucifixion.

The words *crisis* and *certain* stem from the same Greek root meaning for cutting and separating. If blood is drawn in the hour of crisis it is not for wounding, but healing. Crisis cuts us loose from doubt and fear. It clears the head and nerves the will. The heart's fire of torment is extinguished by the cool streams of God's mercy. His angels of mercy minister gladly.

Matthew 26:40 □ *Matthew 26:36-46*

But we have this treasure in earthen vessels, to show that the transcendent power belongs to God . . .

This is our favorite sentimental saying that reveals an almost patronizing attitude toward God: "There, there, it is all right that you have given us clay feet as long as you blot out the messes when we knock things over with them." The text becomes a barbed saying when we have faithfully interceded for someone — not expecting things to fall into pleasant places, but for the glory of God to be manifested. And then, surprisingly, that person falls apart! It seems an insult to us and our Lord.

How can someone let us down especially at the last moment? For months Jesus had discussed His impending crucifixion. Only what we hide can ultimately hurt us, right? He continued to exhibit good mental and emotional health as His time drew near. He demonstrated the gift of tears at Lazarus' death. Jesus was in control at the Passover. "And when they had sung a hymn, they went out to the Mount of Olives." There, Jesus made an appointment to see His friends in Galilee right after Easter. Then He went to a place called Gethsemane and fell completely apart!

What Jesus models makes for the rule, not the exception. That is why intercessory prayer cannot follow certain success patterns, but must be modeled on the person and power of our Lord alone. Paul, who prayed with relentless zeal and urged the practice on all churches, was never able to package and market "the transcendent power of God" as foolproof success formula. He could only share the secret of his sacrificial life, "We are afflicted in every way, but not crushed, perplexed, but not driven to despair, persecuted, but not forsaken . . ."

The practice of God-pleasing intercession never leads to the glow of self-satisfaction, only to continued growth through His all-sufficiency.

2 Corinthians 4:7 □ 2 Corinthians 4:7-15

For God has consigned all men to disobedience, that he may have mercy upon all.

This is galling news to the earnest young believer. He is like an adoring young husband who barely hides his contempt for older men whose ardor has settled into stodgy breadwinning.

To the seasoned saint the saying makes for a knowing smile. This is but one of the alternate spellings for *grace*. To him luxurious peace flows forth from Paul's stern words. The mature believer who has long taken God at His word and consistently acts upon it, has stumbled unto a secret. When through the steady transaction of faith obedience ceases to be a string of acts, but settles into an attitude of the heart, we are home safe.

Active obedience, no doubt, is the key to spiritual fruitfulness. But if we take our polished little acts of dutifulness to hold them up to the light of our Father's beaming approval, we can become too performance-oriented. We are pleased when our small child brings us a flower as a spontaneous gesture of love. But if he decapitates a whole flower bed from greed for approval or uses his discovery of love as a bargaining power, we must curb such performance. Spiritually speaking, if we chalk up an impressive number of identifiable acts of obedience, we unwittingly maneuver ourselves into a position of vulnerability.

If not one single saint has his or her act together at all times, it is not that we have not tried. Heaven knows we try! But God looks on the heart and if our attitude is pleasing to Him, He will engineer those slips that cause our forced free fall through grace. If so, we always land in the soft center of His merciful heart. "Don't be so hard on yourself," He smiles. "I love you for who you are, not for what you do."

Romans 11:32 ☐ *Romans 11:25-36*

Brethren, if a man is overtaken in any trespass, you who are spiritual should restore him in a spirit of gentleness.

Only one caught in the act himself could pack such wealth of grace into such few words. Paul, caught red-handed on the Damascus road, spelled out in no uncertain terms our spiritual responsibilities toward a member of God's family who has slipped.

"Brethren . . ." No earthly father takes pleasure in his children's tattletales. He is most gratified when they work out their own problems. At first it is a noisy process of squabbling. As their sense of justice matures, so does the response of mercy. The parent's finest hour comes when good communication is not only evident in verbal skills, but also in mutual empathy and affection. At this stage in maturity the offender courageously admits to his wrong and asks for forgiveness. The offended brother responds in such a way that mutual respect flourishes once again. Brethren, says Paul, the Father is watching and listening. Please Him!

"If a man is overtaken in any trespass . . ." We want to make a distinction between the little brother who broke our favorite toy and the big brother who stole the affection of our fiancee. The one we are satisfied to reprimand; the other we need to nail! Paul was a murderer, a tormentor of women and children when caught on the Damascus road. Christ instructed Ananias to call this man brother and lay hands on him for restoration. This Paul says "any trespass . . ."

"You who are spiritual should restore him in a spirit of gentleness . . ." The religious communicate their moral outrage even when smiling until their teeth rot. The spiritual are guided by Christ's compassion. They heal the sense of shame and sorrow as fellow debtors to the cross. They restore to fellowship by being the fellowship. Among such God dwells with delight.

Galatians 6:1 ☐ Galatians 6:1-5

I was . . . in prison and you did not visit me.

A number of prison visitation programs are available to churches to get willing members involved in a sorely needed one-to-one ministry to the lonely and abandoned behind bars. So often the product of a broken home, this may be their only chance to discover wholeness through a caring relationship with a whole person.

Just be yourself, the recruiter smiles, and hopes that in the process of becoming a personal gift to the inmate we will allow him to enrich our own life as well. From such mutual respect and trust flows the confidence to return to a productive life instead of becoming the predictable repeat statistic.

How does the score look for repeat visitors? Far too many drop out of the program after a short time for one tragic reason. They are dying to quote Scripture and make a convert out of the convict. One moment he is happily talking baseball and the next he is told of the precious blood of the Lamb. We thrust a black book at him and tell him it contains good news for his situation. Then we leave smugly as courageous witnesses, when in fact we have practiced cowardly abandonment. One does not toss roast beef to a baby.

Christ lived and worked and played among His people for thirty years before He sat down to patiently teach them the great doctrines of the kingdom. He taught by sitting at table with sinners and publicans. He taught by involving Himself deeply in the lives of people who were allowed to discover the singular touch of His loving compassion. And we throw in the towel and walk off in a huff when our prison ministry of three months is a theological disaster! What happened to the gift of our courteous self? I, Jesus Christ, was in prison and you did not visit me.

Matthew 25:43 ☐ *Matthew 25:31-46*

But while he was yet at a distance, his father saw him and had compassion . . .

There is no distress quite as poignant as the godly parent's whose child removes himself to the far country of rebellion. Such distancing may take place right under our roof. At first there is a stunning sense of betrayal. Then we enter into mourning with God for the season of heartbreak that will stretch from our deep wound to the wandering child's pinnacle of self-destruction. We can make this time either a hell of tortured waiting or a wellspring of hope.

From times immemorial, sons and daughters have spurned their parents' ways. Long before Jesus told the parable of the Prodigal to lavish hope on us, the prophets echoed the heart cry of the rejected Father, "Sons have I reared and brought up, but they have rebelled against me. . . . They have forsaken the Lord . . . they are utterly estranged" (Isaiah 1:2,4).

Long before Jesus took us into the prodigal heart of the Father, the seers of old glimpsed His watchful, compassionate eye, "Why will you still be smitten, that you continue to rebel? The whole head is sick, and the whole heart faint. From the sole of the foot even to the head, there is no soundness in it, but bruises and sores and bleeding wounds; they are not pressed out, or bound up, or softened with oil" (Isaiah 1:5-6).

The wandering child laughs at such pathos. For a time his rebellion feels indescribably good. When ego surges and crests in waves of exciting self-discovery, there is an imitation of wholeness. The bold cutting of apron strings is proper indeed. We tremble when the umbilical cord to God's womb of mercy receives violent tugs. In such action is sown insidiously the sorrowful seed of self-condemnation. Our lips are properly silent when our heart is eloquent with His wooing compassion. If we devoutly wait on the Lord, His own watchful awaiting will lay out in our heart's chamber the festal robe and signet ring we shall press on our returned child on the assured day of exceeding gladness.

Luke 15:20 □ Luke 15:11-24

Now his elder son was in the field; and as he came and drew near to the house, he heard music and dancing. And he called one of the servants and asked what this meant.

Greater than the tragedy of the son who squanders his inheritance on harlots in the far country is the travesty of the model son laboring in the field near home — a total alien to his Father's prodigal disposition! Our churches are filled with such dutiful who have never joined the party in God's heart. Picture that tight-lipped dullard who in carping tones asks a servant what the party is all about.

Our sons and daughters want to know the same. Why should I go to church? Why should God who made the sun and surf be mad if I go to the beach instead of sitting in a stuffy room not listening to boring stuff?

Are we the dour son who goes to church because it is there? His unswerving sense of duty was not nourished from springs of joy, but merely expressed his inflexible, passionless character. The young sense such incongruity. Their curiosity and zest for life has not yet been dulled by the routines and conformities pressed on us in the course of earning our bread. Why indeed plod in the field when somewhere there is music and dancing and a fatted calf to be had? God forbid that we drive them into the far country because we have religiously excluded these from our expression of faith.

Before our rebellious children can come to their senses, we have to come to ours. The parable of the prodigal son has not as its moral the folly of wasteful living. Its great central truth is God's "wasteful" love! Instead of wasting words of warning and chiding on our restless young, we should steal quietly into our own heart of hearts. Is there a party going on right now? Have we known God's embrace and kiss? Welcome the music and dancing!

Luke 15:25 ☐ *Luke 15:25-32*

Because this people draw near with their mouth and honor me with their lips . . . and their fear of me is a commandment of men learned by rote; therefore, behold, I will again do marvelous things with this people . . .

What if we apply this biting sarcasm to our custom of saying grace before meals? It is a high privilege to be the church in the home and give thanks at table in the name of our Lord. "Behold . . . if any one hears my voice . . . I will come in to him and eat with him, and he with me." The act of eating together is a celebration of the Father's bounty and the bonds of brotherhood. Our saying of grace is a humble acknowledgement of His goodness, a joyous expression of gratitude for being able to experience it daily. One heartfelt "Thanks!" with a smile would do.

The spoken blessing becomes a priestly function when offered publicly on behalf of a group of people. Here we must ask the hard questions. Should affable Uncle Harry be encouraged to offer thanks to God Almighty even when he has no personal relationship with Jesus Christ? It creates such conviviality and makes for such nice tradition. But what if the Holy Spirit is grieved?

Any degree of intimacy with God is possible only through His Son Jesus. If we do not have His Spirit in us, our brash familiarity by rote and tradition is an offense. How much better to invite the simple thank-you of a little one than to have that child ask one day, "Where are the marvelous things of God in the lives of these 'marvelously' blessed people?" When the prophet says marvelous he really means watch out: God will not be the ceremonial figurehead at your parties! If you are careless with grace you may have to hunger and thirst for it someday!

Isaiah 29:13-14 □ *Isaiah 29:9-14*

For I know the plans I have for you, says the Lord, plans for welfare and not for evil, to give you a future and a hope.

Is that not exactly what we yearn for our children to know and understand? Is that not why we urge them to come to church? If we can only keep them hanging in there long enough until someday, from somewhere a spark will leap out at them and kindle the gift of faith we placed in their cradle!

Someday, from somewhere we receive news of someone's heart attack. The patient is expected to pull through, thank God, but his will be an unhappy life, we conclude in hushed tones. With favorite sports and rugged lifestyle replaced by endless restrictions, how could such a lover of life flourish? Are we aware that in life's unguarded moments we convey unspoken messages to our children that contradict our religious rhetoric full of hope and happy endings?

What kind of God do we hope to bequeath to our impressionable young? The God of our denominational affiliation with its rituals and socials? The God of our fathers with their cherished traditions? The God of our King James Bible with its prose so sweetly imbedded in our ear? Or is it the living God whose future and hope appear bright every day as we take delight in Jesus Christ? We cannot give Him away. Our children cannot take naturally to Him. He is supernaturally born in each believer anew as a fresh gift and unique expression of faith. But we can instill in our young a growing desire to know Him by what they unconsciously see revealed of Him as we live each day in the fulness of His Spirit.

"O Jerusalem, Jerusalem . . . How often would I have gathered your children together as a hen gathers her brood under her wings, and you would not!" This Jesus Christ yearns with the godly parent for his wayward child. Shall we not trust His plans for welfare, to give to both a future and a hope?

Jeremiah 29:11

I know whom I have believed . . .

This blessed modern age that has produced such a wealth of helpful Bible translations and study aids has also spawned new breeding grounds of dissent. From out of left field and right the barbed questions keep coming: What do you believe about the ordination of women, submission in marriage, the date of Creation, the inerrancy of Scripture? Our own personal bias is sniffed out by liberal and conservative as snarling dogs about to fight for the same bone.

If we look at the old guard of staunch King James Bible proponents who consider it the only inspired Holy Writ, and then fix our attention on the nonconformists who clamor for a desexed version of Good News for Modern Persons, the Christian community looks indeed as if it had split into armed camps. How is this new holy war to be fought — while the sick sorrowing world is going to hell on greased skids?

It is a healthy thing when more and more Christians really dig into their Bibles to bring out treasure, not ammunition for arguments. "You search the scriptures, because you think that in them you have eternal life; and it is they that bear witness to me; yet you refuse to come to me that you may have life" (John 5:39-40). What an indictment of human nature that we are right back where it all started. Jesus Himself would run the risk today of incurring the displeasure of extremists for not spelling out His beliefs to the letter of the law.

While we busily testify to our intellectual convictions and argue for our pet point of view, Paul gives in his pastoral letter to young Timothy his clarion call of supreme conviction, "I know whom I have believed." Do we? Do we need to get reacquainted with Him? The deity of Jesus Christ might heal our dogmatic obsessions.

2 Timothy 1:12 ☐ *2 Timothy 1:3-14*

But he did not answer her a word. And his disciples came and begged him, saying, "Send her away, for she is crying after us."

Ah, the bane of women bent on having their way! Just when church business is finally getting under way after everybody has been put into their proper place, this vexing outsider bursts on the scene. We try to ignore her, to shame her, to exclude her by virtue of doctrine. But this Greek woman, a Syrophoenician by birth, has the nerve to fall at Christ's feet in worship, saying, "Lord, help me." And He falls for her faith!

Jesus at this point really had had it with theological arguments. Pharisees and nit-picking scribes had traveled some sixty miles from Jerusalem to argue doctrine and tradition. Worn from the crowds and commotions He then withdrew to the region of Sidon and Tyre along the Mediterranean Sea. "And he entered a house, and would not have any one know it."

"Yet he could not be hid. But immediately a woman, whose little daughter was possessed by an unclean spirit, heard of him, and came . . ." She explained the severe suffering and cried for mercy, but Jesus would not be budged. Go away, He said to her, and defended His unique mission to the lost sheep of the house of Israel. Call me a "dog," she came back at him undaunted, "yet even the dogs eat the crumbs that fall from their master's table." Kneeling, she worshiped the God of all flesh. At this moment her child was healed.

What must the church learn from the woman who defied dignity and doctrine to get her way with Jesus? Perhaps we are like the people who engage in derisive debates over the shortcomings of the telephone system. But when we are stranded, alone and in trouble at night, with one dime and one pay telephone at our disposal, we worship God when the no-nonsense voice of that operator comes on the line!

Matthew 15:23 ☐ *Matthew 15:21-28*

He who conquers shall be clad thus in white garments, and I will not blot his name out of the book of life; I will confess his name before my Father and . . . his angels.

Could it mean this? He who contends to the bitter end for the purity of doctrine shall be marked in pure white, and I will make sure his name stays on the Faithful Subscribers list.

What Jesus said to the church in Sardis must ring with fresh clarity in our ears. They had deeds and a reputation for being alive. But Christ declared them devoid of spiritual life and power, their deeds not completed "in the sight of my God." In our own noisy contentions over what is right and proper for the church, we give the appearance of vitality. But if we neglect our supreme calling to proclaim the Person of Jesus Christ and promote faith in Him alone, our deeds — no matter how well-intentioned and proper — are not completed in the sight of God.

If we engage in continual tug-of-war over correct interpretation of doctrine, we may feel good occasionally when we have scored. But the chronic aggravation will in time force a resigned mood that proclaims: "Well, I stuck it out, but I'm ready to get out." Watch out for sackcloth and ashes in heaven! The festal robe is for those who made their joy in Jesus Christ the focal point of their faith and reproduced it in others.

Old and New Testament agree on the function and witness of the white garment. "Go then, eat . . . in happiness, and drink . . . with a cheerful heart; for God has already approved your works. Let your clothes be white all the time . . ." This prevailing mood of gladness and festivity is echoed in the Book of Revelation where the twenty-four elders, clothed in white, join joyfully with the living creatures "to give glory and honor and thanks to Him who sits on the throne." Let the joy of the Lamb that was slain overcome our striving!

Revelation 3:5 □ *Revelation 3:1-6*

Everyone who acknowledges me before men, the Son of man also will acknowledge before the angels of God . . .

This Son of man, stripped of all divine rights in the course of sacrificial servanthood, intends to make us into the statesman or stateswoman of God. The proposed accreditation before the ministers of heaven carries such weight. If we shift our faith's focus from Christ's person to private, pet views, we favor a career as pork-barreling politicians.

Statesmanship denotes exemplary leadership marked by wisdom and breadth of vision liberated from partisan interests. It is not achieved by ambition. The process is elusive. The formal portraits of Lincoln and Churchill show sober-looking older warriors, not gleeful young fighters. When they took their decisive stands they often stood alone and quite condemned.

Christian statesmanship arises from Spirit-endowed wisdom that weds our "breadth of vision" to the Person of Jesus alone. "For in him the whole fulness of deity dwells bodily, and you have come to fulness of life in him, who is the head of all rule and authority" (Colossians 2:9-10). Our fulness of life is contained in His limitless love. We acknowledge it fully by an authenticating lifestyle. Anybody can argue the fine points of religious bias. How many will convincingly demonstrate the sacrificial life of our joyous Lord? His Holy Spirit alone enables it. Dare we desire Him so single-mindedly?

In the angels we have fellow servants of God keenly interested in our relationship with Him. "Are they not all ministering spirits sent forth to serve, for the sake of those who are to obtain salvation?" (Hebrews 1:14). "Do you not know that we are to judge angels?" (1 Corinthians 6:3). Christ's astonishing breadth of vision betrays our staggering blindness. We receive sight only as we begin by act of will to acknowledge Him before men this very day!

Luke 12:8 □ *Luke 12:1-12*

Just so, I tell you, there is joy before the angels of God over one sinner who repents.

What kind of place is heaven that even one earthling should so dominate the scene? Does earth shed light on heaven? "In the beginning God created the heavens and the earth. The earth was without form and void . . ." We cannot envision such vacuity precisely because we were Creation's crowning glory. Endued with our sense, gifted with intellect and speech, we were the superbly made recipients of God's manifest glory.

Homebound space travelers come closest perhaps to the childlike wonder that surrounded earth's formation "when the morning stars sang together, and all the sons of God shouted for joy" (Job 38:7). Did the angels applaud the creative genius of their Maker? Or was their joy an early measure of man's worth in Jesus Christ? Isaiah says of Creation that God "established" the earth; "he did not create it a chaos, he formed it to be inhabited." Earth was not primarily to be a showcase of creative activity, but an expression of relationship. The Genesis account of Adam naming the animals implies not whimsy of language, but practice in establishing relationships for mutual benefit.

Still, Creation's showcase is evident in our most humble surroundings. Retrieve onion skin, egg shell and banana peel from the garbage! As we compare their amazing functions and trace God's very finger in their distinctive texture, are we not gripped by excitement that we shall explore His creative genius at the highest level? Sadly, man has made a garbage dump of the Visited Planet. By contrast alone heaven must be "heavenly."

Here is where Christ's remark, summing up His parables of the lost sheep and lost coin, must shake us to the core. Seraphic joy is not conditioned by this place called heaven. The angels' transistor radios are not tuned in to heaven's Carnegie Halls. Their only channel echoes the heartbeat of the crucified Lord. When it quickens to the footsteps of even one lost soul coming home, their joy is made perfect. Heaven is not a place of bliss and beauty. It is the heart and home of harmonized relation-ships. Such is the humility of this magnificent God who seeks us still.

Luke 15:10 □ *Luke 15:1-8*

Then I saw a new heaven and a new earth; for the first heaven and the first earth had passed away, and the sea was no more.

John, the Seer on Patmos, would have trouble selling his "theories" today, even in the science fiction market. We would still rather buy little green men on Mars than push our imagination off so steep a cliff and have it set adrift over such impenetrable mist. Abraham, on the other hand, who knew nothing about black holes and other cosmic hypotheses set forth by modern scientists, but did know God and the terra firma between Ur and Canaan quite well, would quickly hail John as kindred spirit and cheer on the truth so simply stated.

Abraham's early convictions? "By faith he sojourned in the land of promise, as in a foreign land, living in tents . . . For he looked forward to the city which has foundations, whose builder and maker is God" (Hebrews 11:9-10). Obligingly, John who obliterates our known universe with one easy stroke of the pen, describes in great detail this amazing city that will dominate the new heaven and earth. Seeing it suspended in "midair," he could easily determine the magnificence of those God-made foundations and recognize promise upon promise made to His covenant people down through the ages. John chose various jewels to express the matchless beauty that met his eye, but when he describes the city street as "pure gold, transparent as glass," we know he was frustrated in describing for mortals the indescribable of eternity's future.

What does it say to us? Simply that God will gladly sacrifice the Swiss Alps, Disneyland, and the solar system to provide an eternal center of unbroken fellowship. Emmanuel — God with us! He tried to tell us as a baby. He will confirm it with His "Big Bang theory"!

Revelation 21:1 ☐ *Revelation 21*

I will write on him the name of my God, and the name of the city of my God, the new Jerusalem which comes down from my God out of heaven, and my own new name.

The first time mother's darling goes to camp, instructions are followed to a tee. From toothbrush to extra underwear (in case you fall into the creek) everything is marked with junior's name. The second year he is less eager for the ritual, being far more concerned if Old Ginger will be there in the corral waiting for him. The third summer Johnny Camper considers it outright sissy to have his things labeled.

The name on the towel says more about relationship than ownership. The label marks him as his mother's son. Wash behind your ears, son. Hang up the towel neatly. I love you, son. I miss you . . . For this one special week Johnny Camper does not want to be his mother's son. For one week he wants to fully relate to this extraordinary world set apart for his enjoyment. In time he will learn that ordinary home is an extraordinary condition of the heart much more than a place for doing homework and hanging up mother's towels neatly.

The Book of Revelation points us to our extraordinary home. If we can remember only one thing about the Apocalypse with its gripping poetic symbolism, let it be the disarmingly simple introduction, "The revelation of Jesus Christ. . . . Blessed is he who reads . . . and blessed are those who hear, and who keep what is written . . ."

This is the blessedly simple revelation of our Lord: Like Abraham we are out "camping" for a time, but destined for the magnificent home founded on God's loving heart. In Jesus Christ His name is undeniably on us, safeguarding for all time and eternity His claims of ownership and relationship. Let Him unravel the mystery while we hold fast to His majesty and exclaim with Jesus, "My God!"

Revelation 3:12 ☐ *Revelation 3:7-13*

One of themselves, a prophet of their own, said, "Cretans are always liars, evil beasts, lazy gluttons." This testimony is true.

How does contemporary Christianity justify the apostle's harsh remark? Paul was no first-century Archie Bunker! He did not pontificate on the shortcomings of minorities with a can of beer facilitating flow of reason. Paul had sharpened his mind by reading the classics. These were filled with allusions to the Cretans' knack of lying. To "act the Cretan" was synonymous to fibbing. Paul quoted the poet Epimenides when he charged Titus to light into the Cretans with the illumination of the Holy Spirit.

Poets stretch truth for effect. If we apply the cosmetics of modern tolerance for human foibles, we can have the ancients come up smelling like roses, "Cretans are fanciful raconteurs, bon vivants, gourmands." With the right twist of sophistication we can project them as God's happy gift to an increasingly gloomy brotherhood. Unfortunately the Holy Spirit does not speak French, only truth. In fact, not many verses later Paul makes the Cretans look good by divulging his fellow Christians' background, "For we ourselves were once foolish, disobedient, led astray, slaves to various passions and pleasures, passing our days in malice and envy, hated by men and hating one another . . ." (Titus 3:3).

Why must this old "ethnic slur" disturb and force us into a decisive re-evaluation of what is ultimately fair to the brotherhood of all men? Sadly, because we have lost our heart for missions, modern thinking having gone to our head. We would rather export cola than this kind of "character assassination," forgetting that we doom whole peoples to spiritual death by denying them regeneration through rebirth in Christ. The brotherhood of men is a fraud if we do not become fellow heirs in hope of eternal life. "The saying is sure" (Titus 3:8).

Titus 1:12-13 ☐ *Titus 1,2 and 3*

Therefore rebuke them sharply, that they may be sound in the faith, instead of giving heed to Jewish myths or to commands of men who reject the truth.

Paul agonized over the Cretan converts because of the Judaizers. These eroded faith in Jesus Christ by preaching salvation with works. Obedience taught by rule and rote sabotaged the fragile process of learning obedience from the heart. Only the Spirit's nurture could vouchsafe the joyous liberty of the convert.

Many of our world's nations are suffering from ambiguous saviors. Western civilization, enamoured with the good life fostered by advanced technology, has sought to share it with less fortunate peoples. But the new shock troops have mostly gone in with soda pop, T-shirts and transistor radios. Some mothers, sold on foolproof fortified infant formulas, are cradling doomed babies today because sterilization and refrigeration eluded their Westernization.

Today's humanitarian is curiously ambiguous about primitive societies. Short of starvation and disease their cultures should be left untouched as living monuments to the irretrievable past, its taboos and terrors stoically endured. The modern-day Titus determined to affect the "local color" with the blood of Jesus Christ is caricatured as prude and killjoy. The golden age of missions is past.

How do we stem the tide? First, by putting our crucified Lord before culture and common sense in our own life first. Secondly, by honoring the Titus in our midst. There is a ground swell of missionary zeal among our Christian youth today. What if we supported them as energetically as we do the National Geographic Society? Their prayer letters will not read like the fascinating photojournalism we so enjoy. But the blood of Jesus Christ they patiently preach will change local color for good. Forever!

Titus 1:13-14

*But if any one has the world's goods and sees his brother in
need, yet closes his heart against him, how does God's love
abide in him?*

Familiar texts brush superficially against the mind
smoothed by easy application. We have immunized ourselves
against the deeper implications by placing our spare cash on
bets surfacing through the mail. Our donation to cancer
research might hit the jackpot of discovered cure. But God lives
in the heart, not the wallet. This verse cannot simply concern
our spare cash.

Our inflationary times have exposed the hoax of loose-
change charity. With a twinge of regret we junk the mail with
the financial appeals we used to honor. The very machinery
that mass-produces such appeals lulls us into a soothing sense
of anonymity.

The problem existed in John's day. Instead of junk mail
there were beggars crying from doorways, roadsides and
temple gates. Hard times exposed them for the nuisance they
were when self-preservation instinct and tender conscience
became locked in battle. Hard questions arise. Who is our
brother? Can we afford to close our heart? What are the
world's goods?

The world's goods are simply material necessities, not
amassed wealth. Spare-cash charity is out! The heart is the
composite of intellect, will and emotions. Indwelled and
empowered by the living God, it expands in proportion to
exposure to His own heart. Enlarged spiritually, it is singularly
suited to take in the needy brother, whether he be missionary
or member of the body locally. Let the world satisfy conventional charity needs. The Christain is called to a higher exercise
of trust and responsibility. Let him enter into the costly caring
relationship where he really sees his brother in need. It forces
us to look to God, not our wallet. Dare we close our heart
against Him?

1 John 3:17 ☐ *1 John 3:11-18*

If one member suffers, all suffer . . .

Mere checkbook-charity is popular because it puts us in control. Risks and benefits are calculated in advance. Generosity pays dividends at income tax time. When God removes the dollar signs from our eyeballs and makes us look at the brother in need, we are catapulted into shocking helplessness.

What if the "brother" turns out to be a woman with five children? Perhaps we are first tapped for rent money when she faces eviction after prolonged illness. We write that first non-deductible check just in time to find out that the children have different fathers. Not every new creation in Christ can neatly tuck away the forgiven past. Intellectually we accept it. Existentially we gloss over it until God challenges us to the costly caring relationship.

When God has us initially hooked He seems to drop a leaking tube of Krazy Glue in our path of righteousness. We step from one sticky situation into another. No sooner are we reconciled to our sister's redeemed past than an old boyfriend shows up and knocks out some of her teeth. A young son is held up at knife point during his lunch hour. The high school senior gets pregnant. God may spare us such suffering and merely involve us with a chaste maiden missionary in a far-off land. Now we merely worry about chronic shortages of all kinds, with political uprisings and natural disasters spicing our prayers.

What is God teaching when the shock waves of existence race our emotions through periods of perplexity, resentment and anguish? He teaches salvation instead of quickie solutions. Commandment in place of pious platitudes. He takes us into the world of the needy brother to acquaint us with suffering. He stretches our heart so we can never close it again. The Suffering Servant's vulnerability becomes ours. We never get quite used to it!

1 Corinthians 12:26 ☐ *1 Corinthians 12:12-26*

Give us this day our daily bread . . .

Unless we enter the fragile world of the needy this classic petition does not ring true when we routinely pray it. Used to freezers and supermarkets we are more apt to be after the grocer for our weekly specials. The idea of living from hand to mouth seems anachronistic until shared misfortune instills in us the desire to take Jesus at His word.

When God yokes us with the brother in need we realize quickly that we cannot foot the bill for two households. In fact, He will tie our hands in peculiar ways to keep us from reaching into our pocket, wanting to cure with cold cash what needs to be healed with patient caring. God is responsible for two hearts. He safeguards the healthy balance between giving and taking. As in all transactions of faith the glory belongs to Him.

"This is the day which the Lord has made . . ." "This day" invites the focus of the here and now in positive acknowledgement of the Giver of life. With Christ's emphasis on personal relationship it is no accident that the petition for daily bread is immediately followed by the one responsibility charged to the believer, "And forgive us our debts, as we also have forgiven our debtors . . ." This is not the pardon of salvation, but the application of grace to favorably affect fellowship.

One of the great blessings coming to the Christian who cares deeply and patiently for a needy brother is fresh discovery in prayer. At first we pray for him in solution-oriented ways. Then we learn to pray with him and this becomes a celebration of the fellowship God intended. When we pray for daily bread where there is no car or job we learn afresh to hunger for our Lord Himself. The Bread of Life is able to deliver manna still. "What is it?" we may ask when His answers puzzle us at times. In time the seasoned saint simply calls it "faithfulness."

Matthew 6:11 □ Matthew 6:9-15

He who supplies seed to the sower and bread for food will supply and multiply your resources and increase the harvest of your righteousness.

Have we courageously hired the Holy Spirit as our financial manager and investment counselor? If we work with a stockbroker, we can follow the game plan through the Wall Street Journal and call the shots as we see them. If we sign on with God, He refers us to ground rules that are binding regardless of circumstances. In essence He says go for broke!

In outlining the adventure of trust Paul speaks of blessing, seed, bread, resources, generosity, obedience, contribution, and "inexpressible gift" (2 Corinthians 9:6-15). Not once does he mention money. Some messengers of miraculous multiplication shock with their blatant faith-bargaining explicitly expressed in hard currency. Send us your twenty-dollar bill and we will pray over it. Then watch for the surprise mail or the next bingo game or the supermarket sweepstakes . . .

Is there a happy middle ground for the responsible Christian who sees his money as security as well as potential? Our investment in God's work cannot be determined by a "safe" actual dollar amount. It starts with the very real measure of faith given to us. The more intimately related we are to our Lord, the larger the measure and the greater our abandonment to Him. The initial leap of faith is as scary whether we give away our first ten or ten thousand dollars! The amount is incidental, the act of trust monumental.

If we mean to make money for the sake of making money, we will feel better with conventional counsel. If we mean business with the Holy Spirit, Hosea contributes splendid advice, "Sow for yourselves righteousness, reap the fruit of steadfast love; break up your fallow ground, for it is the time to seek the Lord, that he may come and rain salvation upon you."

2 Corinthians 9:10 □ *2 Corinthians 9:6-15*

The master commended the dishonest steward for his shrewdness; for the sons of this world are more shrewd in dealing with their own generation than the sons of light.

When it comes to "unrighteous mammon" — plain dirty money — some Christians resemble a satin-gowned dowager with long white gloves sucking on a sour pickle. We stand aloof and disapproving of this tainted worldly commodity. Necessity compels us to endure some of the rules, but we refuse to play the game of money.

Christ commends crook! Savior solicits sharpies! In startling contrast He stands there with His shirt sleeves rolled up, a rugged hero of the new frontier. The same Lord who angrily cracked the whip over the money changers in the temple, vividly educates us in the worldly use of money. He has no admiration for the patsy who ignores that "the earth is the Lord's and the fulness thereof." Ordinary life is not a pox on the spiritually minded. It is God's gift and breathes with the common grace of Him who so loved the world that He gave His only son . . .

A rich man had hired an agent who was found guilty of mismanagement. So he got notice that he was fired. While cleaning his desk he pondered the future. Too old to dig and too proud to beg, he summoned his employer's debtors. One by one he had them state their debt, tear up the original bill, and write a new one for a lesser amount. In doing so, the successful schemer bought himself all the future he needed. Buster, I took care of you, now you'll have to take care of me.

Of course Jesus did not applaud the cheating. But He commended the man's shrewd dealings with his contemporaries. He operated entirely at their own low level. In truth those debtors were the cheaters and as such already at home with their sweet-talking friend. "And I tell you, make friends for yourselves by means of unrighteous mammon, so that when it fails they may receive you into the eternal habitations." It is right to give away money, says Jesus, with the hope of winning friends and reaping blessings. If the law of unrighteousness works for the unrighteous, how much more shall the law of righteousness benefit God's own!

Luke 16:8 ☐ *Luke 16:1-9*

Now concerning the contribution for the saints: as I directed the churches of Galatia, so you also are to do.

Here is comfort for the poor preacher at odds with his flock over finances. Instead of hatching new plots to dramatize the need for regular giving, let him simply no longer hedge on the Word. The people of God must be told, not asked. The Apostle Paul already did the dirty work of blunt confrontation; the timid man of the cloth need only cite his eminent colleague. In fact, this strategy is tinged with such sweet irony that the suffering saint in the pulpit should quietly jump for joy. Worshipers clamor for inspiration. Let them have it!

Many a testy parishioner questions a pastor's propriety to talk money in church. Whole congregations steel themselves against the stewardship drive in the fall. A collective surge of faith may not leap forth, but a collective sigh of relief is heaved when things return to "normal." But while we gather full steam for our personal fall activities, church leaders trim budgets and arrange for loans to tide the family over until Christmas. Then we play Santa Claus to the hilt. Should the next faith pledge drive see our pastor dressed in red costume and beard?

"Lo! I tell you a mystery. We shall not all sleep. . . . For the trumpet will sound, and the dead will be raised. . . . When . . . the mortal puts on immortality, then shall come to pass the saying that is written: 'Death is swallowed up in victory.' . . . Now concerning the contribution for the saints . . ."

One moment we bask in the magnificent resurrection rhetoric — the next we are holding the collection basket! Paul socked it to us long before our leaders gently urged us to be faithful in systematic, regular giving. Our recalcitrant stance dishonors the Head, Jesus Christ, and hinders the effective functioning of the body. What if the last trumpet blows the whistle on our fickle faith!

1 Corinthians 16:1 □ *1 Corinthians 15:51-16:4*

Woe to you . . . hypocrites! for you tithe mint and dill and cummin, and have neglected . . . justice and mercy and faith; these you ought to have done, without neglecting the others.

"Will man rob God? Yet you are robbing me. But you say, 'How are we robbing thee?' In your tithes and offerings . . . Bring the full tithes into the storehouse . . . and thereby put me to the test, says the Lord of hosts, if I will not open the windows of heaven for you and pour down for you an over-flowing blessing" (Malachi 3:8-10).

Will man still rob God? But you say we live under grace, not law. So principled, you do not give a tenth of your earnings as gift to Him who gave His all. Jesus, who ushered in the age of grace, affirmed the tithe. While exhorting the Jewish leaders to honor God from the heart, he encouraged them not to neglect this other expression of devotion. The scribes, always the sticklers for the minutia of religious life, had so "perfected" the tithe that it included a tiny aromatic seed like cummin. Jesus did not correct such zeal.

The believer who puts a dollar bill into the collection plate from "grace" habit is the first to detest money talk as routine family matter. With due respect for his feelings, the invitation to tithe must be given again and again. The household of God demands our best, not least. If all were to pull together in glad response to Christ's sacrificial giving, how worship and witness would be dramatically enhanced!

If the tithe seems coldly calculating, so is the dipping of one's toe in the ocean. If we want to master the turbulent surf and achieve that expert swim, we have to start cold. If we want to unlock the windows of heaven for the sake of the church, why not try it God's way! No tithing Christian is a nag and complainer. In his joy he goes on to bless God with his offerings.

Matthew 23:23

We want you to know, brethren, about the grace of God which has been shown in the churches of Macedonia, for in a severe test of affliction, their abundance of joy and their extreme poverty have overflowed in a wealth of liberality . . .

If tithe and heaven's window test violate the grace-endued conscience, here is cheerful propaganda for the grace principle of successful giving. "And a vision appeared to Paul in the night: a man of Macedonia was standing beseeching him and saying, 'Come over to Macedonia and help us'"(Acts 16:9). "I am going to Jerusalem with aid for the saints. For Macedonia and Achaia have been pleased to make some contribution for the poor among the saints at Jerusalem; they were pleased to do it, and indeed they are in debt to them, for if the Gentiles have come to share in their spiritual blessings, they ought also to be of service to them in material blessing" (Romans 15:25-27).

Prevenient grace, experienced grace, applied grace. In every instance grace appears in the context of close-knit fellowship. Paul then delivers his "gracious" stewardship appeal to the Corinthians and those of us who recoil from legalism, "Now as you excel in everything — in faith, in utterance, in knowledge, in all earnestness, and in your love for us — see that you excel in this gracious work also. I say this not as a command. . . . For you know the grace of our Lord Jesus Christ, that though he was rich, yet for your sake he became poor, so that by his poverty you might become rich."

One tiny matter must not be overlooked. Before the Macedonians pulled off their feat of liberality, "they gave themselves to the Lord and to us by the will of God." Is there a missing link in our chain of amazing grace? Have we given money to the church without giving ourselves to our leaders first? The will of God and law of love demand that vital link!

2 Corinthians 8:1-2 □ *2 Corinthians 8:1-7*

And his gifts were that some should be . . . pastors and teachers . . .

No matter how commanding the credentials of the professional in the pulpit, we are to regard him highly in the first place as a gifted servant of the Most High. He has derived his position by the sovereign will of God, not by climbing the ladder of success. Theologian and country parson are equally dependent on the favor of God. The idea is not to humble the one and exalt the other in men's eyes according to whim, but to base all subsequent considerations on established divine will.

The pastor must be the first one to realize this clear distinction. The will of his people is a formidable force to be reckoned with. The people in the pew can make or break a church. Holding the purse strings, they have been known to manipulate them to effect their preference in program and proclamation. If God's leader sells out to such people, he digs his own grave.

The congregation after God's own heart presents an initial gift in response to His gift of pastor and teacher. It is not natural affection and good will, but a sacred commitment to recognize their position as under-shepherds called to imitate the chief shepherd, Jesus Christ. Dare we present in person this affirmation to our leaders, whether at first we outright admire or barely tolerate them? Agape love is action first, emotion last. Having spoken our binding words of prayerful devotion, we will think twice before condemning as "unresponsive" a busy pastor.

A pastor must make time to be intimate with his people so mutual love can grow and strengthen the body. But God forbid that we should clamor to be the pampered pet sheep. The pastor is not the paid lover to be summoned at whim. By the will of God he has the task of pointing willful children to "mature manhood" in Christ. Will we obey our leaders and submit to them "as men who will have to give account"?

Ephesians 4:11 □ *Ephesians 4:7-16*

. . . to equip the saints for the work of ministry, for building up the body of Christ . . .

The relationship between pastor and congregation is not that of speaker and audience, meeting under the auspices of the Mutual Admiration Society. Yet we carelessly perpetuate that myth. If the preacher is warm, witty and wonderful, we flock to hear him gladly. If he is out of town and a lesser member of the fraternity proclaims the Word of God, we stay home to weed the yard. We think we pay our favorite man a compliment when in fact we break his heart.

What do worshipers whisper to the preacher when they queue up to shake his hand after the service? The man of courtesy and love ponders the words in his heart. Adulation he must hate; affirmation he deserves in ever larger measure. The worshiper strapped for ready inspiration receives help from Scripture, "It is not good to eat much honey, so be sparing of complimentary words." The glory belongs to God!

Isaiah strikes the chord thàt makes for sweet music in the rewarded heart, "For as the rain and the snow come down from heaven, and return not thither but water the earth, making it bring forth and sprout, giving seed to the sower and bread to the eater, so shall my word be that goes forth from my mouth; it shall not return to me empty, but it shall accomplish that which I purpose, and prosper in the thing for which I sent it" (Isaiah 55:10-11).

When have we last thanked our pastor and teacher for equipping the saints, for administrating the work of ministry, for building up the body of Christ? Such compliments arise not from the hearing of the sermon, but from doing the Word of God. There is no higher honor, no deeper love we can bestow on our leaders than to let them behold with their eyes and experience the fruit of their labor in our changed lives.

Ephesians 4:12

For though you have countless guides in Christ, you do not have many fathers. For I became your father in Christ Jesus . . . I urge you, then, be imitators of me.

The senior pastor of a large church has to work with a sizeable staff to cope with the needs of his congregation. We tend to treat such staff as "countless guides." Their very presence causes us to jockey more determinedly for a position in the father's lap. How can the headman make headway if the headstrong and weakened cling near his cluttered desk?

"What is this that you are doing for the people?" Jethro, Moses' father-in-law, was visiting his famous relative. Amazed, he watched a line of people stretched from morning till evening waiting to see Moses. Jethro's reaction? Good grief! Hebrew translation: "What you are doing is not good. You and the people . . . will wear yourselves out, for the thing is too heavy for you; you are not able to perform it alone." The priest of Midian then introduced Moses to the concept of delegation. It worked.

Paul hopes to put us to work. No one understands better than he the problems besetting a beloved pastor and his people. He does not fault us for desiring that extra measure of attention and affection. He now has hit on a fine solution. "Be imitators of me." Get off the pastor's shirttail. Let yours hang out for someone to hold onto for a while. See how it feels! But we have no master's degree in this sort of thing. "Be imitators of me, as I am of Christ." Claim the Master's decree. "And walk in love, as Christ loved us and gave himself up for us, a fragrant offering . . ." If we give of ourselves in this manner, the senior pastor will wish to come and bask in our love!

1 Corinthians 4:15-16 □ *1 Corinthians 4:8-21*

Greet Prisca and Aquila . . .

Chalk one up for the "little old woman"! She gently demonstrates the happy results of being "affectionately desirous" of sharing gospel and self with a fellow Christian who has become very dear. These Christ-imitators, the Apostle and the First Lady of the Epistles, have a surprise in store. Paul is not the woman-eating ogre. Priscilla is quite the woman theologian.

Paul first met Aquila in Corinth. He and his wife were exiled Jews from Rome. Fellow tent-makers, Paul stayed with them. After Paul had left for Jerusalem, they befriended Apollos. This brilliant young Jew, in time to become Paul's co-worker, was well educated and on fire for God. He spoke and taught "accurately the things concerning Jesus." After Priscilla and Aquila heard him in the synagogue, they tactfully took him aside and with love "expounded to him the way of God more accurately."

Paul's correspondence attests to their friendship in his sensitive greetings. In his letter from Ephesus to Corinth in 56 A.D. Paul writes, "Aquila and Prisca, together with the church in their house, send you hearty greetings in the Lord." In the letter from Corinth to the Romans in 58 A.D. he greets "Prisca and Aquila, my fellow workers in Christ Jesus, who risked their necks for my life, to whom not only I but also all the churches of the Gentiles give thanks." In 66 A.D., writing from Rome to Timothy in Ephesus, he repeats his distinctive salute, "Greet Prisca and Aquila."

Priscilla in Latin means "little old woman," diminutive of "old woman" Prisca. Saul alias Paul was keenly name-conscious. The Greek Paulos meant "little one." Because he thought of himself as "the very least of all saints," he insisted on using his Greek name. This Paul honored Priscilla's stature as great friend and admired woman in Christ by calling her Prisca. This lay leader had loved the church professional well and he came to bask in her love.

2 Timothy 4:19

Not neglecting to meet together, as is the habit of some, but encouraging one another . . .

Why is early Sunday morning slumber so sensuously delicious? With the cares of the week behind and a day of leisure stretching out before us, sleep gloriously smooths out the rough edges of living. No wonder church sounds Greek to many when we are "called out" of bed on the Lord's day!

Church — *ekklesia* — "called out," *ek* "out," *kaleo* "to call." The word assumes shape in assembly, popular meeting, religious congregation. On Sunday morning when creature comfort and Christian conscience may clash, it helps to remember this distinction: We do have a choice about removing our body from bed and moving it to the building called church. We have no choice about *being* the church! Christ called us out. On Pentecost we were historically — eternally — united to Him and each fellow believer in the baptizing work of the Holy Spirit. As the historic death and resurrection of our Lord must be worked out existentially in our own personal life, so the historic birth and function of the church must find personal expression.

Here is the crucial responsibility we conveniently overlook when we focus on the church as a building. We were called out to be the church. Paradoxically, precisely because of this mystical process we must follow it up with the mundane and immediate. The sheer body count in the sanctuary affects morale favorably. The pleasure of familiar faces is undergirded by the witness of faithfulness. This kind of roll call is being noted by angels and "powers and principalities." No believer enjoys the luxury of privacy.

The world measures prestige and popularity of dignitaries by the crowds they command at public functions. Is God the Father Almighty, Maker of heaven and earth to be treated with the ho-hum of the negligent believer?

Hebrews 10:25

O LORD, I love the habitation of thy house, and the place where thy glory dwells.

David's "O LORD sounds like a sigh of contentment — several notches up from our frantic, "O Lord, time to get up or we'll be late for church!" Where we deliberate habit, he thinks habitation. Where we are sporadic visitor, he is permanently at home. Where we worship in a brick structure, David acknowledges his God in "the place where thy glory dwells."

David's "place," we must not forget, was the great disappointment of his life. When David transferred his reign from Hebron to Jerusalem, he sent for the ark of the covenant. It was brought into the City of David in joyous procession, with the king dancing before the Lord with all his might. "And they brought in the ark of the Lord, and set it in its place, inside the tent which David had pitched for it."

Interestingly, when David had moved his base of operation to Jerusalem, having won that stronghold in battle, the king of Tyre sent cedar trees and workmen to build him a house. Through this gesture "David perceived that the Lord had established him king over Israel, and that he had exalted his kingdom for the sake of his people Israel." Picking up on this logic, his soldiering days behind him, he told Nathan of his plan, "See now, I dwell in a house of cedar, but the ark of God dwells in a tent." God came back quickly at David through the prophet. Thanks, but no thanks! David's hands had shed too much blood to build God's house. The honors would go to his son. God's remarkable counter offer: "Moreover the Lord declares to you that the Lord will make you a house." Out of that dynasty came the Prince of Peace.

"I was glad when they said to me, 'Let us go to the house of the Lord!'" When will we discover with David the joy of the house that is habitation and glory? What if we danced into church?

Psalm 26:8 □ *Psalm 26*

Thus says the LORD of hosts: In those days ten men from the nations of every tongue shall take hold of the robe of a Jew, saying, "Let us go with you, for we have heard that God is with you."

Imagine getting ready for church and outside the whole neighborhood is assembled waiting to go with you! Imagine interviewing these enthusiasts for membership and asking for letters of transfer from their home church. What if these eager candidates answered in turn: I've never been in a church before! I'm transferring here from the municipal golf course, the tennis club, the African violet society . . .

This brief, exhilarating glimpse into the future is to accomplish two things. First, it should illuminate God's incredible thoroughness in working out His sovereign rule solely through His chosen people. Secondly, it should cause us to examine and rededicate our own ordinary contribution to His extraordinary future.

Revelation 20 and the Thessalonian letters in particular sketch the circumstances surrounding the Millennium. The present church age draws to a close with the tribulation. The rapture and second coming of Christ take place. Believers attain their resurrection body. It is immortal, yet mysteriously bears identity to the one we know now. At the end of the seven-year tribulation Christ reigns on earth 1000 years and we with Him. Then comes the brief final showdown with Satan. Unbelievers will be resurrected and judged. Eternal life from God's ultimate perspective begins.

Endless discussions can be had concerning exact interpretation of these eschatologies. One glorious truth is self-evident. The Millennium is God's gracious provision for His fulfillment of all covenants. After our long, hard childhood of faith the people of God are to relish the exhilarating taste of their adulthood in Jesus Christ!

Zechariah 8:23 ☐ Zechariah 8:18-23

Ascribe to the LORD the glory of his name, worship the LORD in holy array.

This age so fiercely liberation-minded has struck down dress code after dress code and the axe is still swinging. The quest for individuality has carried over into church life. Our Sunday best ranges from "dressed to kill" to tattered jeans.

"Worship the Lord in holy array." It is a recurring Old Testament theme. "Array" refers to rich or beautiful apparel. "Holy" means set apart and dedicated to the worship of God. What if we were to rethink our Sabbath best along these lines? Would nostalgia buffs parade Easter hats every Sunday of the year? How could the male of the species compete? Skull caps? Prayer shawls? King James could have had a field day in England's heyday of ruffles and laces. But his translators rendered the text as, ". . . worship the Lord in the beauty of holiness." That makes for a beauty contest which throws not only thoughts, but judges, into disarray.

In our dilemma we take a look at Him who clothes us with the garments of salvation. How did Jesus dress? In His most definite identification as Son of man He went naked. His seamless robe dropped off at the foot of the cross. In His most explicit revelation as Son of God on the Mount of Transfiguration, "his garments became glistening, intensely white, as no fuller on earth could bleach them." Does heaven's glory really make for dressing "up"?

The James of the King's version of Scripture says we do well if we fulfill the royal law, "You shall love your neighbor as yourself." We are not to fawn over the man "with gold rings and in fine clothing" at the expense of the poor man "in shabby clothing" in our assembly. Where there is uniformity of consideration for our neighbor — beautiful in Christ — we can joyfully conclude with the Psalmist, ". . . and in his temple all cry, 'Glory!'"

Psalm 29:2 □ Psalm 29

And rend your hearts and not your garments.

When the crafty sons of Jacob returned to him their hated brother's bloodied robe, they said, "Joseph is without doubt torn to pieces." Jacob promptly tore his robe. Informed of Saul's death, "David took hold of his clothes, and rent them; and so did all the men who were with him."

The Old Testament is strewn with torn clothes and warnings to mend ways, yet the few references to sewing do not relate to repair. Despair was in Job's words to his needling friends, "I have sewed sackcloth upon my skin."

To nudge the heart of the matter closer to us, the prophets and Ezra expand on the theme. Reacting to bad news, Ezra pulled hair from his head and beard to give vent to indignation not fully spent on his ruined clothes. Who of us has not known the instinct! Isaiah graphically sums up such "hairy" times, ". . . instead of well-set hair, baldness." In startling contrast Jeremiah employs an opposite picture, but the Hebrew language reveals the identical message. It is like saying *fat chance* when we mean *thin chance*. "And you, O desolate one, what do you mean that you dress in scarlet . . . that you enlarge your eyes with paint?" The more telling King James version, ". . . though thou rentest thy face with painting, in vain shalt thou make thyself fair. . . ."

It simply comes down to this. We would rather solve problems by means of cosmetics than character surgery. We are better at facades than facing truth. We are quick to react with external indignation, and slow to act on inner conviction. When violence strikes down a pope or president we tear our hair and angrily claw at the fabric of rotting society. As soon as TV channels are cleared for regular programming, we nonchalantly resume the diversion of watching violence packaged as entertainment. We decry pollution and pollute. We denounce waste and waste. When God cuts in, we want to cut out.

Joel 2:13 ☐ *Joel 2:12-13*

*Look among the nations, and see; wonder and be astounded.
For I am doing a work in your days that you would not believe
if told.*

Habakkuk asked questions we are beginning to ask as our
nation's ills blight our own neighborhoods. We probably ask
not from spiritual sensitivity, but from the sheer inconvenience
of evil's intrusion into our set ways. "O LORD, how long shall I
cry for help, and thou wilt not hear? Or cry to thee 'Violence!'
and thou wilt not save? Why dost thou make me see wrongs
and look upon trouble? Destruction and violence are before
me; strife and contention arise. So the law is slacked and justice
never goes forth." With these complaints so contemporary,
does God's answer to Habakkuk carry weight for our day?

The prophet sealed his own fate with the first strokes of his
pen, "The oracle of God which Habakkuk the prophet saw."
He did not hear an oracle, he saw one. The Hebrew word is
burden, not enigmatic utterance. God said in effect, "See for
yourself!" The cruel Chaldeans are about to rampage into
Judah. Your known violence will pale against theirs. Let the
Babylonian exile decide how close you want your God! To see
such burden was crushing, to write it down, hazardous.
Habakkuk would now have God, the Chaldeans and his nation
on his back, with every scoffer and religious moderate deriding
him for his "burden."

Surely he would have preferred the divine utterance we so
take for granted, "If my people who are called by my name
humble themselves, and pray and seek my face . . ." But no! It
was face the music. Habakkuk did. "To the choirmaster: with
stringed instruments." Those are his prophecy's concluding
words. If God should have a burden for us, will we trust Him
for a song also?

Habakkuk 1:5 □ Habakkuk 1:1-5

For still the vision awaits its time; it hastens to the end — it will not lie. If it seem slow, wait for it . . .

How does one carry the burden of deep inner conviction? Nothing is known of Habakkuk's actual life. His instruction to the choirmaster indicates that he might have been a Levite and temple musician. His name means "embracer." With God's arms securely around him, he embraced the burden.

Facing directly into the storm of his soul, he first braved the Chaldeans. Giving his imagination free reign, he yielded his emotions to the terrors of their known reputation. In the night of his soul he then wrestled with his own will. Forcing aside fear and repulsion, Habakkuk accepted the Chaldeans as God's judgment on Judah. Acknowledging the spiritual bankruptcy of his people and the conditions of chastisement, he now faced the character of God. O Rock!

"Art thou not from everlasting, O LORD my God, my Holy One? We shall not die." Habakkuk knew his God. From the strength of personal relationship he faced into his coming trial of faith. The Chaldean's reign of terror could not last. If God dealt so decisively with Judah's iniquity, how much more would He requite them for their evil arrogance. Then Habakkuk listened to his delivered soul and from it rose a majestic hymn of praise to the person, power, and purpose of the God of his salvation.

The initial battle of the soul fought on the note of triumph, the dread reality of God now breaks to the conscious surface, "I hear, and my body trembles, my lips quiver . . . I will quietly wait for the day of trouble to come upon people who invade us." The rugged life of demonstrated faith must now unfold. It begins and ends with the humility that exalts God's sufficiency alone.

Habakkuk 2:3 □ Habakkuk 2:1-3

Behold, he whose soul is not upright in him shall fail, but the righteous shall live by his faith.

We receive God's promise of deliverance for our burden in a burst of light. Fresh from the battle of the soul — flushed with victory — faith flexes its muscles and savors its strength. Then, without warning, utter darkness. In the drama of faith played against the backdrop of life's routines and distractions, we have unwittingly lost the conscious concentration that at first masquerades as invincibility.

The saint grown wise to the ordeal of darkness knows this much: It is the rule, not the exception, and must be embraced. Picture the places of densest darkness and disregard such dead ends as grave and cave. But march your faith into a pitch-black tunnel and there behold your temporary darkness. A tunnel is essentially a shortcut, saving us circuitous climbs across inhospitable mountains!

It is inherently human to desire a walk by sight and sign. When we carry a burden and inevitably grow faint, the danger of seeing mirages and steering toward them is great. God's deterrent of darkness protects His purpose and in the long run saves wear and tear on the saint. It is no adverse reflection on our obedience, no shadow on the love relationship. On the contrary. "The just shall live by faith." The Pioneer and Perfector of our faith reveals His strength in our weakness. As the human eye adjusts to darkness, so does faith. Our dim vision of the promise grows brighter as we face straight His way.

Psalm 107 points to our comfort. "Some wandered in desert wastes . . . their soul fainted within them. Then they cried to the Lord in their trouble . . . and he led them by a straight way, till they reached a city . . ." We are able to embrace our "tunnels" because God makes His face to shine upon us and gives us peace!

Habakkuk 2:4

Rise, let us be going . . .

Speak to that person! Write that letter! Put yourself in that place of risk! When God's alarm clock shatters the quiet of our soothing meditations, we want to turn away and sink back into our dream world.

It is not easy to stir from the comforting embrace of sleep. Clocks come with "snooze alarms" that cater to our groans for ten more minutes. We always want ten more minutes from God. Unnecessary bed rest leads to atrophy. Strapping athletes become as sick men. The life of faith is positionally one of rest. In practice it requires action. Supernaturally speaking, we have already attained our promise. We merely need to claim it.

"Rise, let us be going." There is no drum roll. God thrusts no printed program at us and excitedly says, "Watch the curtain go up on act one! Watch me play out for you the Drama of Faith, my version of 'This Is Your Life!'" With the shrill buzz of His alarm comes no soothing spiritual exercise to get rid of the sand in the eyes and the fog in the brain. The very action for which we must quickly rouse ourselves is the splash of cold water. Cold it is. The reality of our spiritually hatched forethoughts is never His reality of actual life.

God does not plan His strategies around our spiritual highs. When He cuts our moorings and we unexpectedly rush out toward the open sea, we can only dash for the sail and let it catch the wind of the Holy Spirit. The drama of faith unreels not from our logic or x-hours of prayer investment. God transacts sovereignty from the original contract of faith which we signed in the light. After that we are often in the dark and cold. "Awake, O sleeper, and arise . . . and Christ shall give you light." Unless we rouse ourselves to repeated action, God cannot put the pieces into place.

Matthew 26:46 □ Matthew 26:36-46

Can a man bear a child? Why then do I see every man with his hands on his loins like a woman in labor?

Relax! When God says to relax, we immediately want a spiritual prescription. We haul out Bible and concordance and dig for the perfect peace verse. We exhibit all the grace of the bargain shopper who viciously dives into a pile of sales goods. Relax. When will we help ourselves to God's great sense of humor?

There is nothing quite as deadly as the determinedly spiritual person. If there is compulsion to tack a Bible verse to every thought and action as hygienic protection against the contaminated world, watch out. There is a nut loose among the "oaks of righteousness" and it is not an acorn. God absolutely begs us to claim our gift of holy hilarity. He knows people *are* funny.

Not all of us are born with a sense of humor. But we do not have to watch comedians or memorize jokes to become proficient at laughter. A good look at ourselves will suffice. The next time we are in a tight spot thanks to the high adventure of faith, we ought to look into a mirror, not the Bible. Study body language! We are Awful Grimness personified. We look ridiculous. How does the Father see us?

Consider the "terrible twos" of babyhood when the small tyke turns tiger. He grimly plays grownup in his small world waiting to be harnessed to his control. Watching him struggle, his tongue sticking out, do we not smile and scoop him up into a big hug when silly turns serious? The first fruit of the Spirit is love. Healthy self-love is resplendent with laughter.

When the next tight curve looms, avoid for a change the fear verse and try the funny version. Laughter relaxes. We might just lean into that curve with grace and discover the thrill of God's fast ride!

Jeremiah 30:6 ☐ *Jeremiah 30:1-7*

I was dumb and silent, I held my peace to no avail; my distress grew worse, my heart became hot within me. As I mused, the fire burned; then I spoke with my tongue . . .

In place of such volcanic eruption God wants to give us the gift of gab. Let childhood illustrate. The maladjusted child is typically silent and sullen. The outgoing youngster happily at play keeps up a running commentary even when all by himself. The child's practice of interpreting his surroundings as he sees them can stimulate a whole family's imagination. Think of the stuffed animal that becomes an important personage. When the child balks at something his crankiness is bound to rub off on a tired mother. A bit of sweet reasoning with the toy mouse may just save the day! Idle chatter my eye.

Why should the child of God not be outgoing with the Father who went all out for him? If we communicate in stiff formalities only, we deprive Him and ourselves of vital cement that glues a love relationship. When at first we talk with Him "off the record" in a natural conversational tone, we may feel foolish at the sound of our voice. Fine. We sing God's praise in public, shall we not learn to say it in private. As we progress, we tell Him what strikes us as funny and we discover shared laughter. When sorrow fills us with doubt, it makes sense to describe to God our feelings. In return He shares His tenderness. God is not an inanimate object!

The practice of speaking with Him leads to the healing stillness before God. "Lord, what more can I say?" Tears or humble adoration may flow from such silence. When words no longer suffice to express our deep satisfaction, we step up to the practice of most prized surrender: Take my life, Lord, and make it the expression of my praise!

Psalm 39:2-3 ☐ *Psalm 39*

O Lord, heal me, for my bones are troubled. My soul also is sorely troubled. But thou, O LORD — how long?

But you, O suffering saint — how long? When God slows us down, we just as soon gulp down two spiritual aspirins and get going. There comes a point in the adventure of Christ when even rough seas cannot deter from the excitement of sailing by the wind of the Holy Spirit. When God becalms us, He may well be teaching nothing more than human kindness.

When our physical body receives a blow through illness or injury, we accept the natural consequences. Not enthusiastically perhaps, but realistically. If we break a leg, who can argue with the unwieldy cast?

When the responsible saint first suffers from spiritual battle fatigue or emotional blows, he courts guilt in the worst way. If I am right with God and do things His way, why should I feel so bone-weary and depressed? If an emergency room attendant dealt as roughly with the bleeding man off the street as we sometimes deal with ourselves, he would be instantly fired. If we have joined ourselves to God in obedience and trust for an adventure of faith, our basic assurance is this, "God is at work in you, both to will and to work for his good pleasure." Low moods are no reflection on our walk with Him. To feel worn out is no sin, but a sign that the sufficiency of grace must be freshly applied.

Troubled bones and troubled soul need vigorous spiritual exercise like a moose needs a hat rack. Perhaps you need to sleep or go fishing or eat crepe suzette or read a spy thriller. Give yourself the gift of human kindness you would urge on your dearest friend. Let God be the judge when you are fit for active duty again. And do not mar your R&R by sending up neurotic little prayers every five minutes as if to forestall a court-martial! Do only what is comforting to you. Your life already is an expression of praise.

Psalm 6:2-3 □ Psalm 6

Is there no king in you?

If we are not often in trouble, the answer perhaps is no. If we are not regularly driven to our knees, the living Christ does not reign from within. To the impeccable believer who worships Him from the comfort of the pew, the tear-stained saint is an enigma. How can a person of faith be so emotionally unstable? Why the fervent plea, "Pray for me" — as if Christianity were some kind of "Titanic"?

When the King is worshiped from without, faith is defined by orderly church experience. That may produce a breed of good, moral Christians. But — oh, how the wonder of Christ is missing!

To the Christian satisfied to be spectator, and pleased with what seem obvious rewards of an ordered life, Paul the tear-stained fool for Christ's sake writes, "Already you are filled! Already you have become rich! Without us you have become kings! And would that you did reign, so that we might share the rule with you! For I think that God has exhibited us apostles as last of all, like men sentenced to death; because we have become a spectacle to the world, to angels and to men" (1 Corinthians 4:8-9).

"Is there no king in you?" Are you spectacle or spectator? "The kingdom of God," adds Paul, "does not consist in talk but in power." When the King lives in us, our natural life must trip over the supernatural reign again and again. The frontiers of our faith are extended trouble by trouble, tear by tear, triumph by triumph. Driven to our knees — the safest spot in all of God's kingdom — we take to heart the prophet's question, "Now why do you cry aloud? Is there no king in you? Has your counselor perished, that pangs have seized you like a woman in travail?" Emptied, we receive Him afresh — the Counselor, Comforter, Helper — our Advocate with heaven. In His might we reign and are content to be a spectacle for as long as it pleases our risen Lord.

Micah 4:9 □ Micah 4:6-10

Did you receive the Holy Spirit when you believed?

Forget about the pollster. He deals in curiosity and percentages. He directs the question at our denominational persuasion. Our pastor or prayer partner must aim the question at the jugular and ask from concern over a stagnating church. A positive answer must reveal "the works." A "no" or "don't know" must be followed up with compassionate love.

Why is it not enough to simply say I believe in God? So do demons, answers James, and they "shudder." The church as supernatural expression of God's intervention in human affairs is the restraining force against evil in the world. But our fight is not against "Saturday-night specials" and trigger-happy misfits. The church has to take its stand "against principalities, against the powers, against the world rulers of this present darkness, against the spiritual hosts of wickedness . . ." Mere belief in God is like the diploma on the wall of a physician's home who chooses not to have a practice.

The Holy Spirit is none other than the Person of Jesus Christ. Invited to live and reign in the heart of the believer, He imputes His character and power. When we first believe in our heart and confess with our lips that Jesus died for our sins and rose as proof of our redemption, we are sealed with His Spirit as heirs to eternal life. This is salvation. But the "infilling" of the Holy Spirit must take place again and again as we expend His strength through our ministry to the world. We desire Him with joy because through Him alone can we experience the intimacy and immediacy of God the Father.

The Holy Spirit is a gentleman. He will not enter unless asked. Ask Him, for God's sake and yours! Polls come and go. The power of the church must come and grow. Our times demand that we do the "greater works" of Jesus Christ.

Acts 19:2 □ *Acts 19:1-7*

Then he goes and brings with him seven other spirits more evil than himself, and they enter and dwell there; and the last state of that man becomes worse than the first.

At first "when the unclean spirit has gone out of a man, he passes through waterless places seeking rest, but he finds none. Then he says, 'I will return to my house from which I came.' And when he comes he finds it empty, swept, and put in order." This house is the heart that Christ has cleansed through His atonement. Have we ever wondered why some Christians do not act "saved"?

The God-shaped void in our soul was designed to be inhabited by our Lord. If we do not grant Him His rightful residence, the place is up for grabs. The spiritual forces of "wickedness in the heavenly places" are too cunning to make us into a hell-raiser given to gross sins of the flesh. Their primary options are to preserve their man as a satisfied nominal Christian; to make him so good that he becomes terminally proud; to make him so sour that no fellowship can form around him; or to teach him self-perfection and reward him with despair. This perhaps is the most common form of "demon possession" among believers.

On the surface the tragedy does not appear for what it is. On the contrary. We see an eager-beaver Christian doing everything to live up to his Savior's high expectations. With all his heart and mind and strength he imitates the life of Christ. Sooner or later he resigns himself to an impossible dream and leads a defeated life of mere Protestant ethics.

"Did you receive the Holy Spirit when you believed?" Salvation is based on the completed work of Christ's atonement. In that sense the house of our life stays swept and in order. When we invite the rightful Owner to move in, the squatters must shudder and leave. That is why the question of the Holy Spirit must be aimed at the believer's jugular vein of the will again and again!

Matthew 12:45 □ *Matthew 12:43-45*

Thus Joseph who was surnamed . . . Barnabas (which means, Son of encouragement), a Levite, a native of Cyprus . . .

If Luke's manuscript of the "Acts of the Holy Spirit" had been destroyed at exactly this point, the life of Barnabas would still be an open book to us. What is revealed about him should be said of every man and woman in love with Jesus Christ. We can pay no higher compliment to the Father than to be known as "Son of encouragement." Baptized by the Holy Spirit, Barnabas took His very name. Paraclete!

The specific nature of Barnabas' encouragement is expressed in the Greek *paraklesis*. It denotes comfort, consolation, exhortation, and entreaty. The word for Holy Spirit is *parakletos*. He is our Comforter and Advocate with the Father. Barnabas uniquely modeled the very character and function of the Holy Spirit. The great heart cry of the church today is for such men and women in Jesus Christ.

Barnabas gave strategic leadership to the early church at four vital junctures. When Paul returned to Jerusalem after his conversion, he walked into a wall of hostility. "But Barnabas took him, and brought him to the apostles, and declared to them how on the road he had seen the Lord . . . and how at Damascus he had preached boldly in the name of Jesus." Some nine years later Barnabas went looking for Paul in Tarsus and brought him to Antioch, where he had detected an exciting seedbed of the faith. For a year he ministered there with Paul. He later successfully defended this ministry at the Jerusalem council.

Luke sums up the witness, ". . . beloved Barnabas and Paul, men who have risked their lives for the sake of our Lord Jesus Christ." This is the one risk we can no longer afford not to take. Let the church reveal her sons and daughters of Encouragement now!

Acts 4:36

And there arose a sharp contention, so that they separated from each other; Barnabas took Mark with him . . . but Paul chose Silas and departed . . .

Aha! Do we exclaim in triumph or derision? How do we assess the integrity of the Holy Spirit? How about kudos to Luke, the beloved physician! As the author of Acts, what does his honesty tell us about his confidence in the Holy Spirit? If we see things his way, we shall desire Him more than ever.

The spark that fueled the fireworks lies innocently buried in Acts 13:13, "Now Paul and his company set sail from Paphos, and came to Perga in Pamphylia. And John (Mark) left them and returned to Jerusalem." Later, after their first missionary journey, Paul suggested to Barnabas that they visit their fledgling churches. "And Barnabas wanted to take with them John called Mark. But Paul thought best not to take with them one who had withdrawn from them in Pamphylia, and had not gone with them to the work." And so the fat was in the fire and the heat drove the hotheads apart for a time. In the process, incidentally, Paul discovered Timothy. Barnabas bolstered the self-esteem of his nephew. The "deserter" later wrote the gospel according to Mark. He also joined the imprisoned Paul in Rome. What does it all prove?

It establishes once and for all that the indwelling Spirit does not rob us of our own personality. Some Christians suffer from the irrational fear that the Holy Spirit will violate and subdue their selfhood and reduce them to something of a Casper Milquetoast. How ironic in view of the fact that the Spirit-filled Christian relishes his boldness and bemoans his former bland state! The Holy Spirit does not erase, but enhances our distinctive personality.

Acts 15:39 ☐ *Acts 15:36-41*

Make love your aim, and earnestly desire the spiritual gifts, especially that you may prophesy.

Prophecy has become big business. What God does *not* need is yet another doomsday announcer with the Book of Daniel, the *Los Angeles Times*, and a stopwatch in his hot little hands.

In the rush to batten down the hatches before the waters of judgment come rolling in, some of our pop prophets conveniently forget about the servanthood of the church. Why be so anxious to interpret the signs of impending destruction when the Bible itself teaches the discipline of temperance. "But do not ignore this one fact, beloved, that with the Lord one day is as a thousand years, and a thousand years as one day. The Lord is not slow about his promise as some count slowness, but is forbearing toward you, not wishing that any should perish, but that all should reach repentance" (2 Peter 3:8-9).

"Make love your aim." If we are to save those doomed to perish unless we reach them with the Good News, we must indeed earnestly desire spiritual gifts. In our natural state we lack the boldness to launch such a major offensive. We are mostly good at defense. It is unwittingly reflected in our kind comments heaped on the church. A great many believers express their satisfaction at gratifying intervals. We admire our leaders and love our programs. The organ sounds great, the retreats are organized well and the old gang of regulars gives us a nice homey feeling.

To this gang of good guys Paul says, "Earnestly desire the spiritual gifts, especially that you may prophesy." The church does not exist for itself, but for the purpose of servanthood to the world. We must learn to say things — forthtell them — as God sees them and speak the truth in love.

1 Corinthians 14:1 □ *1 Corinthians 14:1-5*

He who prophesies speaks to men for their upbuilding and encouragement and consolation.

Sentimentalists need not apply for the job. The forthteller is not God's warm-up person so the congregation will sing lustier and pray livelier. The prophet concerns herself chiefly with organic structure built on the cornerstone of her Lord. Her ideal finished product is not a large, famous church, but a body built up "to the unity of the faith and of the knowledge of the Son of God, to mature manhood, to the measure of the stature of the fulness of Christ."

Sentimentalist and forthteller will be hard-pressed to see eye to eye. The first bubbles with enthusiasm over the lovely anthem or wonderful sermon. Church is an "experience." By comparison the prophet is clearly a killjoy. She probes beneath the surface and does follow-up. Did you receive the Holy Spirit when you believed? Are you a minister of the gospel at your place of work? Does your giving reflect your ah's and oh's?

The prophet scandalizes still. The *skandalon* of the cross will not go away. The "stumbling block" of Jesus Christ prevails. In "upbuilding" the body, the prophet must take us down to the foot of the cross and in sanctified stubbornness insist that our enthusiasm must come from there — and from the crushed spirit and contrite heart of the believer as well. God's prophet knows. He meets her there often.

"Make love your aim." This cannot be showy, glad-handing, back-slapping love with a *bon mot* tossed in for good measure. Tough as nails — the *skandalon* again — the prophet loves by gentle example. The very nature of her difficult calling makes her predisposed to encouraging, comforting fellowship. The prophet loves the anthems too and is a fiend for great sermons. But she is scandalized when the people of God do not worship Him in spirit and truth.

1 Corinthians 14:3

Yea, and on . . . my maidservants in those days I will pour out my Spirit, and they shall prophesy.

Aviatrix, authoress, prophetess . . . It does sound labored. Exegesis is problematic also. The critical interpretation of this text hinges on "those days." Joel's prophecy in the strictest sense applies to the Jewish remnant who will rediscover God's favor in the Messiah. Portents in heaven and on earth point to end times. Yet on the day of Pentecost Peter cited this very prophecy as explanation for the disciples' startling conduct. Almost 2000 years later, where does that leave Christ's woman with the burning heart?

Even a superficial glance at Scripture reveals that prophets invariably incurred the displeasure of God's people. The prophetess seemed to enjoy smooth sailing. Beginning with Miriam during Exodus and ending with Anna who exulted in the Messiah on the day of the baby's circumcision, the woman "seer" of God was held in high honor. Deborah of the Promised Land is a feminist's dream of an activist, holding sway over God's people whether judging them under the "palm of Deborah" or marching off to battle with a man not her husband. When temple repairs during King Josiah's reign yielded the forgotten scroll of "our" Deuteronomy, he immediately had it sent to the renowned prophetess Huldah. Not the high priest, but this literate, sensitive woman issued directions and extended consolation.

What leader of male hierarchy — what king invites the ministry of today's capable woman? The questioning maidservant does well to retrace her steps to the place of woman's deepest bereavement, the place of the greatest stumbling block. The crucial stone is rolled away. "But the angel said to the women, 'Do not be afraid; for I know that you seek Jesus who was crucified.'" "Those days" are these days.

Acts 2:18

For we are his workmanship, created in Christ Jesus for good works, which God prepared beforehand, that we should walk in them.

The notion that today's free woman in Christ must blaze new trails is held in check by God's sovereign disposition of His workmanship. We do not carve our specific niche in history. "Lord, thou hast been our dwelling place in all generations. Before the mountains were brought forth, or ever thou hadst formed the earth . . . from everlasting to everlasting thou art God."

The liberated woman in submission to Christ makes a satisfying discovery. Not only has He blazed our trails of glory long before we ached to walk in them, His idea of "workmanship" is ideally suited to a woman's sensitive heart. Together with our English word *poem* it shares exactly the same Greek root *poiema*.

The exciting thing is that this concept of poem and poet is not one of passively dreaming on paper. *Poietes* defines the poet specifically as doer! Deborah's song of deliverance after predicting and directing a successful military campaign is a prime example of such workmanship: "In the days of Shamgar . . . caravans ceased in Israel . . . they ceased until you arose, Deborah . . . Tell of it, you who ride on tawny asses, you who sit on rich carpets and you who walk by the way. To the sound of musicians at the watering places, there they repeat the triumphs of the Lord, the triumphs of his peasantry in Israel."

What if you are more of a Mary? "My soul magnifies the Lord, and my spirit rejoices in God my Savior, for he has regarded the low estate of his handmaiden." Let this be the questing woman's prayer, "Let thy work be manifest to thy servants, and thy glorious power to their children. Let the favor of the Lord our God be upon us, and establish thou the work of our hands upon us, yea, the work of our hands establish thou it."

Ephesians 2:10

If I say, "I will not mention him, or speak any more in his name," there is in my heart as it were a burning fire shut up in my bones, and I am weary with holding it in, and I cannot.

The prophet is commissioned by God. "Now the word of the Lord came to me saying, 'Before I formed you in the womb I knew you, and before you were born I consecrated you . . .'" God's chosen instrument also knows the depths of Jeremiah's despair, "Why did I come forth from the womb, to see toil and sorrow . . .?"

If today's seer of God and doer of His word can intimately relate to Jeremiah, how closely must the church identify with the people of his time? He prophesied "violence and destruction" to his contemporaries and was ridiculed, ignored, or mistreated. They could not see the tree for the forest. They had become so much the product of their destructive times and violent environment it never dawned on them that they themselves were the "burden" of Jeremiah's oracles.

In this particular instance of torment Jeremiah had just come from prison for committing an act of prophecy at Topeth in the valley of Ben-hinnom. In the place where broken pottery was thrown he broke an earthenware jar in demonstration of the ruin about to come on the people and their city. The valley would be known as Valley of Slaughter, a burying place for the victims of the Babylonian invasion. For the squeamish saint never quite happy with this bloodthirsty Old Testament God, this particular valley of the shadow holds a grisly clue, "And they have built the high place of Topeth, which is in the valley of the son of Hinnom, to burn their sons and daughters in the fire."

We are the product of our corrupt times as well. Syncretism is rampant. We compromise flagrantly. We sacrifice our children daily to the violence and destruction practiced on the level of entertainment. "Speak to us smooth things . . ." No!

Jeremiah 20:9 □ Jeremiah 20:7-18

And when they read it, they rejoiced at the exhortation. And Judas and Silas, who were themselves prophets, exhorted the brethren with many words and strengthened them.

Beware of the smug smiler in the natty suit and his flood of doomsday literature. The days of the legitimate loner in the prophecy business are gone. On the whole, any kind of do-it-yourself prophecy must arouse suspicion. Excesses and abuses are common.

The publicity-minded loner eager to sell us his private ecstasies and prophetic warnings — regardless of ample Scripture quotations — must be pressed for a satisfactory answer to this question: How did you grow in the grace and knowledge of Jesus Christ? If he grew in the hothouse of his own private contemplation, he is at best ornamental. God grows His useful servants in the field of experience among those who serve and sing and exchange encouragement and consolation. With such cross-fertilization taking place, a more reliable witness prevails.

Paul and Barnabas, joyously blazing God's trails to the Gentiles, were visiting Antioch. "But some men came down from Judea and were teaching the brethren, 'Unless you are circumcised according to the custom of Moses, you cannot be saved.'" Earnest discussions ensued. Paul and Barnabas, along with leaders from Antioch, were dispatched to consult with the apostles and elders at Jerusalem. The closing arguments were expressed in this manner, "For it has seemed good to the Holy Spirit and to us to lay upon you no greater burden than these necessary things . . ."

A letter was sent to Antioch with Paul and Barnabas, as well as Judas and Silas from the Jerusalem assembly. The letter was publicly read to the congregation and then the prophets continued in daily fellowship until the believers at Antioch were firmly rooted in love and built up in the faith. Here is our model of responsible prophecy.

Acts 15:31-32 □ Acts 15:1-35

We destroy arguments and every proud obstacle to the knowledge of God, and take every thought captive to obey Christ . . .

What makes for spiritual clout? For example, Christians concerned about the effects of television on their children can argue the problem academically. One person might conduct child studies. Another might research programming and contact sponsors. Still a third could comb Scripture for verses supporting a given viewpoint. However, the fed-up parent simply pulls the plug on the family set! Simplistic analogy aside, the church must raise up leaders with the courage of their conviction.

Paul had a tough time maintaining his apostolic authority with the Corinthians. "Superlative apostles" had usurped it. Incensed and sorrowful at the deceit disseminated by artful speech and wishy-washy heart, Paul fired off a stern letter of reprimand. Titus played mailman and Paul sweated blood until he was reunited with the much-delayed messenger. On the whole, thank God, the Corinthians had taken their medicine well. Godly grief had produced indignation, alarm, longing, zeal, punishment. They were still mopping up. But Titus had picked up some barbs as well. Paul purrs in person and barks when absent! "His letters are weighty and strong, but his bodily presence is weak, and his speech of no account."

Paul himself had fed them the line, "When I came to you brethren, I did not come proclaiming to you the testimony of God in lofty words or wisdom. For I decided to know nothing among you except Jesus Christ and him crucified. And I was with you in much fear and trembling; and my speech and my message were not in plausible words of wisdom . . ." Paul was a skilled and persuasive speaker, of course. But he decided against Greek-style oratory so linked to the celebration of human wisdom.

What then was Paul's divine power with his beloved Corinthians — and the hated strongholds of Satan? Quite simply the clarion call of Christ and the courage of his convictions — with sufferings. A leader can only effectively lead to

the point of his or her insight and growth. We must grow up —
here and now! The destruction of strongholds is decidedly not
for children.

2 Corinthians 10:5 □ *2 Corinthians 10:1-6*

Whatever is true, whatever is honorable, whatever is just, whatever is pure, whatever is lovely, whatever is gracious, if there is any excellence, if there is anything worthy of praise, think about these things.

The challenge to take "every thought captive to obey Christ" is not a rodeo. The idea is not to rope in quickly whatever comes out of the starting gate.

We enter the Whatever Exhibit in deep silence. On walls draped with velvet we savor "lovely" and "gracious." On pedestals of marble are shown "just" and "honorable." In a chest lined with silk we contemplate "pure." The masterpiece at the center is "excellence." We step to the souvenir stand in the lobby to see if there is anything worthy of praise. Just then something is whispered to us. The exhibit is a bequest to us in order to fulfill "true." A message is sent home with it, "Do not be conformed to this world, but be transformed by the renewal of your mind, that you may prove what is the will of God, what is good and acceptable and perfect."

We have no velvet walls to create silence. We have forgotten how to think. Radio, TV and stereo are blaring. Ice crusher and garbage disposal are grinding. With the left eye we read cereal box labels and with the right eye the raised print on the dog's flea collar.

How does one learn to think again? Soaking in silence helps. When first we unplug ourselves from our myriad distractions, the noises become deafening: growing fingernails, palpitations of the heart, silent screams of panic. And then the holy hush steals in and we grow strangely content. A flower's delicate architecture holds our gaze. Praise wells up. We meditate on the nearness of the Creator. The adventure of the transformed mind is on. Never expect the Holy Spirit to take the place of self-discipline!

Philippians 4:8

I appeal to you therefore, brethren, by the mercies of God, to present your bodies as a living sacrifice . . .

It is terribly crucial to get this straight. If we have it backwards we are sentencing ourselves to a defeated life. The key word in this passage is not "body," but "present." If we think "body," far too many exotic notions swirl up in our mind.

A preacher, so the story goes, was saying some rather explicit things about man's most notorious "member of unrighteousness." The men fidgeted in their seats and the women became pink-cheeked as he challenged them to think about the evil ways in which they made use of this little member that "boasts of great things . . . setting on fire the cycle of nature, and set on fire by hell." Just when the congregation was ready to quit sex cold turkey, their tormentor pricked the bubble of their vain imaginings. "And the tongue is a fire. The tongue is an unrighteous world among our members, staining the whole body . . ." (James 3:5-6).

Be careful about who or what dictates your living sacrifice. We cannot offer up our reproductive organs or the digestive system and expect to be relieved of their needs. A growling stomach cannot be appeased by an appropriate Bible verse. During a period of low drive the body might well fake spiritual conversion. Do not trust glandular resolutions to quit illicit sex or booze. Conversely, a high energy surge cannot spell the cure for habitual laziness. All these things are effected only by moral decision. The lasting ones come from a regenerated mind.

"Present your bodies as a living sacrifice." Let the body "be at hand" — ready to carry out the mind's new instructions. Do not put the cart before the horse. The mind cannot obey the body. If we try, we will go down in defeat with heartbreaking regularity.

Romans 12:1 ☐ *Romans 12:1-2*

To set the mind on the flesh is death, but to set the mind on the Spirit is life and peace.

Watch the astronaut suit up in cumbersome gear. Why the temporary inconveniences of the complex space suit? It ensures perfect adaptation to a sojourn in space.

Simplistically speaking, the flesh is our "earth suit." As such it is not evil, but inherently practical. We owe it every consideration and respect. Our body was endued with its functions to complement those of our temporary habitat. Observing the natural laws governing flora and fauna, we marvel at ordered interrelationships and delicate balances. Our insensitivity to those natural laws has unleashed a chain reaction of adverse repercussions for which all pay.

Humans are distinct from their fellow creatures on earth as a spiritual creation destined for eternity. Plants and animals return to the earth for good, nourishing the soil by their disolution. "To set the mind on the flesh is death . . ." This is nothing more than natural law extended to the natural body. No need to freight the thought with sinister implications. Sex is not dirty! A full belly is not evil! A good snooze even in broad daylight is not of the devil! We are to use our "earth suit" responsibly and enjoy its benefits. Cooperation with the demands of our earth mission is imperative.

"But to set the mind on the Spirit is life and peace." Of course it makes sense to cater chiefly to the spiritual reality because it is our hearth and home! Our life is not biological function, but eternal existence. This "mind over matter" is much more a practical issue than a moralistic one. God, make no mistake, expects us to live in harmony with our body. But as the space suit does not mastermind the mission just because it has a self-sustaining air supply, so our "earth suit" must submit to eternal law.

Romans 8:6 □ *Romans 8:1-8*

For sin will have no dominion over you, since you are not under law but under grace.

As realistically as the nails penetrated the flesh of our crucified Lord, so must this Good News penetrate our thick skull. If it sounds too good to be true, we have not realized the Atonement in our flesh.

While visiting his urologist, an octogenarian said somewhat wistfully, "Doctor, I wish you could lower my sex drive." The doctor looked in shocked disbelief at the wisp of a man and blurted out, "It must be all in your head!" "Exactly," said the man sadly.

That is exactly our good news! When through self-discipline we yield more and more of our mind to the regenerating work of the Holy Spirit, He actualizes in the flesh our conceptual understanding of the Atonement. The same Spirit that brooded over the waters at Creation and raised Jesus from the dead, invades the living tissues of our brain. The same power that overshadowed the Virgin Mary and activated the reproductive processes of her body, intervenes in ours. The Holy Spirit breaks the very connectors that carry negative impulses. He activates circuits that aid the flow of the positive energy we call grace. Jesus Christ must reign victoriously where His power holds sway.

"The death he died he died to sin, once for all, but the life he lives he lives to God. So you also must consider yourselves dead to sin and alive to God in Christ Jesus." This "must" is not one of our grim appeals to willpower, but a firm invitation to faith. We cannot fully grasp the meaning of the Good News. Like falling in love, it must be experienced. When God Himself is at work in us, "both to will and to work for his good pleasure," we learn to cherish our body as the temple of the Holy Spirit. God's pleasure in it becomes ours. Is there a Christian plagued by persistent sex sin? Let him have his head examined!

Romans 6:14 □ Romans 6:1-14

He who did not spare his own Son but gave him up for us all, will he not also give us all things with him?

At times the most experienced saint doubts it! When we are too perplexed to praise Him, too grieved to muster any kind of strength, let us simply sigh, "Selah." It is the peculiar notation found in the Psalms that indicates a pause or shift in musical accompaniment. With our Selah we stake the claim that our song of faith will flow again. Richer, purer . . .

We are particularly vexed when habits earnestly yielded to God will not become dislodged quickly. The friend who chain-smoked to the point of coughing blood might be delivered from her bondage instantly. When we are still enslaved by nicotine months later, self-doubts are excruciating. One thing about habits: God is not so much against cigarettes as He is *for* us. Where we want Him to work quickly against our problem He longs to have us get more deeply in touch with Himself — for the sake of wholeness. Then, too, easy success may become the "faith formula" we are tempted to press on others. We are never to institutionalize the nuts-and-bolts of what worked for us, but to praise Him who works individual deliverance by His sovereign will.

When we are down in the dumps and need to know afresh that God is irrevocably for us, His Word speaks to that need. The written self-revelation of the Father flows directly to the hidden life of Christ forming in us. We inhale the quickening breath of God as if an oxygen mask were pressed to our blue face. No need to stop and analyze the texts we read. The person receiving emergency oxygen does not care about its atomic weight and specific gravity. The lungs get the message.

"Likewise the Spirit helps us in our weakness; for we do not know how to pray as we ought, but the Spirit himself intercedes for us with sighs too deep for words." Selah. Praise God!

Romans 8:32 ☐ *Romans 8:31-39*

And lead us not into temptation, But deliver us from evil.

Not enough is said from the pulpit today about the inherent power of God's Word. It creates spiritual life and shapes it to our Creator's scope and intent. It awakens the need for redemption and satisfies it with the Redeemer. Natural man and his finite mind cannot grasp the eternal God apart from His Word. "It is the spirit that gives life, the flesh is of no avail; the words that I have spoken to you are spirit and life" (John 6:63).

Devotional reading must not supplant personal Bible study. A daily verse is fine for meditation or memorization. But reading whole chapters establishes context and stimulates curiosity. The habit of looking up cross references leads to the satisfying discovery that the Bible is its own best commentary. Good habits aside, the Christian is mandated to feed voraciously on the Bread of Life. Poems and pep-talk pieces by writers hedging on the deity and atonement of Christ are mere nibbles on a fortune cookie. Let God's own be resolved to do away with sophisticated inspiration that is "holding the form of religion but denying the power of it" (2 Timothy 3:5). The power — our life — is in the blood of Christ alone!

This was precisely the issue when Satan went for Christ's jugular in the wilderness. Could He be tempted to exhibit saving power that would bypass the cross? Because of His deity Jesus could not yield to the tempter, ". . . for God cannot be tempted with evil . . ." (James 1:13). But in His humanity He endured the fury of testing and authenticated the sinless nature demanded of the Savior. "It is written . . ." Christ's repeated stand on God's Word sent the devil packing his bags. Today's text from the Lord's Prayer should demonstrate clearly the interrelationship between God's spoken Word and written Word that makes for inherent power.

Not enough is said either about what the inherent power of God's Word is *not*. It is not magic formula to be exploited by manipulators of faith. We have no right to pull texts out of context to force our will and wishes on God in the name of religious grandstanding. Christ's injunction stands today,

"Again it is written, 'You shall not tempt (test) the Lord your God" (Matthew 4:7). The litmus test of "inherent power" is our willingness to rest on the reality of our redemption.

Matthew 6:13

Let what you say be simply "Yes" or "No" . . .

The Mount of Beatitudes. Jesus is teaching the crash course on the Amazing New Life. "You have heard that it was said to the men of old . . ." But I say! Yet the old ways hold fascination. The law as "schoolmaster" made clear that we must take God by His Word, even as He holds us to ours. "And you shall not swear by my name falsely, and so profane the name of your God: I am the LORD" (Leviticus 19:12).

Jesus made mincemeat of oaths. Among other things, they had become ridiculous. To swear by the temple was nothing; to swear by the gold of the temple was for God to pay attention. The contemporary Pharisee frowns, of course, on the neophyte who peppers his earnest conversations with "I swear to God . . ." Let the indignant one think back to the last time he hit a snag with the Eternal One. When in the face of His silence we are in abject need of reassurance, watch how subtly we tug at His sleeve. "God, if you will do just this one tiny thing for me, I will do *all* that for you." "I swear I didn't do anything wrong!"

By the same token we want people to know where we stand with the Almighty, especially when immersion into the Amazing New Life has landed us in hot water. Paul, servant by the will of God, lapsed into our human pattern more than once, "For this I was appointed preacher and apostle (I am telling the truth, I am not lying) . . . (In what I am writing to you, before God, I do not lie!)" This was the problem with the old system of oaths. People became two-faced. Elaborate phrasing invoking the name of God gave the solemn appearance of godliness. Under that guise ordinary speech could be deployed as vehicle for deliberate distortions.

Christ's revolutionary cure: When the name of your God — "I am the Lord" — is imputed into your life by my Holy Spirit, a simple Yes or No will inherently identify you as a person of integrity before heaven and earth.

Matthew 5:37 □ Matthew 5:33-35

We are of God. Whoever knows God listens to us, and he who is not of God does not listen to us. By this we know the spirit of truth and the spirit of error.

What is truth? Every age of sophistication asks afresh. Thinkers, poets, artists, the drunk at the bar, the guy struggling with tax forms, the virgin in the back seat of a car suffering her first pangs of passion — they all wrestle with the question according to the need of the hour. Every age darkened by human wisdom blunders anew.

What is truth? Let no mature Christian fall into the trap of awkwardly describing and defending it. Truth is a person. To the doubter Thomas, Jesus said, "I am the way, and the truth, and the life." Anything less for the Christian is to miss the boat. Anything more violates Christ's command, "Let what you say be simply 'Yes' or 'No'; anything more than this comes from evil."

"We are of God." Such is our incredible confidence by the inherent power of God who makes us truth incarnate. No writer in all of Scripture used the word "truth" more than John. Consider his classic, "And the Word became flesh and dwelt among us, full of grace and truth." Or his correspondence, "The elder to the elect lady and her children, whom I love in the truth, and not only I but also all who know the truth, because of the truth which abides in us and will be with us for ever . . ."

This gentle John was once the son of thunder who yearned to rain fire down from heaven to consume the "deaf." This transformed seer of truth does not use the word as such in Revelation. Now he triumphantly calls Him Alpha and Omega, the Amen, the Witness, the Beginning of God's creation. In John's vision of the culmination of history — His story — no listener will have to strain to catch the truth. "And I heard a voice from heaven like the sound of many waters and like the sound of loud thunder . . ."

1 John 4:6 ☐ 1 John 4:1-6

His voice was like the sound of many waters . . .

Revelation was written in code by the imprisoned John partly to evade Roman scrutiny, but mostly to convey to the suffering believer the most profound kind of consolation. With known symbolism he established the astonishing congruity of God's culminating Word with His witness down through the ages, beginning with Eden.

John's vision of "Jesus Christ the faithful witness" matches Ezekiel's description set down 600 years earlier. Ezekiel testified to the sound of His coming as that of "many waters." It was wide-ranging biblical practice to symbolically link water with man's afflictions.

"O that my head were waters, and my eyes a fountain of tears, that I might weep day and night for the slain. . . . Save me, O God! For the waters have come up to my neck. . . . They surround me like a flood all day long. . . . I am poured out like water. . . . We must all die, we are like water spilt on the ground." To the soul swept away by the torrents of sorrow John now announced the waters of God's healing presence.

Ezekiel, stationed by the door of the temple that faced east, describes in chapter 47, ". . . and behold, water was issuing from below the threshold of the temple toward the east . . ." Read for yourself the majestic vision of the many waters gathered into God's mighty river of gladness, lined with trees, pouring life even into the Dead Sea. Now face east with the Genesis perspective, "And the Lord God planted a garden in Eden, in the east. . . . A river flowed out of Eden to water the garden . . ." Finally, face the rising sun of Revelation's thundering conclusion, "Then he showed me the river of the water of life . . . flowing from the throne of God . . . also, on either side of the river, the tree of life . . ." Shall we not thrill also to the decoded message of God's inherent integrity!

Revelation 1:15 □ Revelation 1

About this we have much to say which is hard to explain, since you have become dull of hearing.

The writer is clearly frustrated — caught in the vicious cycle of dull believers. On the surface they have accepted the basic doctrines of faith, but having said "I do" to Christ, they "don't"! As a result there is no enthusiasm, no imagination, no sharp delight in living on the growing edge of discovery. Worse, by avoiding the stretching experiences of Christ, they plod along without Him.

Trying once again now, surrounded by his books, the writer freshly explores his challenge to quicken the sheep so anesthetized by complacency. Leafing through his notes, looking up ancient texts, an air of excitement suddenly grips him. Aha! Melchizedek, the priest-king of Salem! In him he has the perfect illustration to give grace and old Abraham a new twist. Hurriedly he reaches for the pen and then — in midair — drops it and crumples back in his chair. Melchizedek who? Salem what? The code is meaningless. These Hebrews with their baby bottles cannot handle meat!

Are we weaned? When in the course of Christian fellowship our testimonies of praise are invited, what fresh currents of rejoicing are unloosed? People always give pious thanks that Jesus died for them. After a while it sounds like a wake. We owe our Lord far more than dull acknowledgements of Calvary. Where is our resurrection life? Where is the exclamation point of Pentecost? "Little faith will bring your soul to heaven; great faith will bring heaven to your soul."

"Therefore let us leave the elementary doctrines of Christ and go on to maturity . . ." The writer's pen is flying now. Let the children be bored or whimper for milk. He is going to carve meat and — by Abraham — they will taste it. Better to chew long and hard than to lose teeth from nonuse. "For this Melchizedek . . ."

Hebrews 5:11 ☐ *Hebrews 5:11-14*

You may freely eat of every tree of the garden; but of the tree of the knowledge of good and evil you shall not eat . . .

Why? Because God said so! Before we descend on mysterious Eden as on a press conference with poised note pads and eager questions, we must be admonished, "Have this mind among yourselves which is yours in Christ Jesus, who, though he was in the form of God, did not count equality with God a thing to be grasped . . ." His holiness commands our humility.

No question about it. The small child rushing toward a hot flame must be stopped instantly. Obedience comes before understanding. The parent takes no chances. If the warning is not heeded, swift and stern punishment is applied. It is really an act of mercy. Parent and child are spared tragic consequences.

Those children at history's dawn, Adam and Eve, rushed headlong into the open flame of God's consuming fire. "For the Lord your God is a devouring fire, a jealous God." He guards with good reason His holiness for His protection and ours. How significant that the first ray of illumination from the forbidden fruit of light fell on man's genitals. Apart from the full instruction of the Creator's harmonious design, immediate distortion resulted. Adam and Eve, ashamed of their nakedness, pulled away from each other as well as from God. Their death sentence was both punishment and provision of mercy. Plunged into death's darkness, mankind was saved from the hell of living forever in the distorted illumination engineered by Lucifer.

As the tree of knowledge begins to yield to us its fragrant promise, we shall understand better. The "faithful witness" in Revelation testifies to God's original intent, "To him who conquers I will grant to eat of the tree of life, which is in the paradise of God."

Genesis 2:16-17 ☐ *Genesis 2 and 3*

. . . in the day that you eat of it you shall die.

The rivers flowing from the source of God's delight place Eden somewhere in modern Iraq. This ancient Mesopotamian cradle of civilization began in a dim age. Adam and Eve wore animals skins. Fire was obtained laboriously. Candles, matches, batteries and lasers were a long time in coming. In view of eternity's foreshadowed brightness, our present powers of illumination are still in the Stone age. At His consummation of history Christ is to appear as the "bright morning star."

The glory of God's sovereignly timed self-revelation was manifest in the fruit of Eden's tree of life. Adam and Eve as the primal parents of nations were to rest their faith in the sheltering shade of God's promises. Blinded to His ultimate purpose by the shock of forced disclosure, they forfeited the intimate learning walk with their Maker. Their immediate lot became the world, the flesh, and the devil. Adam had carnal knowledge of Eve and she bore Cain who would baptize with fratricide the darkened brotherhood of man.

Our inability to handle instant light is borne out by the fact that prophets over many centuries had to foreshadow the incarnation of Jesus. "And we have the prophetic word made more sure. You will do well to pay attention to this as to a lamp shining in a dark place, until the day dawns and the morning star rises in your hearts" (2 Peter 1:19).

Lucifer, the son of Dawn, could not compete with the Light of the world. Before self-styled equality with God spelled his doom, Lucifer appeared as counterfeiter of intimacy and divine disclosure before Adam and Eve. His proposed instant gratification produced unwholesome genital fascination instead of wholesome sexuality lived out in concert with the Author of love. Unless the Morning Star has risen in our heart, we are still trapped in that pattern.

Genesis 2:17

Then he showed me . . . the tree of life with its twelve kinds of fruit, yielding its fruit each month; and the leaves of the tree were for the healing of the nations.

Scratch that silly image of wearing a nightgown and languishing on an oversized cotton ball with a golden harp and tremulous memories of Monday-night football! The Bright Morning Star is the unending source of abundant creativity and original life.

The reference to nations indicates the spice of variety. No cookie-cutter Christians rolled out from bland earnestness, thank heavens! Rich in diversity and distinctive in character, "nations" will flourish and flavor the commonwealth of heaven. Because the tree with its leaves "for the healing of nations" has its roots in the mainstream of God's sustaining life force, there will no longer be withered dreams and patterns of decline. What we build will not suffer decay or sudden destruction. The things we cherish shall cheer others; the adventure of individual and mutual discovery will be unending.

The twelve kinds of fruit for each month symbolize completeness and renewal without stale repetition. Knowledge and resources will be ours at the right season of learning. Life will be punctuated with rhythm and changing scenery. The God who filled this fleeting earth with His majesty and whimsy will delight in our creative expressions. We might just form that committee and come up with our own camel!

Ultimately, however, we are not headed for the glorified free-for-all of a tinkerer's dream of paradise. Our essential celebration of life eternal will center on the worship of our magnificent God. Ours will be the joy of meaningful service; the satisfaction of exercising responsibility. The thrill of secret lovers who whisper "I love you" in a 1001 delightful ways will become ours. Our adoration of God is eternity's greatest gift and fulfillment of glory.

Revelation 22:1-2 □ *Revelation 22:1-5*

You are already made clean by the word which I have spoken to you. Abide in me, and I in you. As the branch cannot bear fruit by itself, unless it abides in the vine, neither can you, unless you abide in me.

Every saint in Christ aches to be fruitful. The inherent snare is our determination to work for Him. Instead, He patiently goes to work on us. He wields His pruning shears with astonishing regularity and deadly precision.

"You are already made clean by the word which I have spoken to you." Catch the hint of impatience. We mistake the Gardener's pruning shears for the surgeon's knife. Grabbing our own biopsy, we race to the lab of fierce introspection, looking for the cancerous cells that would identify God's objection to us. Such futility. The cancer of guilt was excised at Calvary. The slicing into our psyche with the sharp objective to become antiseptically clean is an insult to our Physician who healed us. Of course we are crawling with germs! But a heart yearning to be fruitful is a heart right with the Savior. To be in touch with our feelings is helpful; to be in touch with faith through His Word is to know restoration.

"Abide in me." Before discernible top growth and fruit can be reality, our roots must push through crusty layers of earth-impacted soul until they draw the moisture of God's river of mercy. When the root system has grown deep and strong, Christ's own original life wells up in us and ripens into fruit. No longer do we anguish about specific gifts and ministries. The vine of Jesus is inevitably in God's planted vineyard. Our stifling self-consciousness would have us be plastic grapes in someone's hapless tray. To be Christ's expression of fruitfulness is to be naturally in the right place at the right season, caressed by the leaves of His healing presence.

John 15:3-4 □ *John 15:1-11*

Let it alone, sir, this year also, till I dig about it and put on manure. And if it bears fruit next year, well and good; but if not, you can cut it down.

God demands a fruitful people! The church branching out in religious programming for the enjoyment of members is in for shocking news. "Bear fruit that befits repentance, and do not presume to say to yourselves, 'We have Abraham as our father'; for I tell you, God is able from these stones to raise up children to Abraham. Even now the axe is laid to the root of the trees; every tree therefore that does not bear good fruit is cut down and thrown into the fire" (Matthew 3:8-10).

The church is debilitated with complacent believers today. They treat Christ as one treats a country-club membership. Church is the cultural extra garnished with a sprig of virtue and a slice of goodness. "I tell you, God is able from these stones to raise up people that sit in pews and fidget with their program."

Recognizing our natural tendency to settle into comfortable patterns, responsible church leadership must press for continuous growth. When have we last participated in a church retreat or renewal conference? How faithfully have we availed ourselves of ongoing equipping-and-enabling ministries? If self-satisfaction or unordered priorities have kept us away, we court far more than our leaders' heartaches and headaches. At some point we shall know God's burning anger, the season of cutting off.

When God enters the vineyard to give His withering look to the fruitless tree, Jesus pleads for one more year. Brace yourself for His spade's decisive blows to your hardness of heart. Suffer the stench of manure. When in shock you turn to the Vinedresser, know that it is not sweat running down His face. He is handwatering you with His own tears! Such is His passionate love.

Luke 13:8-9 □ *Luke 13:6-9*

Son of man, behold, I am about to take the delight of your eyes away from you at a stroke; yet you shall not mourn or weep nor shall your tears run down.

Quite cold-blooded for a God reputed to be love. "God is love." Perhaps it is the most virulent form of apathy. The image of the zealous Old Testament God has been blurred by the cultured Jesus of our careless Sunday Christianity. "Jesus Christ is the same yesterday and today and for ever." Just how cold-blooded might the Vinedresser get in His passion to restore God's vineyard to full productivity?

"Son of man, behold. . . . So I spoke to the people in the morning, and at evening my wife died. And on the next morning I did as I was commanded." Ezekiel groaned silently, but excluded himself from all outward expressions of mourning.

Ezekiel's cold-blooded composure was such that the shocked people pressed for a clue to his crass behavior. His withering blow was delivered swiftly, "Thus says the Lord God: Behold, I will profane my sanctuary, the pride of your power, the delight of your eyes, and the desire of your soul . . . you shall not mourn or weep, but you shall pine away in your iniquities and groan to one another."

Ezekiel had spent his early years in Jerusalem, the pride and joy of Israel. "God is love" — their magnificent temple seemed ample proof. For their sin of neglecting true worship, God inflicted the Babylonian exile on His people. The sudden death of Ezekiel's wife signaled the destruction of the temple by pagans. In restoring His cold-hearted people to fruitfulness, the Jesus Christ of yesterday dug the pit of captivity, fertilized it with death, then watered it with the tears that Ezekiel was forbidden to shed. Who or what is the "delight of our eyes"? Who or what do we take for granted because "God is love"?

Ezekiel 24:16 ☐ *Ezekiel 24:15-27*

And he said to me, "Son of man, eat this scroll that I give you and fill your stomach with it." Then I ate it; and it was in my mouth as sweet as honey.

"The fear of the LORD is clean, enduring for ever; the ordinances of the LORD are true . . . sweeter also than honey and drippings of the honeycomb" (Psalm 19:9-10). "Thy words were found, and I ate them, and thy words became to me a joy and the delight of my heart; for I am called by thy name, O Lord, God of hosts" (Jeremiah 15:16). "I took the little scroll from the hand of the angel and ate it; it was sweet as honey in my mouth, but when I had eaten it my stomach was made bitter" (Revelation 10:10). God obviously has Ezekiels — the name means "God will strengthen" — in every age. Those whom God strengthens feed on His Word as for dear life, in order to stomach His passionate love that will not settle for second best!

When Ezekiel had feasted himself on the perspective and promise of God's living Word, His "tough love" flooded his heart and coursed through his veins. "All of the house of Israel are of a hard forehead and of a stubborn heart. Behold, I have made your face hard against their faces, and your forehead hard against their forehead . . . Son of man, all my words that I shall speak to you receive in your heart, and hear with your ears." Of course Ezekiel trembled at the prospect of having to eat his own words. Certainly his "stomach" was bitter with the death of his wife.

"Greater love has no man than this, that a man lay down his life . . ." "So I arose and went forth into the plain; and lo, the glory of the Lord stood there, like the glory which I had seen by the river . . . and I fell on my face. But the Spirit entered into me, and set me upon my feet." That is the "plain" explanation of Ezekiel's courageous compassion for God!

Ezekiel 3:3 ☐ *Ezekiel 2:8-3:11*

And when I passed by you, and saw you weltering in your blood, I said to you in your blood, "Live . . ."

Newspaper headlines: Newborn baby girl abandoned in vacant lot — Young woman of mysterious background to marry royalty — Prominent wife of nobleman accused of prostitution; cult involvement and child abuse implied. — Trial separation announced — Surprise move confirmed by husband; reconciliation effected.

Reporter: Ezekiel the priest, son of Buzi, in the land of the Chaldeans by the river where "the hand of the Lord was upon him" and gave him this major scoop. Ezekiel had done extensive background reading involving the scandal. When the Husband granted him private interviews to rescue the honor of His wife, Israel, the reporter simply had to go public with the story. It presents a fascinating look behind the scenes of this incredible "marriage."

The story is not for the squeamish. A literary masterpiece, the 16th chapter of Ezekiel is "weltering" in blood and sex. It contains "our" proverb, "Like mother, like daughter." Above all it proclaims: How much like God to show such long-suffering and compassion! Through Ezekiel's words we are taken into His "bitter stomach" and forgiving heart. "Son of man, make known to Jerusalem her abominations . . ."

"And as for your birth . . . your navel string was not cut, nor were you washed with water to cleanse you . . . nor swathed with bands, — And you grew up and became tall and arrived at full maidenhood . . . — You were at the age for love . . . and I covered your nakedness: yea, I plighted my troth . . . and you became mine. Then I bathed you with water and washed off your blood from you, and anointed you with oil. — You grew exceedingly beautiful, and came to regal estate. — But you trusted in your beauty, and played the harlot . . . — And after all your wickedness (woe, woe to you! says the Lord God). . . . I forgive you all that you have done."

Ezekiel 16:6 □ *Ezekiel 16*

What is this thing that you have done? You fasted and wept for the child while it was alive; but when the child died, you arose and ate food.

"Then desire when it has conceived gives birth to sin; and sin when it is full-grown brings forth death." This is the drama of disobedience we share with David. No glamorous plot of adultery and murder required. The forceful conclusion centers on these essentials alone: "David said to Nathan, 'I have sinned against the Lord.' And Nathan said to David, 'The Lord also has put away your sin.'"

The prophet announced God's pardon. At this point David was home free. The process of his full restoration to sonship was successfully launched. But practically speaking, God's judgment was just now unfolding. Bathsheba's baby fell gravely ill. By Levitical code David's crimes against society deserved death. By God's grace not even man's condemnation could touch him.

David lay prostrate before God. So dramatic was David's withdrawal during the time of anxious waiting that when the child died on the seventh day, he was considered too suicidal to receive the news. The servants' whisperings roused him to the sad truth. To their consternation he got to his feet, washed and perfumed himself, changed into fresh kingly garb, worshiped God in His house, then went to his own and demanded food.

We must do exactly as David. Jesus Christ is our prophet who pronounced God's pardon through His death and resurrection. At the time of our confession we acknowledge that He took our punishment on Himself. The "judgment" of God is not punishment. Rather, it points to His intrinsically righteous character which feeds into our restoration to sonship. First we are perfumed with the fragrance of the knowledge of our Savior. Then we strengthen ourselves to become fit for service once again.

2 Samuel 12:21 □ *2 Samuel 11:1-12:23*

Create in me a clean heart, O God. . . . Then I will teach transgressors thy ways . . .

David's "clean heart" bears investigation. Did his plea center on body chemistry? In the leveling-off days of his sordid affair with Bathsheba, was the demon Lust still doing the dervish dance in him? Hardly . . . Even lust requires a modicum of energy. David was just about worn out from plotting the cool logic that cost Uriah his life.

David might well have forgotten about the pleasant diversion. But the lady sent a reminder, "I am with child." David sent a message to his military chief, "I am with headache." Send me her husband on the double! Uriah arrived at court and briefed the king. As a reward, David suggested he go home and make himself v-e-r-y comfortable. The dutiful dullard did not catch on, preferring to sleep with his soldiers at David's doorstep. With Uriah's paternity thus ruled out, David had to make a widow of Bathsheba so he could officially move her in with him and silence the gossips.

Pregnancy, childbirth, illness, death. "Create in me a clean heart, O God!" David cried not from sexual immorality but from self-condemnation. If we picture the need for a clean heart in the context of sex sin and self-interest, we tragically miss the point. David's "clean heart" needs to be associated with the "clean fear" of the Lord! The clean heart must shield us from insidious self-condemnation. It is the chief interest of our Redeemer!

David's clean heart did not save him from the consequences of his sordid acts. Incest, murder and rebellion in his own house marred his later years. But delivered from self-condemnation he was able to turn from the negative and invest his energy positively. In his instruction of transgressors he did not teach how to stay away from married women, but how to turn to God as forgiven sinner!

Psalm 51:10,13 □ *Psalm 51*

He said, "What have they seen in your house?"

What happens when God relents? How are his interests served when deathbed miraculously becomes child bed by way of a blessed marriage bed? Illustrious Hezekiah makes for an interesting case study. It does not prove more than the premise that God has every right — and much good reason — to reign sovereignly.

Hezekiah succeeded his vacillating father Ahaz to the throne of Judah (c.B.C. 715-687). God-fearing, he held down God's fort courageously during a period of history when the Assyrians made mincemeat of opponents all over geography. Hezekiah pushed for vital reforms. He took down the "high places" and centralized worship of the living God in Jerusalem. He had not yet produced an heir when he fell mortally ill. The prophet of God instructed him to set his house in order. "You shall not recover."

The king wept bitterly and reminded God of his good deeds. "And before Isaiah had gone out of the middle court, the word of the Lord came to him: 'Turn back, and say to Hezekiah . . . Thus says the Lord . . . I have heard your prayer, I have seen your tears; behold, I will heal you . . .'"

Babylon sent envoys with a gift to cheer the recovered king. After their visit Isaiah paid a call. "He said, 'What have they seen in your house?'" Surely the Lord's mercy and majesty? No! The might of Hezekiah's treasury — much to the spies' delight. During the Babylonian invasion the looters would know where to look! When informed of his stupidity of pride and the deeper implications of Judea's future captivity, the egotist shrugged it all off. Let the tough times come — as long as they come after my time. The king's heir, Manasseh, ascended the throne at the age of twelve. Reverting to pagan influence, he rebuilt the high places. "And he burned his son as an offering . . . He did much evil in the sight of the Lord, provoking him to anger."

2 Kings 20:15 □ *2 Kings 20:1-21:9*

Do not rely on your own insight. In all your ways acknowledge him. . . . Be not wise in your own eyes. . . . It will be healing to your flesh and refreshment to your bones.

A strong whiff of autocracy? Will it sell in the consciousness-raising market where the nectar of sweet self-reliance is hawked? The newfangled harmony of "encountered" psyche, massaged ego and cocoa-buttered flesh is baptized in the instant-intimacy of the shared hot tub. When ritual sips of Chablis lend a silvery edge to soft laughter and mellow conversation, heaven on earth is sweetened with just the right dab of mystery.

The hedonist is not the only one who prefers a God of poetic mystery to one of pragmatic mastery. We like divine wisdom as a dollop of cream on our dessert, but not as bran-flavored steady diet. Our ambivalence stems from innate distrust of self. Deep down we despair of our inability to be as much for Him as He is for us. By keeping Him on an ornamental level, we spare Him and us the repeated disappointments of one-sided relationship. The God of our mental projection is the Perfectionist we would like to be.

Watch for Him when your "trenchant insights" end in a foxhole while all around you harmless presuppositions explode with a whine in the face of advancing crisis. Do we hold on to our "helmet of salvation" for dear life while ducking? No, we scratch around like mad for the perfect instructions we failed to heed earlier. How awkward to sit in a pit in the midst of one's own civil war — showered with the confetti of a thousand SIN CANCELED notices.

In all your ways acknowledge Him as the God of perfected mercy! It will be healing to your "navel" and "marrow" to your bones. The Hebrew speaks of God's "natural juices" that flow through the umbilical cord to our womb of contentment. We are fed the very lifeblood of Christ's humility. God is not the Father of autocracy, but the Mother of mercy.

Proverbs 3:5-8 ☐ *Proverbs 3:1-8*

*But the wisdom from above is first pure, then peaceable,
gentle, open to reason, full of mercy and good fruits, without
uncertainty or insincerity.*

Our nation obsessed with youth and push-button
knowledge cares little about sagacity that comes only with age,
much to the detriment of alienated senior citizen and youth
alike. The world's wisdom, says James, is tainted with jealousy
and selfish ambition. In marked contrast, divine wisdom is
meek. Yet wisdom is perhaps the most neglected virtue in the
Christians' repertoire. We make love our chief tool, but unless
we have wisdom, we cannot make it stick as truth.

What is the difference between sage and sapling? The
mature saint has time, experience and reflection on his side.
The young firebrand blitzes his would-be converts with unpro-
cessed information. When "pure," "peaceable" or "gentle" are
mere theological buzz words tumbling from the lips of one who
is not open to reason, not full of mercy and good fruits, he is
shunned as dogmatist and not welcomed as wise man bearing
gifts to hail the new life.

How does the eager young reconcile his passion for
usefulness with the need to grow in the *grace* and knowledge of
Jesus Christ? What if the characteristically revolutionary really
started a revolution? What if today's Christian youth began to
reverse the trend of neglect that afflicts our elderly and shames
the nation? What if they learned to cherish and respect these
first before lusting for the quick, prestigious conversions
among contemporaries? What if the sagacious saint wore his
wisdom with such obvious grace that he could be "open to
reason" — mutual listening and learning — without
uncertainty or insincerity? God made Jesus Christ our wisdom.
In Him there is no generation gap.

James 3:17 ☐ *James 3:13-18*

Behold, wise men from the East came to Jerusalem, saying, "Where is he who has been born king of the Jews? For we have seen his star . . . and have come to worship him."

Nasty Herod got the magi to Bethlehem. Nice "Christians" like us might have blasted Eastern wisdom in general and wicked stargazing in particular. We could have thrown the Book at them. But the Bible's peaceable wisdom bids us to keep the wise men coming.

"And men will come from east and west, and from north and south, and sit at table in the kingdom of God." A Roman centurion had challenged Jesus to "only say the word" and his servant would be healed. His basic understanding of delegated authority led him to faith. Such wisdom had triggered Christ's remark about the global influx of believers who would shame "the sons of the kingdom" with their rigid religiosity.

Speculations about the magi range widely. It matters little whether the "wise men" were Chaldeans notorious for their augury, or kings alerted to the rising star of a precedent-shattering dynasty. Importantly, they journeyed from their time and place with an innate desire to worship the truly worthy. When the star of their exceeding great joy led them to a baby in humble surroundings, they fell down and worshiped at once.

The study of stars requires time, concentration and disregard for creature comforts. Credit the wise men for focusing on majesty where they first perceived it. "When I look at thy heavens, the work of thy fingers . . . what is man that thou art mindful of him . . .?" Witness Job's remarkable kinship of spirit as he praises the God "who made the Bear and Orion, the Pleiades and the chambers of the south . . ." Perhaps there is an Eskimo with a deep yearning for God gazing at his northern sky right now. Sheep, vine, well, or bread he might not recognize. The mystery of star and baby are within his familiar grasp. May God keep the wise men coming from their own time and place in the east and west, north and south. May our peaceable wisdom welcome theirs!

Matthew 2:1-2 ☐ *Matthew 2:1-12*

Ask, and it will be given you; seek, and you will find; knock, and it will be opened to you. For every one who asks receives, and he who seeks finds . . .

"Every one" — categorically so! Next excuse, please. Faith, not extremism, unlocks the secrets of the kingdom. We either try a bulldozer or expect to simply peel off a label and — presto — instant glory hallelujah. The King James antidote? "In your patience possess ye your souls." Even as we are not popped into our skin fully grown, so we "acquire" our soul by progression. The wise men from the East illustrate the spiritual pilgrimage.

Ask! They were not three peas in a pod discovering the star under identical circumstances. Whatever their actual number or fraternal ties, we can safely assume that the phenomenon was first a matter of private calculations and speculations. Their questions developed naturally along professional and spiritual lines. The way they set out on an unknown journey with their own kingly gifts for an act of supreme worship tells us something about the depth of their pointed asking. God clearly listened and guided at once.

Seek! What distances were traveled, what danger encountered and how many discomforts endured? As seekers we blithely opt for the scenic Inspiration Drive. What if God has mapped out our route of perspiration? Perhaps hardship, not holy haste, needs to crystallize the true worth of our proposed worship.

Knock! Five miles short of their destination, the star simply quit on the stargazers. There was Jerusalem with its dazzling sights and distractions. Instead the magi went knocking. God used no waiting Simeon, no devout Anna to point the way to the Messiah. Their knocks unlocked malicious Herod's dark intentions. Only then did their star speed them directly to the King of kings. Is the bright Morning Star our exceeding joy? How could He possibly fail you and me!

Matthew 7:7-8

If any of you lacks wisdom, let him ask God . . . But let him ask in faith, with no doubting . . .

No spiritual pilgrimage is easy! None is designed as a guilt trip! Every stern exhortation is cushioned with compassion. Like the traveler with known medical problems we should wear a spiritual "Medi-Tag" around our wrist for on-the-spot reassurance. "Bless the Lord, O my soul; and *all* that is within me, bless his holy name. . . . For he knows our frame; he remembers that we are dust." If nothing in all creation can separate us from the love of God, shall the butterflies in our stomach undo Him?

Every journey begins with the one crucial small step that has us scared silly. Our humanity is no sin. Emotions of fear and doubt are inborn. The sooner we nudge them to the surface and "own" them, the quicker God can dismiss them. The gift of faith is His responsibility. From the moment we acknowledge our inherent lack and confess our abject need of God Himself, it is His sacred duty to aid and comfort us greatly!

The grave responsibility in the believer's life is action. When doubt does not yield to prayer and becomes a tormenting demon instead, leading us down the road to despair, it is not that prayer has failed. Prayer can become a convenient cop-out when practical action is needed, no matter how drastic or seemingly insignificant. We hardly ever feel like doing the precise things we must do! It is entirely futile to deal with this kind of reluctance in prayer. God will turn a deaf ear to our pious fussing. He does release courage and supernatural provision at the precise moment we exercise our will into decisive action. Faith is active cooperation.

On spiritual odysseys God does not act the travel agent. We receive no detailed itinerary, confirmed reservations or ready foreign currency in our pocket. He simply promises to travel with us, one scary, liberating step at a time.

James 1:5-6 ☐ *James 1:2-8*

So Peter got out of the boat and walked on the water and came to Jesus; but when he saw the wind, he was afraid, and beginning to sink he cried out, "Lord, save me."

As comic relief to those who waver we have Peter who makes waves. "O man of little faith, why did you doubt?" What look does Jesus wear on His face? How do we perceive the sound of His voice? If we smell a rebuke, we might be one of the wavering cowards. If upon reflection we have sunned ourselves in His affectionate smile, we are Christ's own brave fool on the go.

Thank God Peter avoided the dull script that would have assigned him a flawless feat. Because he fell flat on his face with such flourish, we can light out after our risks without thought of decorum. We can attempt the spectacular and gleefully imagine the very worst that might happen. "Lord, save me." The world says sink or swim. Jesus saves us the swim. Immediately He "reached out his hand and caught him, 'nice going there, Peter. Next time I worry and you walk. Meanwhile, let me pull the plug on this storm. You, brave friend, deserve a breather.'"

Peter, mind you, had not blundered or paid with defeat for boasting. This beloved disciple paid Jesus the grandest compliment of his apprentice career. Let every "iffy" Christian take notice of Peter's noble *if*. "Lord, if it is you, bid me come to you on the water." Such boldness was in direct response to Christ's ever present *if*. "If any man would come after me, let him deny himself . . . and follow me." Peter was brave beyond measure when in growing trust he did walk on water — and did cry for help when fear pushed the "down" button.

Nothing ventured, nothing gained. Expect the distressing realities temporarily robbing us of our concentration of Jesus! Before the cry forms on our lips His hand is near. Catch His smile as He catches you! It is His badge of honor for bravery.

Matthew 14:29-30 □ *Matthew 14:22-33*

. . . Peter went up on the housetop to pray, about the sixth hour. And he became hungry and desired something to eat; but while they were preparing it, he fell into a trance . . .

Fall in love with God and falling becomes a way of life. You fall short and you fall hard and you fall into the Sea of Galilee. You fall in with new people and fresh ideas fall into your head. And when you stand bolt upright in prayer at noon with mostly hunger pangs on your mind, you fall into a trance!

The word is *ekstasis* — "a displacement of the mind." Try the do-it-yourself version some time. Come home hungry and spend a spiritual "happy hour" shut in the bedroom while dinner is being prepared. Be enchanted by the heavenly smells that come from the kitchen. Go out of your mind trying to puzzle together the menu while your mouth waters and stomach growls. Such was the agony and ecstasy of Peter's prayer time.

How fitting that his somewhat displaced mind should be receptive to the vision of a tablecloth descending from heaven just loaded with ham, pork chops and Italian sausage. Peter, being Jewish, could not quite see it that way, of course. Three times the flying menu made a pass over his stomach and under his eyes. Each time a cheerful voice rang out, "Rise, Peter; kill and eat." Three times Peter turned green and pleaded kosher restraint. Each time he was told to forget it. When the agony of his *ekstasis* had ended, three Gentiles stood at the door and spoke of their master's hunger for the living Lord.

The next time we suffer pangs of indecision and our iffy Christian walk leaves a hollow feeling in our stomach, let us stand and pray near the barbecue where steaks are cooking. Forget about eating, but do take a long, hard look at the tablecloth spread out before your inner eyes. Who will not be at table in the kingdom of heaven because we have refused to be broken bread and poured-out wine for the God-hungry around us?

Acts 10:9-10 □ *Acts 10:9-16*

About the ninth hour of the day he saw clearly in a vision an angel . . . saying to him, "Cornelius. . . . Your prayers and your alms have ascended as a memorial before God."

Cornelius, centurion of the Italian cohort, was an uncircumcised proselyte to the Jewish faith. Wholly devoted to God, he was instructed in his vision to send for Peter. With clockwork precision the Spirit had prepared the apostle through his "displaced mind" to share Christ with the God-hungry Gentile. While Peter was preaching, the Holy Spirit fell on the Gentiles "just as on us at the beginning." An unprecedented age of harvest had been doubly confirmed by God.

The Book of Acts contains twenty-eight chapters. It ends with a pause, not a period. We pick it up on this note of promise, "To be continued." We are God's people chosen to write the twenty-ninth chapter now!

Peter and Cornelius are *not* the patron saints of the ecumenical movement. That is where the church is bogged down today. The two men with their precedent-shattering experience of the Holy Spirit typify the "first fruits" of the ancient harvest festival of Pentecost. In the language of old, Cornelius represents the freewill offering; Peter, suffering death for his consuming faith, typifies the burnt offering.

Having witnessed the sample of the new grain of God's "later crops," we must acknowledge that time of harvest now. The fire will fall afresh. Consuming passion in Christ must be demonstrated. Today's ecumenics managed by conventional wisdom are nothing more than a great sheet with cleaned-up food for thought on display. The fire of the Holy Spirit must in actuality process and consume all reservations; our sacred cows must go! Such offerings by fire release "a pleasing odor to the Lord." From such harvest celebration God stills His people's hunger.

Acts 10:3-4 □ *Acts 10:1-8*

And the priest shall burn the whole on the altar, as a burnt offering . . . a pleasing odor to the LORD.

Long before Christ gave Himself up as a fragrant offering, God signaled His desire to be approached by liberal use of perfume! Leviticus is partly butcher's manual, but the "pleasing odor" keeps you hooked. Both you and Moses have fond memories of backyard barbecues. And then the fire of the Holy Spirit falls and you suddenly recognize the logical link between the anicent priest's primitive rite and God's powerful self-manifestation at Pentecost.

"Do you smell fire?" Let someone pop the question and we immediately sniff the air. Fittingly, our verb *smell* has traceable roots in such words as "to smolder," "scorch," "fire" and "glow." The Hebrew interpretation of *ruach* embraces such meanings as "to blow," "to breathe," "to anticipate," "to accept," "to make of quick understanding." As identical noun it relates to mind, wind, spirit. The Pentecost phenomena of forceful wind and individualized fire were precisely based on the realization of *ruach!* Leviticus was already perfumed with the promise of the divine Presence breaking through the time and space barrier.

Perfume itself is rooted in smoke. Fragrant herbs and oils — frankincense for instance — helped fumigate the place where a compassionate God agreed to meet with His contaminated people. The seeming crudity of primitive sacrifice reflected on the pagan culture of that day. By regulating rites and setting limits, God weaned His people from demonic influence and educated them and us toward the day of Jesus Christ. On Pentecost the disposition of the Lamb's perfect sacrifice was burned into the believer's consciousness in such a way that it could be "breathed out" as new life into others. Leviticus is as contemporary as our own Pentecost! Do you smell fire?

Leviticus 1:9 □ *Leviticus 1*

With golden bowls full of incense, which are the prayers of the saints . . .

Look what happens when real life goes up in smoke! To primitive man far more at the raw mercy of his natural world, the mystery of fire spelled comfort because God involved him in the control and benefit of it. And the believer was comforted because his prayers were visibly ascending into the presence of God.

Smoke is a gaseous product visible due to the presence of carbon particles. Incomplete combustion results in soot. When we have the nagging conviction that our prayers stick to the ceiling of our house, we may have a point. The fire of God burns clean and releases energy in such unhindered flow that in terms of prayer it travels in full concentration straight to the mark. Prayer unfueled by the Holy Spirit lacks the "updraft" of the risen Lord.

Revelation as harmonious sequel to Leviticus imparts peace to our faith struggles now. Every seemingly primitive symbolism serves as a reminder of God's willingness to meet us at our point of need and understanding. During Exodus, when Moses went up to receive the law, "Mount Sinai was wrapped in smoke, because the Lord descended upon it in fire; and the smoke of it went up like the smoke of a kiln, and the whole mountain quaked greatly." Through such vivid imagery God fueled His people's imagination, which is a prerequisite to faith.

When God subsequently invited and regulated His people's sacrificial offerings (from a root meaning "to draw near"), He reiterated the basic premise that He is intrinsically holy, merciful and mighty. From the fire originating and culminating in heaven, we can imagine His initiating love and sustaining power. Through His Holy Spirit what we know becomes "know-how" at both ends of the channel.

Revelation 5:8 □ *Revelation 5*

The LORD answer you in the day of trouble! The name of the God of Jacob protect you! May he send you help from the sanctuary. . . . May he remember all your offerings . . .

Good luck! Why? Why wish on our fellow Christian a purposeless, unpredictable, uncontrollable force when in fact we are privileged to invoke heaven's own blessing! The psalmist offers no mere figure of speech. These are powerful words of experienced faith; the underlying imagination firmly fixed in divine reality. The reciprocal nature of the blessing is in harmony with the function of the Holy Spirit as Advocate. He represents God and believer.

How does heaven deal with our petitions, we wonder. We are torn between God as ultra-personal Lover or super-sophisticated Computer. We need not be. Scripture is generous with illustrations. If we pick up the clue in Revelation, we might say that general prayers of a like nature are kept for a specific time of witness. In the case of the "golden bowls full of incense," our adoration will give rise to a "new song" at the end of the age, "Worthy art thou . . ."

A contrasting passage seems to deliver the corporate clout of our cries for God's forceful intervention. "And another angel . . . was given much incense to mingle with the prayers of all the saints. . . . Then the angel took the censer and filled it with fire from the altar and threw it on the earth; and there were peals of thunder . . . and an earthquake" (Revelation 8:3-5).

Meanwhile, back on earth, we have eyewitness accounts of heaven's individualized messenger services. "Four days ago, about this hour, I was keeping the ninth hour of prayer in my house; and behold, a man stood before me in bright apparel, saying 'Cornelius, your prayer has been heard and your alms have been remembered before God.'" No more good luck, please. Let us invoke the blessing and get on with Acts 29!

Psalm 20:1-3 □ Psalm 20

They said to her, "You are mad." But she insisted that it was so. They said, "It is his angel!"

Peter's angel missed a terrific show. Pure comedy in the midst of tragedy. Herod Agrippa I, grandson of the Herod who ruled at Christ's birth, played quite the public charmer and religious patriot. His zeal branched out into persecution and James, beloved son of thunder, became the first apostle to suffer a martyr's death. Herod's popularity surge caused Peter's arrest just before the Passover. He was to taste the sword's blade right after.

The classic line now following must be read with an absolutely straight face, lest it come back to haunt us. "So Peter was kept in prison; but earnest prayer for him was made to God by the church." The night before his untimely demise and while he slept, the believers were gathered for prayers designed to storm the very gates of hell. Peter's angel promptly engineered a magnificent prison break. The prison gate swung open on its own accord. One block away God's secret agent vanished and Peter headed for the comfort of friends. Hard at prayer, they refused to be budged by the knock. Rhoda the maid ventured out to the gate door, heard Peter's voice, and in her wild joy forgot to let him in. While the speedy answer to their earnest prayer kept knocking, the believers argued back and forth with the maid that it could not possibly be Peter!

"It is his angel!" Do we have such earnest confidence today? Jesus believed in guardian angels. "See that you do not despise one of these little ones; for I tell you that in heaven their angels always behold the face of my Father . . ." (Matthew 18:10). Peter, finding himself in a "little" bit of trouble now and then, never argued with "Peter's angel."

Acts 12:15 □ *Acts 12:1-17*

The saying spread abroad among the brethren that this disciple was not to die; yet Jesus did not say to him that he was not to die, but, "If it is my will that he remain until I come, what is that to you?"

"This is the disciple who is bearing witness to these things, and who has written these things; and we know that his testimony is true. But there are also many other things which Jesus did; were every one of them to be written, I suppose that the world itself could not contain the books that would be written." *This* is John, beloved son of thunder, ending his illustrious interpretive gospel on this endearingly human note.

John was uneasy about His Lord being misquoted or quoted out of context. John gently admonished the reader to add up the works of the Savior and measure them against His words as mark of authenticity.

In a singularly touching scene on the beach one morning after the Resurrection, Jesus restored Peter to fellowship with Him. The disciple's three denials were offset by three professions of love. Each affirmation was crowned with the Lord's commission to feed His sheep. Peter, undoubtedly in his glory, was then taken into an even deeper camaraderie with His beloved Master. Jesus prophesied that he was to glorify God by death on a cross "when you are old." (He was crucified around 67 A.D.) "And after this he said, to him, 'Follow me.'" Peter turned and saw John following at a distance. "Lord, what about this man?" None of your business, Peter. Just concentrate on following me!

The "saying" that spread abroad among the brethren that John was to be exempted from dying would naturally raise a host of speculations. New doctrines might have to be formulated to answer questions satisfactorily. Such works take time and energy. Meanwhile, who is doing the "greater works" of Christ? The "sayings" should be solely stretched along that line!

John 21:23 □ *John 21:20-24*

Truly, truly, I say to you, he who believes in me will also do the works that I do; and greater works than these will he do, because I go to the Father.

In a Bible-believing church where witness clicks with proclamation, there should be miracle workers! The deity of Christ, not doctrinal juggling, determines their ranks. We take our clue neither from holy roller nor scholar who relegates miracles to the apostolic age. Our text reveals no labels, no qualifiers. Truly — the one "string" attached is the umbilical cord of the Holy Spirit that links the child of God to His workings.

"Truly, truly, I say to you, the Son can do nothing of his own accord, but only what he sees the Father doing; for whatever he does, that the Son does likewise. For the Father loves the Son, and shows him all that he himself is doing; and greater works than these will he show him, that you may marvel. For as the Father raises the dead and gives them life, so also the Son gives life to whom he will" (John 5:19-21).

The word *miracle* comes from the Latin "to wonder," "to smile." Watch young children during a puppet show! Their faces perfectly mirror the "marvel" of our birthright in Christ. They know the characters on stage are "worked" by their creator. But as the puppets "live and move and have their being" in the storyteller, they miraculously overcome their inherent limitations. Bursting into an exciting life of their own, they have the small fry on edge as they identify with the struggling hero. Such relief to know that one tug of a string by a powerful grownup can halt the antagonist's antics. Miracle workers promote the art of wondering. I wonder what Jesus could do in this situation? I wonder if I should go lay hands on my sick co-worker? I wonder if someone from church would pray with me for guidance? Is anything too hard for God?

John 14:12 ☐ *John 14:1-14*

What must we do, to be doing the works of God?

Jesus forced their question. The crowds dogged His every footstep hoping to be regaled with signs. A new spectator sport had evolved around His person. Jesus had to stop their fascination with performance and challenge them to faith in His person. He invited active participation in His kingdom. He still does!

Christ's simple answer was a shocker. It turned gleeful gawkers into grumblers who left Him by the thousands.

"Truly, truly . . . you seek me, not because you saw signs, but because you ate your fill of the loaves. Do not labor for the food which perishes, but for the food which endures to eternal life, which the Son of man will give to you; for on him has God the Father set his seal." Now the crowd's curiosity peaked, "What must we do, to be doing the works of God?" The simple answer, "This is the work of God, that you believe in him whom he has sent." Their evasive reply, "Then what sign do you do, that we may see, and believe you? What work do you perform?" They boasted of the manna given by Moses to their wandering forebears. My Father gave it to them, Jesus gently corrected, and offered Himself as the true bread from heaven. A mass exodus followed.

What about the "greater works" Christ has challenged us to embrace? "Whatever you ask in my name, I will do it, that the Father may be glorified in the Son." Jesus is asking for prayer. It is not prayer as preparation or prelude to work. Prayer is the "greater works." Our Lord asks for nothing more — and nothing less — than such intimate oneness with Him that He might continue through us His love relationship with the Father; "for the Father is greater than I." No greatness, no proven worth, no ambitious plans on our part, just costly prayer. Jesus awaits our yes or no, now. We have exhausted the safe middle ground.

John 6:28 □ *John 6:22-40*

And he could do no mighty work there. . . . And he marveled because of their unbelief.

Could this be a decisive factor in our impotent church of today? Do we worship prestige and position? What if we had a Department of Miracles and called for a team of experts to assist with a special need? In order of preference we would expect the following: The naturally winsome pastor; the dynamic businessman-elder; the charming couple well known for their gracious home; the attractive deaconess radiating quiet completeness. What if a "bunch of little old ladies" convened on our doorstep instead?

Instant dismay! A little old lady's place is in the kitchen. The church kitchen. Stick her with the missionary tea and the hospital gift shop. Let her send used clothes to Indian reservations. But don't send little old ladies to the home reeling from leukemia, job loss or sex scandal! How Christ must sorrow for His "Gray Panthers" who could constitute a major power cell of any congregation because He has gained all of their time and devotion. What if any of those nondescript saints gave a "sign" and nobody came?

When Jesus came to His own country, contempt was heaped on Him because He had neither the prestige of higher education nor the advantage of exotic background. He was merely regarded as hometown kid putting on airs — an embarrassment and nuisance.

As the family of Christ in the home country of His church we unwittingly carry on with faithless familiarity. Those "little old ladies" stuffing hospital bags could do footwashing and marvelous signs — if by faith we opened ourselves to their ministry of prayer. Look around at the nondescript saints of any congregation! "Can anything good come out of Nazareth?"

Mark 6:5-6 □ *Mark 6:1-6*

Again I say to you, if two of you agree on earth about anything they ask, it will be done for them by my Father in heaven. For where two or three are gathered in my name . . .

The "sleeping giant of the church" will not fully stir to life until we mobilize into strategic prayer clusters. Jesus-style intimacy calls for our own "Peter, James and John." Gethsemane and the Mount of Transfiguration are for sharing. The valley of frustration demands companionship. Easter and Pentecost cry out for existential witness. Where two or three are conscientiously gathered in Christ's name, pious pretense or lazy ignorance cannot last.

No matter how pressing the needs and how frenzied the pace imposed by seekers, our Lord resolutely made time for fellowship with His disciples. As the professional church staff meets faithfully, so the congregation should know the power and satisfaction of regular "staff of life" meetings. The Bread of Heaven is at stake!

"Do not labor for the food which perishes, but for the food which endures to eternal life . . ." Consider how unquestioningly we follow the rules to obtain perishable food. The more demanding and rewarding our job, the more we invest our energy in it. We subscribe to trade publications, attend sales seminars, submit to tests and enroll in ongoing education programs. If nurse and accountant have to move along with the time, how can any Christian justify his stagnation with its paralyzing effect on the whole body?

No significant growth occurs in an individual's faith until he is exposed to the discipline and encouragement of fellow strugglers. If we say we love God and go it alone, we are an anomaly. Our Lord mandates the small, strategic prayer cluster. "Follow me!" He urgently needs to meet with the Peter, James and John that is today's man and woman of daring trust.

Matthew 18:19-20 □ *Matthew 18:15-20*

And immediately. . . . And immediately. . . . and immediately. . . . And at once his fame spread . . .

It pays to study Mark's gospel for the word "immediately" alone. It is used over forty times. Mark gives the distinct impression that where Jesus is actively involved there is nary a dull moment. Or do those honors go to Peter? Mark was in a small group with him! In fact, Peter's reminiscences of life with Jesus evolved into the gospel according to Mark.

There is something infectious about "immediately" that must be savored and explored. There is a contagion of "action with accountability" that will save our small fellowship group from dying of dullness or terminal decorum. Perhaps we should drop all pretensions to religious propriety and like Peter and Mark — zestful kids at heart — operate straight from the principles of a fan club. Imitation is the sincerest form of flattery.

How do energetic youngsters run their fan club devoted to a movie idol? They discuss the star's various pictures, referring with affection to vintage films, and arranging to go see the latest work. They gladly sacrifice differences to identify as closely as possible with their adored subject and each other.

Jesus Christ is worthy of such eagerness and excitement! The "vintage footage" of the gospels fuels our imagination sufficiently to picture His newest works. In fact, we can have starring roles; Mark's action-packed script contains a fully developed servant theme. Jesus is always the leading man of action. Our prayer group holds us accountable. Immediately after announcing our good intentions, we carry them out. Immediately Christ's joy floods us. Immediately we long to report back that "it worked." And at once Christ's fame spreads and we cannot share His works enough!

Mark 1:18,20,21,28 □ Mark 1:1-31

Therefore every scribe who has been trained for the kingdom of heaven is like a householder who brings out of his treasure what is new and what is old.

Why is there no gospel according to Peter? He had the position and disposition to write one. Peter was uniquely treasured by his Lord. He was the historic preacher and interpreter of Pentecost. His prominent leadership in the church steered the course of inclusiveness so essential to Christ's command to go into all the world.

His two epistles exhibit the broad sweep of his pastoral heart. They tip us off to his passion for sharing his personal knowledge and experience of Jesus. "I think it right, as long as I am in this body, to arouse you by way of reminder, since I know that the putting off of my body will be soon, as our Lord Jesus Christ showed me. And I will see to it that after my departure you may be able at any time to recall these things."

How? Mark, Peter's son in the faith, wrote a unique portrayal of the Servant King. Was Peter aware to what extent his reminiscences were "worked" into a lasting memorial? He could not possibly envision that in all four gospels he would become the most prominently featured disciple in terms of recorded dialogue with Christ and give-and-take in personal relationship.

Whatever Peter had in mind for his memorial, of this he could be confident: His life had found the mark. The mark was Jesus Christ. Who is our Mark? Has our life found its mark? The "scribe who has been trained for the kingdom of heaven" may well be the minister who conducts our memorial service. What treasure will he reveal to the assembled household and guests on behalf of the "householder," who is the Lord God Himself?

Matthew 13:52

. . . he called to the man clothed in linen, who had the writing case . . . "Go through the city . . . and put a mark upon the foreheads of the men who sigh and groan . . ."

Aaron the high priest wore linen garments. From his linen turban hung a sign of pure gold that touched his forehead proclaiming, "Holy to the Lord." In Ezekiel's vision of Jerusalem's destruction, such a priest anointed with salvation all who sorrowed over sin. To the executioners following the man with the "writing case," the Lord's instructions were unsparing and pitiless, "Slay old men outright, young men and maidens, little children and women, but touch no one upon whom is the mark. And begin at my sanctuary."

The mourners gathered in the sanctuary know they are vulnerable. Death is looking them over. Who will be next? How will the mortal blow be struck? As the priest lays eternal life on the line for the sad saint and struggling sinner, what distinguishing mark do we want attached to our life? Shall he glorify the Christ of the Jerusalem confrontation or the corpse of the "Tyre" self-exaltation? "Now you, son of man, raise a lamentation over Tyre. . . . 'O Tyre, you have said, "I am perfect in beauty". . . . Of fine embroidered linen from Egypt was your sail, serving as your ensign. . . . The merchants among the peoples hiss at you; you have come to a dreadful end and shall be no more for ever.'" The proud coffin ship!

If we have set sail to the wind of the Holy Spirit, let the good news be extolled! Let there be just enough of "our" Peter to honor the love affair with Jesus. Hail above all the mark of the cross so that life will spread out from the sanctuary! Let this be the mourner's parting cry, "May we shout for joy over your victory, and in the name of our God set up our banners! May the Lord fulfill all your petitions!" A priest in grave linen? Yes, Jesus Christ!

Ezekiel 9:3-4 □ *Ezekiel 9*

Be the more zealous to confirm your call and election . . . so there will be richly provided for you an entrance into the eternal kingdom of our Lord and Savior Jesus Christ.

Is "natural" death an option like natural childbirth? Is our birth into heaven a labor of love worthy of our positive participation? To what extent do fear and drugs inhibit the spontaneous process? Can exercise and correct breathing aid a smooth passage? Having zealously confirmed our call and election, are we the "full-term" child of God ready to be delivered to Him? Is the "entrance richly provided" for us the fully dilated birth canal that signals nature's eager cooperation?

The rebellion leading to natural childbirth was not only against the drugs that depress the respiratory center in the baby's brain, but against the Genesis curse of fear and pain. The natural birth process as such is a marvel of cooperation. Maternal blood volume is up as much as twenty-five percent; the heart becomes slightly larger. The mouth of the womb grows soft; muscle fibers in the birth canal become elongated for maximum elasticity. The baby's head bones slide to adapt to narrow passage. The Fall did not annul the Creator's "engineering" marvel. Removed from God's harmonious intent and healing presence, Adam and Eve inflicted their dis-ease of mind on the delicately tuned body, much to its detriment.

"Perfect love casts out fear." Because of our Redeemer's atoning work, "natural" death is a viable option. The expectant mother is counseled to regard labor as work, not primarily pain. Our "birthing" into heaven should receive similar positive encouragement. There is the strengthening work of prayer; the concentrated breathing in and out of the Holy Spirit; the conscious focusing on the loving, waiting hands of God. "Father, into thy hands I commit my spirit!" The supreme joy will not delay!

2 Peter 1:10-11 □ *2 Peter 1:3-11*

O death, where is thy sting?

The young pregnant wife is sooner or later struck by the awesome realization that there is no turning back. Powerful forces are sculpting an unknown future right under her eyes. One brief act of self-surrender has imposed a bondage for life. In a climate of love, the mystery of bonding takes place. Where emotions are starved, a woman feels trapped. Without Christ, death is to be dreaded as the ultimate trap. Loved by Him, the reality of bonding translates into succinctly stated truth, "For me to live is Christ, and to die is gain."

Nominal Christians are especially fond of quoting the twenty-third Psalm. Beware, let not "valley of the shadow of death" lore become the "hard labor" lore of old wives' tales. Balance the poetry of subtle palpitations with the hard-nosed reality of Paul's passion, "My desire is to depart and be with Christ, for that is far better. . . . We are of good courage, and we would rather be away from the body and at home with the Lord." There are subtle shadings that can make us stick with the status quo or break new ground of sacred discovery!

"O death, where is thy sting?" If the macabre corpse-and-casket circus gives us the creeps, we have intelligent choices today. Is the sting our fear of the unknown? "I am the resurrection and the life." A vigorously maintainted focus on His person anchors us firmly to Christ's companionship. Do we agonize over the actual moment of death? "And as they were stoning Stephen, he prayed, 'Lord Jesus, receive my spirit.' And he knelt down and cried with a loud voice, 'Lord, do not hold this sin against them.' And when he had said this, he fell asleep." Take a deep breath of the Holy Spirit and ask yourself, "O death, where is thy sting?"

1 Corinthians 15:55 □ *1 Corinthians 15*

LORD, let me know my end, and what is the measure of my days; let me know how fleeting my life is!

Forget the poetic musings. Be a pragmatist. Home, family, career, community, country — they all convey an illusion of solid investment. There is a sure test to measure the shaky ground we walk on. Take Paul's classic statement, "For me to live is Christ, and to die is gain." In place of Christ insert the more common passions of sports, music, travel or gardening. Restate to yourself your own favorite pastimes in this manner: For me to live is golf, and to die is loss. For me to live is politics, and to die is loss. For me to live is family, and to die is loss.

Join the gathering of friends at the home of the new widower. It is alive with the dead wife's touch. You expect her to step out of the kitchen momentarily. Such eerie flashes of unreality evaporate quickly. Conversation naturally turns to braces, elections, restaurants, weed killer. The next gathering celebrates a first wedding anniversary and the next the birth of a grandchild. And always life hums its busy tune and our laughter and tears are swept under in the headlong rush of time.

Asked how he would spend the day before Christ's assured return, a serene Martin Luther replied, "I would go right ahead and plant my little apple tree." To be deeply centered in Christ is no morbid fixation that heaves lead into the joyously spinning wheels of life endowed with His common grace.

"None of us lives to himself, and none of us dies to himself. If we live, we live to the Lord, and if we die, we die to the Lord; so then, whether we live or whether we die, we are the Lord's. For to this end Christ died and lived again, that he might be Lord both of the dead and of the living" (Romans 14:7-9).

Psalm 39:4

He charged them not to depart from Jerusalem, but to wait for the promise of the Father . . .

Wait! "It is not for you to know times or seasons which the Father has fixed by his own authority." Wait, said Jesus, for the Honored Guest at the surprise party planned by God.

W-a-i-t a minute! With us in Christ's shoes on the day of Ascension, no gift of completeness would have been promised. Grimly rolling our eyes heavenward, we would have groaned, "Okay, fellows, back to the drawing board!" Consider their parting gift to the long-suffering Teacher, "Lord, will you at this time restore the kingdom to Israel?" At this pivotal point the King headed a party of bungling politicians.

Wait. At the "surprise party" the bungling learners (disciples) would become the decisive delegates (apostles) of the King. Before ascending He restated His revolutionary rule, "Thus it is written, that the Christ should suffer and on the third day rise from the dead, and that repentance and forgiveness of sins should be preached in his name to all nations, beginning from Jerusalem. You are witnesses of these things." On Pentecost the harvest of His teaching would become activated and discernible in His followers.

Wait! Three days from Good Friday to Easter; 50 days from Passover to Pentecost — a mere snap when measured against most seasons of waiting. Employing the mode of worship, the mood of joyous expectance expands. When whittling away at time, strange things can happen. Take triskaidekaphobia! The fear of number 13 originates in the thirteenth apostle who replaced traitorous Judas. Waiting, itching for action, Peter worked completeness from where he perceived obvious lack. An election was held to restore the image of "the twelve." Scripture is silent on this particular "thirteenth." Where does Matthias, the ignored apostle, fit in with us?

Acts 1:4 □ *Acts 1*

And the twelve . . . said, "It is not right that we should give up preaching the word of God to serve tables. Therefore, brethren, pick out from among you seven . . ."

The seven deacons all had Greek names; the Hellenist widows would no longer suffer discrimination during food distribution. Selected for practical service, the seven made for their own surprises. "Stephen, full of grace and power, did great wonders and signs among the people." Philip "the evangelist" completely obscured Philip the apostle.

After the Ascension the disciples returned to the upper room and engaged in prayer. Peter, emerging as leader, studied the Word. The very humanity governing Peter's next move is evident in the writer of Acts. His studies convinced Peter that Judas Iscariot needed to be replaced. "Let his habitation become desolate. . . . His office let another take."

Well-meaning Peter suggested an election in which lots were to be cast. Two candidates were put forward, prayers said, and Matthias emerged as the winner. Recognition begins right here. How often do we engineer circumstances, tell God to bless the *fait accompli*, and off we go — into the wild blue yonder! Did He quietly bless Peter's blunder? The man must have worked out in his own, unassuming way. If a "Simon the Zealot" never made it as household word, the Bible's silence on Matthias should not be taken as ominous sign.

Scripture, however, is emphatic in its witness that Christ personally chose His apostles. Of Saul of Tarsus He testified, "He is a chosen instrument of mine." Paul, often having to defend his authority, would pointedly call himself "an apostle of Jesus Christ by the will of God." Peter surely jumped the gun on Matthias. Undoubtedly he qualified by virtue of having witnessed the Resurrection. He was first and foremost a forgiven sinner. Is not that what ultimately counts? Being a legitimate apostle did not save Judas.

Acts 6:2-3 □ *Acts 6*

Jesus answered them, "Did I not choose you, the twelve, and one of you is a devil?"

Careful now. Judas may find himself in good company still. Jesus addressed the paragons of respectability in our crowd when He warned, "Not every one who says to me, 'Lord, Lord,' shall enter the kingdom of heaven." Our concept of mighty works and name-dropping might backfire as well. The prospect is not pretty. "Depart from me, you cursed, into the eternal fire prepared for the devil and his angels; for I was hungry and you gave me no food . . ." Jesus also was thirsty, a stranger, naked, sick and in prison. His lowly sisters and brothers are all around us. The unwelcomed stranger may be called Matthias, or have a Russian surname, or be an illegal alien. An occasional can of fruit cocktail does not still hunger. Diatribes against lenient judges do not comfort Jesus in prison. Charity balls bring no cheer to the nursing home patient.

Although we might well be "sons of disobedience," we treat the "son of perdition" as an isolated, cut-and-dried case. He is perceived as an actor predestined to play his part in a fixed plot. Or else he is portrayed the misguided patriot who hoped to force his Master's hand in overthrowing the Romans. Not quite.

As a member of Christ's elite team Judas was given "power and authority over all demons and to cure diseases . . . to preach the kingdom of God and to heal." From Kerioth in Judah, he was the only non-Galilean. Yet he was elected treasurer of the group. In their solidarity, conscious of their own frailties, his comrades never voiced suspicion when Jesus hinted at betrayal. When Mary anointed Him with her costly nard and Judas shrilly decried the waste on behalf of the poor, John identified him as known thief. Yet at the Passover when Jesus forced the issue of impending treachery, giving Judas his last chance to come clean, the sorrowful disciples "began to say to him one after another, 'Is it I, Lord?'"

Ambition and avarice soured Judas on Jesus' modest kingly goals. The novelty of being different wore off. An empty man hanged himself. Come Friday, the 13th, we better not think of bad luck. The hungry, the sick, the oppressed await our attention.

John 6:70

And the twelve were with him, and also some women . . .
who provided for them out of their means.

How was that again? "Soon afterward he went on through
cities and villages, preaching and bringing the good news of the
kingdom of God. And the twelve were with him, and also
some women who had been healed of evil spirits and infirmities: Mary, called Magdalene, from whom seven demons had
gone out, and Joanna, the wife of Chuza, Herod's steward, and
Susanna, and many others, who provided for them out of their
means."

Some women! Time to explode some myths about the
women in Christ's life. We picture them a pious, nondescript
lot in their drab Palestinian garb — blending in with the sand
and shadows — self-effacing sheep. It comes as a shock to discover that Jesus delighted in His women and saluted their self-
esteem. They have everything in common with today's vibrant
woman who asserts herself in becoming broken bread on
behalf of her Lord.

Take Joanna, the wife of Chuza, Herod's steward. If we
could only interview her! But she is off to the bank, withdraw-
ing more money to help finance the traveling show of the
Galilean who is attracting such notoriety that his own family is
up in arms. Yet Joanna is traipsing right after him, along with a
bunch of adoring females who are also neglecting their duties
and friends at home. Is a husband not entitled to some consideration? Joanna talks about God every chance she has while at
home, but what happened to fun? One of these days this independent wife's shenanigans will cause her husband problems at
work!

God knows Chuza has a rough job being Antipas' business
manager. God knows Chuza could use a devoted wife at home.
The Galilean talks about love and good news. Ever since
Joanna came under His spell, Chuza's comforts have been going down the drain. When will she get tired of dusty roads and
smelly crowds? When will she stop throwing her money away?

Luke 8:1-3

Now when the Pharisee who had invited him saw it, he said to himself, "If this man were a prophet, he would have known who and what sort of woman this is who is touching him . . ."

"And Jesus answering said to him, 'Simon, I have something to say to you.'" What the sinless Son of man said to the Pharisee He needs to repeat to the paragon of perfection today who practices slavish adherence to the letter of the law regarding the status of women. High moral standards, yes. Cold, religious blackmail, no. The churched wife is put on a pseudo-pedestal as her husband's adornment. The chaste single is relegated to a desexed sub-group from which nothing but quiet good deeds are to issue. The sexually active woman suffers instant condemnation.

The woman touching Him was a "sinner" — a euphemism for "sexually active." Was she prostitute, nymphomaniac, or the daughter of prominent people living with her boyfriend? Scripture is silent. But Simon the Pharisee can be read like an open book. He stereotypes her as a loose woman. As he watches her every move, the way her hands glide and her body gracefully bends, he knows she has a way with men. He can tell, because Mrs. Simon displays none of the lady's obvious sexual charms. With Mr. Punctilious passionately performing his righteousness, he is a perfunctory lover. There is little warmth or spontaneity, no true intimacy to enable Mrs. Simon to risk herself fully in love. Simon despises the "sinner" for two reasons. He yearns for the touch of those experienced hands. Deep inside he cries for his own emptiness. Jesus, the Perfect Lover, is so much at ease with the woman!

Hear, coldly correct one: "I tell you, her sins, which are many, are forgiven, for she loved much; but he who is forgiven little, loves little."

Luke 7:39 □ *Luke 7:36-50*

And he whom you now have is not your husband . . .

"The church is not a museum for saints, but a hospital for sinners." Beyond the triteness — and smugness — what truth emerges? The hospital exists as diagnostic facility and aggressive treatment center. The surgeon — with the patient's consent — attacks cancer.

Every person enters church at such calculated risk. The moment we enter God's house we signal both our weakness and longing for perfect health. As "consenting adults" we sign away our right to self-determination. The Holy Spirit diagnoses our specific ills. Jesus Christ is the surgeon who must make the life-saving recommendation, "If your right hand causes you to sin, cut it off . . ." The hospital is a hurting and healing place.

Cohabitation — the new darling of consenting adults — is a cancer of lawlessness that continues to spread. As societal problem it seemingly dead ends in the dilemma of what to call the "roommate." The accurate term is "fornicator." Fornication — sexual intercourse other than between husband and wife — is closely linked with idolatry in Scripture. Playing the "harlot" we are in effect telling God to His face that He is unwilling or incapable to satisfy our needs. It is not a crime committed with genitals, but with unbending knees and self-ruled heart.

The Perfect Lover does not force His way. He gently creates the climate of intimacy that allows truth to penetrate and bear fruit. Jesus enabled the woman at the well to thirst for ultimate satisfaction. When she asked for it, He confronted her with the unlawful lover. Christ cannot condone sexual sin; will not compete with self-rule that allots Him our manhood or womanhood from the neck up. For the sake of wholeness and holiness we must choose between committed Lover and uncommitted sexual partner sooner or later!

John 4:18

No one born of God commits sin; for God's nature abides in him, and he cannot sin because he is born of God.

The language is explicit. Spiritual rebirth — the process of growing into the likeness of Christ — begins with an act of love. When we surrender our will to His wooing, God's reality penetrates deeply and deposits His seed within us. The Greek word is *sperma*! From that point in time we reproduce with the family likeness favoring God's side. "No one born of God commits sin" means that we no longer deliberately engage in habitual sin. Sin is not moral laxity per se, but separation from God. Because the Holy Spirit has mastered "genetic engineering," the seed of God in us guarantees that His nature will abide and prevail.

The rising phenomenon of "living in sin" has cut across all social strata and achieved a modicum of respectability at a time when skyrocketing divorce undermines the validity of marriage. Perhaps it is not so much a matter of casual sex as a frantic commitment to make the most of the tasty morsels snatched from crumbling life in general. It is indeed crumbs when held up to the living Bread of Jesus Christ. How can the church communicate such stern, sacred truth to starry-eyed young lovers, decent senior citizens sharing bed and board from financial consideration, or the winsome, sensitive "consenting adults" who have survived divorce or other forms of rejection?

"By this it may be seen who are the children of God, and who are the children of the devil: whoever does not do right is not of God, nor he who does not love his brother." In loving the struggler whose guide can no longer be a culture-conditioned conscience, we must imitate Jesus, the perfect Lover. Where there is resistance, let us not commit spiritual rape with our forceful convictions. Let the cross penetrate gently. God is for the sinner!

1 John 3:9 □ *1 John 3:1-10*

Let those who have wives live as though they had none . . .

Let temperate Peter reintroduce us to Paul, the oft maligned and misquoted marriage counselor. "Therefore, beloved . . . count the forbearance of our Lord as salvation. So also our beloved brother Paul wrote to you according to the wisdom given him, speaking of this as he does in all his letters. There are some things in them hard to understand, which the ignorant and unstable twist to their own destruction, as they do the other scriptures."

Some religionists make sport of growing in the grit and knowledge of monolithic Pauline teaching on the battle of the sexes. Their canon law of womanhood resembles a cannonade. Retaliating militant feminists burn their spiritual bras for shock value. The Jesus of the Good News throws a monkey wrench into the meticulously crafted "chain of command" so dear to paragons of male virtue. To the bristling feminist who defiantly prays, "Our Parent who are in heaven . . ." the Person of God might well say, "If your right eye causes you to sin, pluck it out and throw it away . . ."

In Galatians, the Magna Carta of Christian liberty, Paul makes his most revolutionary statement, "For as many of you as were baptized into Christ have put on Christ. There is neither . . . male nor female, for you are all one in Christ Jesus." As the Gentile did not have to wear a foundation garment of Jewish prerequisites, so the woman who has put on Christ does not have to squeeze herself into the corset of male chauvinism. As for the tone of Paul's letter to Corinth, we do well to remember that it was the Los Angeles of his day. In a polluted climate of "anything goes" a measure of stringency was needed.

What is the gist of Paul's text? "For the form of this world is passing away!" Wear it lightly! Whoever you are, whatever you do, be above all passionately in love with Jesus Christ.

1 Corinthians 7:29 □ *1 Corinthians 7:25-38*

For no man ever hates his own flesh, but nourishes and cherishes it, as Christ does the church . . .

"'For this reason a man shall leave his father and mother and be joined to his wife, and the two shall become one flesh.' This mystery is a profound one, and I am saying that it refers to Christ and the church." Some men grow up as orphans. Not every woman marries. The ideal script cannot always be followed. No matter what the mate or no-mate situation, every human being has a resident need to belong and give of self in an intimate setting. To the lonely seeker Paul makes a startling proposal: As Christ's lover, become married through Him to His church!

Many of us carry on a permanent engagement. We have a date once a week and feel fondness. We go for the "flowers and candlelight" mood of church as an end in itself, never dreaming that it should be the prelude to real passion. We are not "pure" in that sense, only incredibly dull. There *are* marital delights to be had. Never mind the basic "missionary position" of staid church life. The cherishing and nourishing of the body invites joyous creativity.

In this mystery of marriage to the church, two imperatives are at the heart of Paul's teaching. One comes double-barreled out of the canon of First Corinthians: "I urge you, then, be imitators of me." "Be imitators of me, as I am of Christ." Our primary identification must be with Jesus as Lord of the church; His person alone merits passion. The second heart cry of Pauline writing is, "Be filled with the Spirit." It implies a continuing process. Keep falling in love with Christ. Keep submitting to Him or you cannot joyfully present your body "a living sacrifice."

Marriage, humanly speaking, entails tedium, loss of privacy, and bondage unimagined by the yearning unmarried. For the privilege of shared bedroom there are mushrooming responsibilities ranging back and forth between the trivial and traumatic. Marriage keeps being a celebration only if we purposely keep falling in love with our mate and draw strength from this essential commitment. This mystery of mundane, marvelous union translates into our relationship with Jesus and His body, the church. How He yearns for those who will nourish and cherish it as their own!

Ephesians 5:29 □ *Ephesians 5:21-33*

Come away by yourselves to a lonely place, and rest a while.

Where is our lonely place? Our quiet apartment? The crowded restaurant? The bus bench after church on Sunday? Perchance the marriage bed? No human being is exempted from loneliness. Instead of plotting escape, what if we embraced it?

Few people enjoy their primitive fear of the dentist. Most opt for Novocain to deaden the nerve-racking ordeal of drilling. But once in a while a favorable doctor-patient relationship allows for timidity to venture forth into trust and by mututal agreement the anesthetic is dropped. With our defense-mechanism shifted from automatic to manual, an adventure of self-discovery develops.

Pressed into the plastic embrace of the lounge chair, we receive a rare anatomy lesson. The heart is a heavy sloshing mass spiked with jumping beans. Its native range is between fluttering stomach and pounding ears. An apprehensive mind makes for rigid muscles and cramps. By the time we wonder about rigor mortis, the grinning professional tells us to gargle and glory in great cooperation. Glorious good riddance to wooden jaw and foam rubber lips!

We all want to come into our own and be fully at home with the right person, place and position in life. Married or single, young or old, our unfulfilled yearnings trigger feelings of inadequacy which we swathe in loneliness. What if we discovered rest in it? Stretch out consciously and put your defenses on manual. Sift through the wishful thinking, the built-up resentments, the outward things that cannot be changed. Befriend yourself in the sorrows that become more gentle with time, but will never quite go away. Strength and self-respect flow from endurance salted with wisdom. Courageously lonely, we discover the ministry of silent identification with our Lord. "He came unto his own, and his own received him not." How eloquent the heart language that can quietly say, "Lord, I know."

Mark 6:31

Whoever humbles himself like this child, he is the greatest in the kingdom of heaven.

The traveling salesmen for the Kingdom Co. are restless. Their very product indicates that lower-echelon jobs can be traded for top-management positions. Scurrying up and down imaginary ladders to explore the heights within the corporate structure, exciting promotions are spotted. A meeting with the president is requested. Picture the salesmen in their smart suits and correct ties, jutting out the jaw at just the right angle to convey an image of executive caliber. "Sir, we were wondering about those juicy plums at the top as the crowning fruit of our labor . . ." While they discreetly dab at their moist brow and the chin stained by imaginary plum juice, an executive vice-president happens to be nearby and is introduced to the salesmen. "Gentlemen, this is what executive caliber looks like!" A hug and a wink confirm his superior status.

It is easy for us to laugh now at those salesmen jockeying for position in the plum orchard. They deserve credit for asking an honest question, not afraid to risk their humanity with the Lord who knew and loved them so well. These men had sacrificed family, friends and jobs to trudge all over the countryside in proclamation of a kingdom at once powerful and yet shaky. Jesus talked about suffering and death with increasing urgency. A favorable peek into the future, if not the vying for plums, was understandable.

Where does the demonstration of humility check our ambitions? What does the child so honored by Christ teach us? The little boy was available. He allowed himself to be loved without questioning. He had nothing to offer in return except his innate eagerness and trust. He lived exuberantly in the here and now. We can have a splendid second childhood for the asking!

Matthew 18:4 □ *Matthew 18:1-4*

But to all who received him, who believed in his name, he gave power to become children of God . . .

The child born into a loving family takes an awful lot for granted. Food, shelter, clothing, schooling, vacations, spending money, future inheritance — the inalienable right to think of himself as the pride and joy not only of his parents, but all the generations of the extended family.

The joke goes that on Sunday we pray "Our Father" and during the week we act like orphans. We should laugh so hard until we cry. In Jesus Christ we have been offered adoption into the family of God. "Truly, I say to you, unless you turn and become like children, you will never enter the kingdom of heaven." Within the natural family setting, do we use a ladder and squeeze in through a window to get to our second-story room? Do we starve when we are little because we cannot reach the food on the table? Are we not enthroned in a high-chair and waited on with consummate skill and loving devotion? If Jesus asks us to "turn" and become like children, He addresses our sin of separatism that mocks our natural sonship.

England's royal weddings should not so much awe as jolt us into a fresh realization of our own infinitely superior royal heritage. Believing in the name of the House of Windsor and receiving its heir apparent, the bride naturally submitts to her new privileged status. Neither household nor the adoring, skewering public will let her forget the pleasure and pain of irreversible choice.

With the models of common family life and royalty in a contemporary setting, we can certainly draw parallels to our existence as children of God. Do we have the confidence of a cherished child or a celebrated princess? Do we resemble groveling beggars or conniving outsiders? We either call God "Abba! Father!" or "Liar." Shall we not turn from pretender to heir apparent?

John 1:12

Blessed are those servants whom the master finds awake when he comes; truly, I say to you, he will gird himself and have them sit at table, and he will come and serve them.

Let us assume that we received a personal invitation for a weekend at Windsor Castle. At Heathrow airport we will see the *Concorde* for starters. At Windsor we will marvel at the musket ball that killed Admiral Nelson at Trafalgar. The King's Closet houses Rembrandts. There is stunning St. George's Chapel with the tomb of Henry VIII and Lady Jane Seymour. From Norman conquest to Victoria's reign to twentieth-century gossip all will come alive at the historic castle. Enough pomp and circumstance to cry blimey and go bananas. Yankee enthusiasm must be reined; the Queen is to be addressed as "Ma'am."

On the Great Day a horse-drawn carriage awaits us at the outskirts of Windsor for the romantic approach to the castle, glorious with Gothic adornment. We are escorted to our private suite which rivals in splendor the State apartments. Then comes the call to dinner and our first glimpse of the Queen. Will she make a grand entrance in Waterloo Chamber, every inch the monarch of renown? We are ushered into a handsome private dining room. A friendly woman, dressed in pastel set off by a strand of pearls, assists the butler and serves the meal. Some of those present simply say, "Thank you, Mum." Some address her as "Aunt Lilibet." We never quite manage to stammer our "Ma'am." Memories of the historic setting and grandeur remain blurry forever. In shocked disbelief we keep pinching ourselves: I was personally served by the Queen of England!

Farfetched and silly? Not really. Come Thanksgiving time at heaven's family table the Lord of lords and King of kings will personally serve us!

Luke 12:37 □ Luke 12:35-40

And will not God vindicate his elect, who cry to him day and night? Will he delay long over them? I tell you, he will vindicate them speedily. Nevertheless, when the Son of man comes, will he find faith on earth?

Does it take the spectacular to convince us of God's Word of honor? Take a look at an average Thanksgiving menu: jellied gaspacho, sesame wafers, roast turkey with sausage-rice stuffing, fluffy stuffed sweet potatoes, creamed onions, broccoli *beurre noir*, cranberry-Waldorf salad with fruit dressing, rolls, butter, mincemeat pie, pumpkin tarts, coffee and milk of magnesia.

Such a meal is symbolic of God's bountiful goodness but — goodness gracious — we could not live by such promise day after day! And yet, the offering on the table teaches vital spiritual lessons. Nature itself attests to God's vindication of His own.

Take the apple sliced into the salad. It had to be brought from the north to lend its crunchy texture. The tree could not have yielded its excellent fruit had it not endured a season of severe cold. Does it not teach us to take our season of chilling sorrow in stride? Consider the patience of the tree that grew nut-meat in its hard shell. When we vainly hammer our fists against the hardness of God, could He be protecting a secret investment bringing delight to a special season? The lowly potato is of comfort to people who are rooted in God's love without concrete evidence of usefulness and feel "grounded." Tubers happen to thrive in dark, rich soil. Think of all the spiritual meat-and-potato men who will be fed. Tom Turkey may be the glamour boy of the feast, but look at the price of meteoric rise to fame. Who wants to be fattened — and flash-frozen!

When the Son of man comes, will He find faith on earth? Only if His elect keep gathering at His table, giving thanks for extraordinarily common bread and wine. Sacrament means pledge. If we eat and drink it we taste indeed that the Lord is good!

Luke 18:7-8 □ *Luke 18:1-8*

And when the town clerk had quieted the crowd, he said, "Men of Ephesus . . . you ought to be quiet and do nothing rash."

The town clerk talked turkey! He addressed himself in a practical and direct manner to the threat of spreading riot and broke it up single-handedly. A pagan and perhaps a bureaucrat, he saved "our boys" from harm and further inconvenience. What if we made the town clerk part of our Thanksgiving tradition?

To really get our act together on the big day we ought to set up some extra chairs in the place where we do our leisurely thinking and there enjoy people we have not "seen" in a long time. Do we ever really look at the unsung heroes who hold our world securely together — the anonymous men and women behind counters and in other places of routine service and dull duty? How quick we are to blast the sullen, inept clerk! What if we learned to quietly bless him or her? "And if you salute only your brethren, what more are you doing than others?" When have we last saluted the sanitation worker, the dry cleaner, the meat cutter, the civil servant and, yea, even the uncivil public servant?

How we take them for granted — the telephone operator, the street sweeper, the desk officer at the police station, the woman who scrubs toilets at the airport. Are some of our "servants" who offend with bored looks and lackluster performance the victims of a dehumanizing process to which we contribute? A smile, a small compliment, an exhibit of patience as the fruit of the Holy Spirit might splash some color into a drab world made more discouraging by the dour, demeaning people they are stuck with. A despised tax collector wrote the gospel according to Matthew! As we learn to give thanks for the overlooked people, let us recover courtesy as the overlooked Christian virtue. As Jesus Christ's band of initiative lovers we are to wear discernibly the fragrance of His name.

Acts 19:35-36 ☐ *Acts 19:23-41*

For he makes his sun rise on the evil and on the good, and sends rain on the just and on the unjust.

Christians sometimes deserve public hostility. Rejection on Christ's behalf is one thing, to catch hell for thinly veiled bigotry quite another. No Christian has "favorite pet" status before God; we are His unique possession to declare His perfection.

Isaiah recorded basic truth for God's ancient chosen people. God not only made the earth, he said, but specifically formed it to be inhabited. (Isaiah 45:18) Indeed, from Genesis to Revelation writers push the idea of nations, an "inhabitant" concept that clashes with Lone Ranger religion. God, it seems, takes pleasure in people and created them with enough diversity to confound a cookie-cutter mentality. Peter, unaffected by secular humanism, but infectious with Christ, learned to say, "Honor all men" (1 Peter 2:17).

It is a timely admonition to guard against counterproductive us-against-them thinking. We need to laugh at ourselves more and take "them" more seriously. Our intensely introverted Christianity must convert to inclusive humanity — "for God so loved the world." In Christ He listened to people from all walks of life. He spoke their language, stayed at their places, and ate their food. The common bread and wine of common man became foremost sacrament.

Common grace calls for common sense. God forbid that His name should be dragged through the mud because we arrogantly promote sectarianism instead of saving grace. God does send rain on the just and the unjust. Guess who gets wetter? The just. (The unjust has the just's umbrella.) Let's laugh a little, love a bit more, and lavish God's sunshine on people from every nation, every tribe, every tongue. "Honor all men." Why give and catch hell when heaven clearly means to bless?

Matthew 5:45 □ *Matthew 5:43-48*

Therefore come out from them, and be separate from them . . .

A mother-in-law sweeps into her weak-willed daughter's wedlock on the train of her satin gown. She plops herself down in the couple's apartment like a piece of mahogany furniture with claw feet and Argus eyes — a sort of TV that watches you. In her opinion the daughter has made a poor choice and she stays there to rub it in until something gives.

"Do not be mismated with unbelievers." God clearly cares about our partnerships in private or public life. We are to love the world in terms of people. But we cannot become identified with its value systems. Whenever carelessness makes for divided loyalty, God must initially bear the brunt of rejection. But when we have come to the end of our rope and, by a frantic tug on His tether, signal our need to be back in His good graces, the acute suffering begins. After the exile many of Israel's finest took for themselves foreign wives and the cycle of misery — compromise, apostasy, judgment — was about to begin again. In a national move of repentance the troublesome alliances were dissolved and the women and children banished. What an incredible toll in suffering, yet from the historical perspective the cruelty was entirely justified. A similar kind of misery awaits the contemporary believer who does not separate himself from predictable traps and temptations.

The tenor of God's intervention is markedly different from that of a surly mother-in-law bent on a breakup. "I will live in them and move among them, and I will be their God, and they shall be my people." In Jesus Christ we know exactly what such grace-filled vigilance looks like. When will some of us drop the role of battle-axe?

The fragrance of Christ is "to one a fragrance from death to death, to the other a fragrance from life to life." We need not exude vinegar to announce our precious purity to the world.

2 Corinthians 6:17 □ 2 Corinthians 6:14-18

You are the salt of the earth . . .

Salt in the ancient East was a valuable trading commodity and as such heavily taxed. Shared freely, it was symbolic of hospitality and friendship. Of enduring nature, it signaled faithfulness and assumed a sacred role in ancient Hebrew worship. "With all your offerings you shall offer salt" (Leviticus 2:13).

Too much salt contributes to hypertension which the world does not need. Take the self-appointed "law enforcer" who religiously observes the maximum speed limit in the fast lane of the freeway. SMILE, GOD LOVES YOU! urges the bumper sticker. Choice epithets are hurled at him as nervous, angry drivers try darting in front of him. The seasoned saint will take his preaching act into the space next to the exit lane. Even there "grace enforcement" will cause him to cooperate with traffic. Salt and self-righteous obstinacy do not mix.

How do we get our salt into the world as purifying agent and preservative? Perhaps the vice squad is conducting a prostitution sweep and a few innocent bystanders land in the net. With whom does the embarrassed victim discuss her ordeal and what recourse should she choose when bail has been set? Forget the hassle and pay the fine, says a cynical world. But what if a Christian support team stands by her and makes it possible to "infiltrate" the system with prayer and empathy all around? Not only does God protect His own, but He delights in those who purposefully embrace the risks of mingling with "publicans and sinners." How can we know? Jesus Christ infiltrated His world in a hundred different ways to open our eyes to need and opportunity.

As God's New Covenant people we are to impart zestful flavor to our world in a hospitable manner. If we honor the shed blood of our Savior, we will cause no one high blood pressure. Salt does not call attention to itself!

Matthew 5:13

Blessed be he who enters in the name of the LORD!

Entry implies a point of departure and a purported destination. For the Christian it means to quit an empty, impotent life and through Christ infiltrate an evil world through His redeeming power. Scripturally speaking the progression in the name of the Lord might look like this: 1. "Let every one who names the name of the Lord depart from iniquity." 2. "I am the door; if any one enter by me, he will be saved, and will go in and out and find pasture." 3. "But you shall receive power when the Holy Spirit has come upon you; and you shall be my witnesses in Jerusalem and in all Judea and Samaria and to the end of the earth."

Paradoxically, many Christians never "enter." They are nominally identified with the "Door," but have not entered into personal relationship with Him. As a result they cannot enter into His peace and, from there, through the gate of His righteousness into the world. Consequently no risks, no conflicts, no contests, no races are entered into.

What plea do we enter to justify our stagnation which so pollutes the blessed name of our Lord? Lack of interest or time? Lack of understanding? To understand the abnormality of not "entering," consider marriage. A splendid wedding may have taken place with all the legal signatures in place. But if the bride's hymen has not been penetrated, the marriage is a put-on and not legally binding. If "entering" can be that crucial in the natural development of human affairs, how much more shall it matter in the kingdom of God!

Happy is he who enters in the name of the Lord! Outwardly we enter into the Christmas mood by going through certain motions. We put on Christmas music, put up decorations, and put out holiday invitations. If we hope to enter the heart of Christmas, we must rouse our will and put our faith into action.

Psalm 118:26 ☐ *Psalm 118:21-29*

I will proclaim the name of the LORD.

What is it that hinders our exercise of will in this most crucial of matters? We all have a hundred good excuses from A to Z; atrophy from disuse of spiritual muscle to zenophobia, which is the fear and hatred of anything strange or foreign. What if we had a hundred or so excellent reasons to overrule them? "O Lord our Lord, how excellent is thy name in all the earth;" Go ahead, choose some from among these appellations of our Lord Jesus Christ:

Advocate, Almighty, Anointed, Author and Finisher of Our Faith. Beginning and End of the Creation of God, Beloved, Bread of Life, Bridegroom, Bright Morning Star, Brightness of the Father's Glory. Carpenter, Chief Shepherd, Chosen of God, Consolation of Israel, Counselor. Day Star, Deliverer, Desire of All Nations, Door. Elect, Emmanuel, Eternal Life, Everlasting Father.

Faithful and True Witness, Foundation, Fountain, Forerunner, Friend of Sinners. Gift of God, Glory of Israel, God With Us, Good Master. Head of the Church, Heir of All Things, High Priest, Holy One of God, Hope. I Am, Image of God, Jehovah, Jesus of Nazareth, Judge. King, King of Kings, King of Glory. Lamb of God, Lawgiver, Leader, Life, Light, Living Stone, Lord of All.

Man of Sorrows, Master, Mediator, Messiah. Nazarene. Offspring of David, Only Begotten Son, Only Wise God. Passover, Physician, Prince of Peace, Prophet, Propitiation. Rabbi, Ransom, Redeemer, Resurrection, Righteous Judge, Righteous Servant, Rock of Offense, Rose of Sharon, Ruler. Salvation, Sanctification, Savior, Scepter, Servant of Rulers, Son of the Father, Son of Man, Sun of Righteousness, Teacher, Truth. Unspeakable Gift. Vine. Way, Wisdom, Wonderful, Word of God.

If we can match a good excuse to each of these "excellent reasons," we can indeed be excused.

Deuteronomy 32:3

*Let the words of my mouth and the meditation of my heart be
acceptable in thy sight, O LORD, my rock and my redeemer.*

"The Queen's Most Excellent Majesty" merits no more than
a cursory glance as a news item while sipping our coffee, unless
we drink tea as a loyal subject of the crown. Our interest
quickens even more if she is a friend — and if she happens to be
our mother . . . Lord, Rock, and Redeemer are nothing but
titles. As mere words of the mouth they have all the appeal of a
printed form letter. But as an expression of the heart, the words
"O Lord, my rock and my redeemer" are literally earthshaking.
How do we come into such power?

The psalms in particular offer vital clues. "Blessed is the
man who walks not in the counsel of the wicked, nor stands in
the way of sinners, nor sits in the seat of scoffers; but his
delight is in the law of the LORD, and on his law he meditates
day and night" (Psalm 1:1-2).

The thought of spending day and night in the Bible is a
boring prospect to most. Few people manage to read a chapter
fully alert. The idea of meditation is strange and foreign to us.
We envision saffron yellow robes and mantras. Eastern mysti-
cism aside, let us remember the testimony of others who
discovered bodily refreshment and expanded mental capacity
through discipline. Should not the Christian lay claim to a heritage of strength that has given songs to the saints of old?

Meditation takes time and initially hard work. Few of us
are naturally geared toward deep, continued reflection on a
single theme. Find a quiet place and lean back into a comfortable chair. Pretend to rest in the arms of God. Close your eyes
and picture a rock. Tether your wandering mind to this focus
and discipline it to produce positive mental images springing
from it. Thank your Redeemer for enabling you to say, "My
God! My Rock!" That is the secret power of sacred reflection.

Psalm 19:14 □ *Psalm 19*

The Preacher sought to find pleasing words, and uprightly he wrote words of truth.

"Besides being wise, the Preacher also taught the people knowledge, weighing and studying and arranging proverbs with great care." Writing down our thoughts of God is a skill well worth recovering. As the priesthood entrusted with the proclamation of His excellent name, we must avail ourselves of the disciplines that vitalize our witness. If quiet contemplation causes discouragement, we may have to make time for paper and pen.

Make time! The "habit" of God does not simply happen. If we say we have no time to develop it, we are less than honest. Intellectual laziness is rampant in an age where television spoon-feeds us a steady diet of mediocrity. How quick we are to pop a tape into the cassette player! Such enslavements keep us from getting to know God and, ultimately, ourselves. If we keep a spiritual journal even with only one entry every few days, we will look back in amazed gratitude on a record of steady growth. The habit of God must be cultivated one way or another. We cannot give Him our will and expect His Spirit to put us on painless "automatic control." Our will is ours for keeps — to be exercised regularly!

"But I cannot write!" While being spoon-fed as babies, we could not hold a spoon either. Practice with the pen may not make perfect, but it does work wonders. Did Jesus select His learners for their literary promise? Look what their habit of God and the Holy Spirit did for those Galilean fishermen! Our task is not to produce literature, but to toughen and enrich our thought life. Good News will inevitably come from it.

"For to us a child is born . . ." What if we sacrificed the specials on TV and surprised Him with a written gift of our mind? Perhaps a dear friend would not mind receiving our meditation for Christmas, instead of trifles.

Ecclessiastes 12:10 ☐ *Ecclessiastes 12:9-10*

My heart is steadfast, O God, my heart is steadfast! I will sing and make melody! Awake, my soul!

"I've got it! I've got it!" cried David as he grabbed a staid member of his startled war council and gave him a hug. At exactly the right moment, preparing for battle, David's disciplines came home to him as God's delight. Having practiced them diligently to proclaim His name in action, the psalmist received an immovable anchor of peace.

"I've got it! O God, I've got it!" The sooner we say it the better. "Why is your grandma staring into her Bible all day?" inquired a little guy of his friend. "She is cramming for her final," replied the precocious grandson. If during our heyday our Bible studies ranged between boredom and stopgap measure, a yawning gap may well open up at the end when life's final hurdle needs to be cleared. Choose now between anguish and anchor, panic and peace.

The Christian's last-minute cramming is wasted effort. We have no test scheduled and cannot be flunked. Jesus Christ took on our behalf the obedience course with its grueling finals. He passed them with flying colors — the blood-stained banner of Calvary. By neglecting our spiritual disciplines, we cheat Him out of our usefulness. Equally sad, we deprive ourselves of songs. How good of God to grant us the gift of an awakened soul in the morning watch. How great our growing repertoire of songs as we journey through the day of our life. Joyous songs, sad songs, funny and grand ones — all gathered into a jubilant paean of praise when heaven's trumpet flourish bids our soul to be united to the Day Star.

Stroll with your lover at night and look at the heavens. At first they appear as a blur. But then your eye becomes fixed on one particular brightness and from it you take your bearings. Now the firmament comes alive with the romance of the constellations. "My heart is fixed! O God, my heart is fixed!" Let it be fixed on the Christmas Star all the days of your life.

Psalm 108:1 ☐ *Psalm 108:1-4*

His tail swept down a third of the stars of heaven, and cast them to the earth.

"And the dragon stood before the woman who was about to bear a child, that he might devour her child when she brought it forth . . . but her child was caught up to God and to his throne. . . . And the great dragon was thrown down, that ancient serpent, who is called the Devil and Satan, the deceiver of the whole world — he was thrown down to the earth, and his angels . . . with him."

Why look at Satan during Advent? Because he means to have us coming *and* going. If he can enter us into the holiday rat race, our soul cannot rest in the Holy Day. When he and his sullied stars were evicted from heaven, they set up shop on earth to sell us their quick fix. To these "red devils" Christmas is their "Fourth of July" — the granddaddy of all independence celebrations — if they can tug at the right heartstrings. For this, Satan plays Uncle Sam with a sprig of holly and a dab of bayberry fragrance behind each ear.

Watch for the "stands" with patriotic bunting where the quick pops and bright flashes and smoke screens are pushed. Love and peace as seasonal sentimentality are perennial show-stoppers. Guilt erasure through gift extravaganza makes for nice glow. If Satan can accent mood and create dependence on it, his merry Christmas is in the bag. If Santa, decorations and parties can do the job, why be a stickler for the sacred? Church programs are supposed to take up the slack. The Christian tampering with tradition in search of a joyous Christmas appears un-American. Satan will accuse him of heresy. Unless we are fixed on Christ, we will fall into the guilt trap. The sacred cows of tradition have singularly soulful eyes, and their lowing rivals siren song. Holiday trappings are lovely, but not if they trap us into x-ing out the cross at the heart of Christmas. Christ was born to die for the sinner, not delude him.

Revelation 12:4 ☐ *Revelation 12*

On earth peace among men with whom he is pleased!

What makes for peace? Ask ten vocal people to contend for their precise definition and a war can be had on the spot. To the communist, peace means a piece of Asia, a piece of Africa. Because of him we have the militarist. Because of him we have the pacifist. Because of the two we have an inflamed home front. On the home front we have the card shop doing a landslide business in Christmas cards with a peace theme.

"Blessed are the peacemakers, for they shall be called sons of God." The number of people involved in court litigation has reached astronomical proportions. Any minor accident or mis-understanding has the potential of "recovering damages." Bah humbug on "Vengeance is mine, says the Lord." So much for peacemaking.

"In those days Jesus . . . was baptized by John . . . and a voice came from heaven, 'Thou art my beloved Son; with thee I am well pleased.'" To such, and to such alone, belongs the promise of peace heralded by the angels! In a sorrowful spirit of repentance we are to identify with our sinful world. If we wish to be identified with peace, the Prince of Peace must become incarnate in us. God's peace is a Person!

"And let the peace of Christ rule in your hearts . . ." Indwelled by the Holy Spirit, God "umpires" the things that disturb us. Some He removes with the peace that passes under-standing. Some He puts on our refreshed mind as catalyst for change. Entering "into" God's peace might well mean entering into human conflict, but guided by His wisdom and mercy. Perhaps we need to toss out the glamorous cards with their meticulously crafted symbols of peace. We may have to appear crumpled before God on our knees — crying to be made into the prince of peace with whom He is well pleased.

Luke 2:14 ☐ *Luke 2:8-14*

And you shall love the Lord your God with all your heart, and with all your soul, and with all your mind, and with all your strength.

You must love the Lord your God! We love Christmas. Awash in good feelings we affirm the many gestures of goodwill. But when weighed against Christ's foremost command, our activities reveal a hollow ring.

Why does the Lord's "must" reveal the hollow nature of our love just when we are doing our neighborly thing with a flourish? Our Christmas shopping and mailing tax mind, body and budget to the utmost. We help with bazaars and musical programs. Holiday entertaining is a must. How can we love God any harder? Are we not exhausting ourselves and our resources? Precisely, says Jesus Christ the Lord for all seasons.

"I am the way, and the truth, and the life; no one comes to the Father, but by me." Christ's chief commandment can be fulfilled by no one but Himself! Only the Holy Spirit can impart to us the nature of His loving. At Christmas, of all times, we must not be blackmailed into favoring counterfeit sentimentality over authentic love. Christ's sacrificial love seeks to give glory to God in the highest. "And I, when I am lifted up from the earth, will draw all men to myself." The one glory God yearns for is Christ's passion actualized in the believer. Only by the repeated infilling of His Holy Spirit do we receive power to give gifts that outlast the paltry conventional trinkets.

The seasonal outpourings of goodwill are reminiscent of the occasional newspaper story of a hungry family that triggers a bright flash of sympathy. But few people venture beyond the initial quickie response. When the reporters leave, hunger and hopelessness return with a vengeance. In tribute to the Lord our God, Jesus Christ invites us to run the Christmas race as His second-milers.

Mark 12:30 ☐ *Mark 12:28-34*

And if any one forces you to go one mile, go with him two miles.

In Christ Jesus we are to become a gift for all seasons to the Father's delight. How then do we rethink our conventional gift-giving? Kindness and custom force us to go the first mile of shopping for slippers, juicers, and popcorn poppers. How can the second mile tie in with the first?

"You shall love the Lord your God with all your heart . . . soul . . . mind . . . strength." If we do, we have no trouble drawing up a shopping list from the wealth of His Word. The next step is to giftwrap His promise in our own flesh. Then we are to give it away in a spirit of power and love. Perhaps the regular gift list will launch us on the "second mile" of adventure that follows hard on the heel of Advent.

Grandpa needs slippers. Christ wants him to have feet shod "with the equipment of the gospel of peace." The teenage dare-devil hints at a "brain bucket." Give him the "helmet of salvation," smiles Jesus. One daughter is smitten with jewelry. He is anxious for her to delight in the "imperishable jewel of a gentle and quiet spirit." Another daughter hankers for hang-glider lessons. Let her "mount up with wings like eagles." The budding musician moaning for amplifiers has an accomplice in Christ, "Sing to him a new song, play skillfully on the strings, with loud shouts." Somebody need a lamp? "Yea, thou dost light my lamp; the Lord my God lightens my darkness." Membership in a gym? "Yea . . . by my God I can leap over a wall."

Perfume? Try the fragrance of "the knowledge of him." Puzzle? "Ask . . . seek . . . knock." Aftershave lotion: "Your God has anointed you with the oil of gladness above your fellows." Sweets? "How sweet are thy words to my taste, sweeter than honey to my mouth!" The possibilities are endless, the promises sure. In Jesus Christ we can be all things to all people at the good pleasure of our glorious God.

Matthew 5:41

Be angry but do not sin . . .

Let the Christian be known by the quality of his anger as well as his love. The refreshing rain that washes the air of stifling heat knows flashing skies and thunderclaps.

Hot seasonal anger smolders in the long lines of fretful shoppers. The short-fused set off the sparks that trigger ugly flare-ups. The conscientious objector to store wars is known by his stony face. How blessed are Christ's peacemakers who have His compassion on crowds. No Christian worth his salt ignores the privilege of front-line duty while waiting in lines. A warm smile, a kind word, a funny observation can perfume a dozen shoppers with the presence of Jesus Christ.

Silent anger is unhealed anguish crusting over with indecision. The world's walking wounded as well as the saint can fall victim to it. Despair and despising may assault us at home where Christ is not real to those whom we love. Sacred hymns carelessly pumped into the "high places" of Mammon worship make us abjectly homesick for the God of our inner heart. At the same time we are heartsick over the garbage spreading its foul heat in our soul. Compressed layers of anguish and anger make for the combustion that is vented in rash words during our unguarded moments. Dare we unleash thunderbolts that clear the air of murky magnanimity?

"God is a righteous judge, and a God who has indignation every day" (Psalm 7:11). Sensitized to His righteous anger, we must endure the times of gathering storm. Let such anger burn brightly and make for the thunderclaps that release oppressed emotions. They need to be expressed in the clarifying compulsion of Christ's lordship. God's own anguish drives us back to the foot of the cross where forgiveness and positive action spring forth afresh. The cross never heals at the expense of buried feelings. Anger can be the glinting steel sunk deep into foundations where God means to build His kingdom from gritty courage, not sugar-laced gingerbread.

Ephesians 4:26

Then Paul said to him, "God shall stike you, you whitewashed wall!"

This definitely was worse than the Christian caught saying "dammit" during Christmas! At first Paul literally got carried away by Romans who rescued him from murderous Jews. The tribune mistook him for an Egyptian whose gang of 4000 called themselves The Assassins. Paul explained in Greek his Jewish roots. To the Jews he restated his Christian roots. Paul's love of roots paid off in evil. The confused tribune ordered him "examined by scourging." Out came Paul's Roman roots. Out came the Sanhedrin. Let his own kind get to the real root of the remarkable rabblerouser.

"And Paul, looking intently at the council, said, 'Brethren, I have lived before God in all good conscience up to this day.'" The high priest unceremoniously ordered him slapped on the mouth. Paul shot back at supercilious Ananias, "You stink to high heaven!"

The moment the stinging rebuke was out of his smarting mouth, Paul was struck by his own offense, "You shall not revile God, nor curse a ruler of your people." I did not realize, he said lamely, that I was talking to the high priest. Had failing eyesight or flaring temper impaired his judgment? His fighting instinct still intact, Paul quickly launched into the resurrection from the dead. Now he had the Sadducees and Pharisees at each other's throats. The Romans removed Paul by force from fear that the opposing factions would shred him in half. All this in the name of God and for the sake of the brethren in and out of the faith! Was Paul reprimanded?

"The following night the Lord stood by him and said, 'Take courage, for as you have testified about me at Jerusalem, so you must bear witness also at Rome.'" That is the shocking anger that earned Paul the promotion to Rome.

Acts 23:3 □ Acts 21:27-23:11

But you, gird up your loins; arise, and say to them everything that I command you. Do not be dismayed by them, lest I dismay you before them.

"And I, behold, I make you this day a fortified city, an iron pillar, and bronze walls . . ." (Fasten your seat belt, turn on the ignition, and I make you this day a tank.) His is the strong stuff that will brace and guard us against dismay. The unbelted, flowing garment of biblical times evokes images of comfort and leisure. When gathered at the waist with a "girdle," we recognize that the squeeze for action is on. God's Word demands work.

One learns best to gather courage and buckle down to confrontation by not second-guessing the outcome. The Holy Spirit fulfills the convicting ministry that honors Christ whether we taste success or defeat. Thanks to vindictive Jews and vacillating Romans, Paul arrived in Rome as Caesar's prisoner. After three days he sent for the local Jewish leaders. His soul-winning streak would simply not quit; the risk-taking had to continue. His notoriety had not preceded him, but Paul was perfectly willing to stir up a fresh batch of decision-forcing dissent. A day long appointment was made.

Predictably, emotions were stirred and the fires of dissent fanned. Paul, God's fortified city at the heart of the Roman Empire, appealed to the Holy Spirit. He struck the Jews with "thoughtfulness." Leaving quietly, each one was forced to contemplate within himself the dull ears, blind eyes, and willful heart of Isaiah's prophecy. From that day on Paul received a stream of eager visitors and shared Jesus Christ "quite openly and unhindered." To that glorious end God needs to press us on to our own Rome. He yearns for us to discover the comfort of Christ's garment of grace. It is girded with praise.

Jeremiah 1:17 □ *Jeremiah 1*

She followed Paul and us, crying, "These men are servants of the Most High God, who proclaim to you the way of salvation," And this she did for many days. But Paul was annoyed . . .

At Philippi two women prevailed upon Paul. One invited salvation, the other incurred his hot displeasure. They illustrate genuine conviction — the personal apprehending ministry of the Holy Spirit — versus "false arrest."

From Luke's brief account we discern the pattern of conviction that attests to Lydia's authentic conversion. Baptism implies that sins were confessed, repentance was sought and Christ's cleansing accepted. The references to Lydia's household and hospitality speak of honest interrelationships and genuine caring.

The scenario is reenacted with a different woman and an outcome that has us mystified for a few moments. "As we were going to the place of prayer," reports Luke, "we were met by a slave girl who had a spirit of divination and brought her owners much gain by soothsaying." Uninvited, she followed Paul's team like a sandwich board, advertising their ministry. In exasperation Paul finally spun around and arrested her unclean spirit on the spot. "I charge you in the name of Jesus Christ to come out of her." With this the free advertising stopped abruptly. Instead, all hell broke loose and the girl's enraged owners caused Paul's and Silas' arrest.

In similar incidents during Christ's ministry (Mark 1:25;5:8), we encounter the mystery of demons volunteering selective truth and making an outward show of worship. In each case Jesus arrested the false spirits and ended the demon-possession. We need only go into our own heart to become demystified. When we are bent on hiding a dark secret, do we not put on a show of exaggerated cheerfulness and busywork — lest someone grow wise during an unguarded moment and ask leading questions? In seizing the offensive outwardly, we confess our inner defenselessness. That is where the Spirit searches and finds us out — and delivers His ultimatum.

Acts 16:17-18 □ *Acts 16:11-24*

Preach the word, be urgent in season and out of season . . .

We make our preaching a matter of target practice instead of prevailing. We look at our fence-straddling friends and select for immediate consideration the most urgently looming problem. Joblessness, cussing, migraines. Then we rehearse for the suitable season. It never comes! Meanwhile we die the ten thousand deaths of the coward. In the process we become so guilt-infested that we are useless as bearers of good news.

If we could only cram enough Christ into our head, we rue-fully figure, then we would have some ready lines to toss to the fish in our pond. But Paul simply shared his love affair with Jesus. If he had any special nerve it was the kind displayed by those tenacious people who bore us to tears with their turgid tales of relatives.

If an uncle died and left us a million dollars along with a villa in Palm Springs, we would have no trouble sharing the news with our friends. We could "bore" them at length with minute details of his life and our earliest childhood memories of him and his family — and still strike the gushing attention so mutually satisfying. How? By casually mentioning that the villa and related amenities are to be shared with appreciative friends.

Paul never tired of sharing the story of how he came into his incredible wealth. We may not have the dramatic hook of his Damascus road, but we were all drastically apprehended along Calvary's Way. Our conversion followed at some time, in some given place, or else we have never fallen in love with the Savior. That might explain some witnessing problems. Not everybody falls for the villa in the desert country. The mountain afficionado would delight in modest shelter high in the Sierras. Preferences can change with the seasons. But if the season of witness prevails, the Holy Spirit tips off the bored-stiff and secretly-enthralled as to where they need to come into the story of Jesus Christ. How hard can it be to retell an exciting love story often!

2 Timothy 4:2

How is it that you have agreed together to tempt the Spirit of the Lord? Hark, the feet of those that have buried your husband are at the door . . .

Heart disease is a merciless killer. We are shocked when the trim athlete is struck by the crippler. With a diagnosis of hereditary predisposition to such disease, he faces a lingering death sentence. The chilling story of Ananias and Sapphira needs to be rethought in terms of our hereditary inclination toward cardiac arrest. In case of an autopsy that is what the puzzled pathologist would have noted on the death certificate.

In Christ we are offered a heart transplant complete with a blood supply uniquely designed to minimize the possibility of rejection. The Holy Spirit is the monitoring agent who assesses spiritual health and regulates medication. The new life cannot be run on the old heart. The old heart is unfit for the new life. Deliberate, cunning halfheartedness is suicidal. With the threat of spontaneous rejection, the Holy Spirit released a powerful checking agent into the bloodstream of Ananias and Sapphira. Foolishly routed by them through the old heart, the dosage proved fatal.

Their story is a classic. Barnabas, beloved "son of encouragement," sold a field and laid the proceeds "at the apostles' feet." It was a gesture of humility and wholeheartedness. The believers showered affection and honor on him. Ananias and Sapphira liked what they saw and sought to duplicate the feat. But when the money from the sale of their land was counted out into their hands, the sacrifice seemed unduly heavy. They schemed to proceed with their show of largess, but to keep the "fat" of the offering for themselves. Instead of the pleasing aroma, a charred witness to pious fraud resulted. Peter, filled with the Holy Spirit, immediately smelled it. He so shocked the pair with his deadly diagnosis of advanced heart disease, that cardiac arrest promptly confirmed it.

We cannot feign wholeheartedness when "dis-ease" is written all over us. The athlete recovering from near-fatal heart stoppage does not perform stunts for the sake of old times. We all suffer from halfheartedness at one time or another. To boast of it is deadly, to submit to the healing regimen of the Holy Spirit prudent.

Acts 5:9 □ *Acts 5:1-11*

But you, gird up your loins; arise, and say to them everything that I command you. Do not be dismayed by them, lest I dismay you before them.

"And I, behold, I make you this day a fortified city, an iron pillar, and bronze walls . . ." (Fasten your seat belt, turn on the ignition, and I make you this day a tank.) His is the strong stuff that will brace and guard us against dismay. The unbelted, flowing garment of biblical times evokes images of comfort and leisure. When gathered at the waist with a "girdle," we recognize that the squeeze for action is on. God's Word demands work.

One learns best to gather courage and buckle down to confrontation by not second-guessing the outcome. The Holy Spirit fulfills the convicting ministry that honors Christ whether we taste success or defeat. Thanks to vindictive Jews and vacillating Romans, Paul arrived in Rome as Caesar's prisoner. After three days he sent for the local Jewish leaders. His soul-winning streak would simply not quit; the risk-taking had to continue. His notoriety had not preceded him, but Paul was perfectly willing to stir up a fresh batch of decision-forcing dissent. A day long appointment was made.

Predictably, emotions were stirred and the fires of dissent fanned. Paul, God's fortified city at the heart of the Roman Empire, appealed to the Holy Spirit. He struck the Jews with "thoughtfulness." Leaving quietly, each one was forced to contemplate within himself the dull ears, blind eyes, and willful heart of Isaiah's prophecy. From that day on Paul received a stream of eager visitors and shared Jesus Christ "quite openly and unhindered." To that glorious end God needs to press us on to our own Rome. He yearns for us to discover the comfort of Christ's garment of grace. It is girded with praise.

Jeremiah 1:17 ☐ *Jeremiah 1*

Have pity on me, have pity on me, O you my friends, for the hand of God has touched me!

Stop analyzing me, cries Job. Be satisfied to see me sick. Comfort me. There are 1064 compelling reasons why you and I should not jump to conclusions when illness strikes. God has the first and last word, warn the 1064 verses of the Book of Job. "And even if it be true that I have erred, my error remains with myself. If indeed you magnify yourselves against me, and make my humiliation an argument against me, know then that God has put me in the wrong, and closed his net about me."

"Oh that my words were written! Oh that they were inscribed in a book!. . . . For I know that my Redeemer lives . . . " God has indeed seen to it that Job's anger and frustration with self-appointed "experts" stand as a witness against their kind forever. Affliction calls for bracing friendship. Let Job's hell of abandonment sink in!

"He has put my brethren far from me, and my acquaintances are wholly estranged from me. I call to my servant, but he gives me no answer; I must beseech him with my mouth. I am repulsive to my wife, loathsome to the sons of my own mother. All my intimate friends abhor me, and those whom I loved have turned against me."

Who is our Job, covered with "loathsome sores" from head to toe? What if the hidden record testifies of him, ". . . and that man was blameless and upright." Consider the fine irony of the three self-serving spiritual surgeons who butchered Job in their obsession for the perfect object lesson. "My wrath is kindled against you . . . for you have not spoken of me what is right, as my servant Job has. Now therefore . . . go to my servant Job, and offer up for yourselves a burnt offering; and my servant Job shall pray for you, for I will accept his prayer not to deal with you according to your folly."

Job 19:21-22 □ *Job 19:13-24*

You hypocrite, first take the log out of your own eye, and then you will see clearly to take the speck out of your brother's eye.

The cat's symptoms had the waspish old maid fly to the phone. "Come at once," she demanded of the veterinarian. "My cat has been poisoned and is suffering terribly!" The doctor had no choice but to make the dreaded house call. He took one look at the "victim" and announced crisply, "Madam, this cat is about to have kittens!" "You incompetent," cried her enraged owner, "How can she have kittens when I have never let her out of the house?" Just then a big yawning tom came crawling out from under the sofa and the vet triumphantly pointed to him. "Don't be ridiculous," snapped the old maid, "that's her brother."

The splinter in the brother's eye has us jump to alarming conclusions. Doctor, I am just about blind with tears and rage that it has come to this. Do something drastic! Something drastic, Madam? I don't think that's necessary. You see, it's just nature's way. Don't be ridiculous, doctor. I've been having my way all this time. Timber! The big log has just crashed into the picture. It explains all the little splinters — yes! — in the very family of God.

Never dissect the ridiculous for neat logic. Put it as a poultice to your afflicted eye and let it draw truth. Ah, the stuff we discover under our own sofa! Take the chip off the old block. Why are we so hard on our teenagers? Is it not because they so audaciously display what we so expertly hide? Is it not easier to take our frustrations out on a target not yet obscured by hypocrisy, than to plumb the depths for the source of our self-despising?

"Judge not, that you be not judged." In the matter of judging, the "evil eye" is definitely in the eye of the beholder — while he stares at himself in a mirror. The only reason we can see the speck is because our log draws attention to its own kind. It is undeniable fact sweetened only by two things: a saving sense of humor and a sincere "God be merciful to me, a sinner!"

Matthew 7:5 □ Matthew 7:1-5

Is any among you sick? Let him call the elders of the church, and let them pray over him, anointing him with oil in the name of the Lord . . .

". . . and the prayer of faith will save the sick man, and the Lord will raise him up; and if he has committed sins, he will be forgiven . . . The prayer of a righteous man has great power in its effects."

The cat is out of the bag. There literally are "big cats" who must take responsibility for our suffering. A slang term denoting "elders" may seem sacrilegious, but we profane the office of presbyter more if we regard it as pantomine of Properly Pious Pillars. When body and soul cry out for God's personal healing touch, we must not picture remote officialdom. What does the "righteous" man or woman in Christ's employ ideally look like? With Peter a model elder, why not look for the fisherman in the crowd! His raw-boned humanity is visibly sticking out, but his intimate walk with the Galilean has clothed him with rare grace and dignity.

It makes sense to entrust the ongoing healing ministry to gifted church leaders. The formality that must prevail to some extent assures our privacy. If we must bare our innermost self, let God provide the listener who will pray for us. With the elder we share our need for a healing experience of God's love. The main emphasis is not on our condition, but on His exalted character. If we insist on prayers for physical symptoms, we forfeit praise in favor of paranoia: Does it still hurt? Has the swelling gone down? Is the cancer healed or merely in remission?

The oil of our anointing symbolizes the power and joy of God's presence. As His Spirit causes us to realize sin, so the oil helps us to realize His desire to heal. The Helper guides us into all truth, and truth sets us free. If the soul enjoys freedom in Jesus, not even physical disability can hinder our experience of genuine wholeness.

James 5:14 ☐ *James 5:13-18*

Trophimus I left ill at Miletus.

A crisp one-liner in the closing paragraph of the letter which is Paul's "swan song" from Rome! Where is the frantic footnote offering plausible reasons for the failure? Paul had a reputation to protect. There was a time when he could raise the dead with a mere snap of fingers, it seemed. Why no miracle at Miletus?

"Trophimus I left ill at Miletus." There is no hint of resignation. On the contrary, a mood of supreme confidence pervades the closing paragraphs of his final communication, "For I am already on the point of being sacrificed; the time of my departure has come. I have fought the good fight, I have finished the race, I have kept the faith."

Today's Paul and Trophimus need to reclaim this secret of confident quitting. Never waste emotional and spiritual energy on the petulant question: Why is God not healing me when He has healed others? Why did I have the gift of healing then, but not now? Only one pointed question needs to be answered with a clear yes or no: Am I in right relationship with God? If by grace we can answer yes on the spot, we can walk away from any unsolved puzzle with these words in mind, "And this is the confidence which we have in him, that if we ask anything according to his will he hears us."

"His will" is first and foremost a matter of absolute trust in His sovereign wisdom. We have no right to bend it into the shape of our personal bias. If we insist that anything less than a glowingly healthy Christian is an insult to God, we deny the reality of redemptive suffering. If we decree suffering as a "must" for the humble saint, we may act the callous neurotic more than the wise prophet. Paul asked God three times to deliver him from his thorn in the flesh. God defined His will in terms of blind faith, "My grace is sufficient for you, for my power is made perfect in weakness." If we make this our supreme confidence, no healing service will ever disappoint us.

2 Timothy 4:19

Now I rejoice in my sufferings for your sake, and in my flesh I complete what is lacking in Christ's afflictions for the sake of his body, that is, the church . . .

Emergency surgery discloses widely scattered cancer. The incision is closed and the wife informed. Choking back tears, she opts to withhold the news from her husband to spare him anguish. Her brave show of pretense turns into a grim ordeal. A climate of growing suspicion requires mutual acts of deception. Loneliness tears away at the flesh more agonizingly than the cancer. When death ends the nightmare, the hell of regret begins in earnest.

No suffering person deserves living death. The hopelessly ill must not be put on a crash diet of pills and pity when he craves dignity and affection. He has the capacity for continued growth and enrichment. When shock and raw grief give way to the gentle sorrow that weave in and out of normal life, it becomes mellow and sweetly pleasing as daily gift. There are smiles and jokes and embraces to be shared — insights to be treasured that triumphantly press to the bright surface after each night of the soul has been endured. When death offers its restful embrace to such a peacemaker, there is quiet rejoicing that the celebration of life prevailed.

"Blessed be the God and Father of our Lord Jesus Christ, the Father of mercies and God of all comfort, who comforts us in all our affliction, so that we may be able to comfort those who are in any affliction, with the comfort with which we ourselves are comforted by God. For as we share abundantly in Christ's sufferings, so through Christ we share abundantly in comfort too."

Are we — the family of God — resolved to cherish our afflicted and dying who long to give away the gift of their selfhood so priceless in Jesus Christ? We show Him our honor and love by treasuring those who complete in their body His afflictions.

Colossians 1:24

*For I am sure that neither death, nor life, nor angels, nor princi-
palities, nor things present, nor things to come, nor powers,
nor height, nor depth, nor anything else in all creation, will be
able to separate us from the love of God in Christ Jesus our
Lord.*

Our proposed itinerary suggested mental impairment. But
with a convincing show of valid passport and bank references,
the travel agent did bow to our wishes. Consider the carefully
mapped-out places that were ultimately visited:

Hiroshima; Bethlehem; Mother Teresa's Calcutta; Uganda
and Cambodia; Washington, D.C.; Middle East; Moscow and
Beijing; Lhasa, Tibet; Death Valley, California; Houston's
space center; Hollywood's movie studios; plus major universi-
ties and headquarters of religious, political and cultural organi-
zations across the nation.

Impossible? Not at all. It took considerable time and
resources, but the investment certainly paid off. We had a
secret wager going and played for incredibly high stakes. The
powerful challenger insisted that such an exhaustive adventure
would cause us to lose personal orientation and identity. But
keeping in regular touch with home by letter and telephone, we
knew every step of the way where our true heart was
anchored. Even when nothing more was mentioned than the
weather or garbage strike, the closing words kept us centered,
"We love you always! Hurry home!"

Researchers, explorers, military people and many others
sacrifice their ordinary home life for the call of duty and adventure. In like manner, Paul suggests no armchair travelogue in
describing his actual journey of faith. He had been to Death,
Life, Angels, Principalities — and nothing had ever robbed him
of his anchor in Jesus Christ! In Him we have wealth, open
doors that no one can shut, and unlimited time and power
drawn from eternity's sources. What keeps us from fully
exploring His high road of discovery?

Romans 8:38-39 ☐ *Romans 8:31-39*

So let no one boast of men. For all things are yours, whether Paul or Apollos or Cephas or the world or life or death or the present or the future, all are yours; and you are Christ's; and Christ is God's.

Focus in your mind the famous pulpits whose occupants ride the crest of popular acclaim. You who gently row your boat in the wake of your "dreamboat" of a preacher, prepare for real turbulence! Paul is about to launch his torpedo boat against such.

Facetiously speaking, Paul had his community church, Peter his glass cathedral and Apollos his Golgotha chapel. Each man had built a following and reputation of his own. Paul actively wooed supporters, recommending himself as a father, not merely a guide, in Jesus Christ. He relentlessly urged people, "Be imitators of me, as I am of Christ." Out of his deep loyalty to God, and from a profound sense of responsibility for His family, he cautioned the Corinthians against their denominational boasting. It had become a matter of chauvinism whether one had been converted by Peter or Paul or Apollos. Baptism became less an initiation into the new life with Christ than into a famous apostle's fan club.

How did Paul refocus the church — as the bride of Christ — on her Lord rather than on some dreamboat of a human leader? "This is how one should regard us, as servants of Christ and stewards of the mysteries of God." The "service" that Paul implies is no longer required anywhere in the world, except in the church where it must be modeled afresh by our leaders. The word "servant" is the rarely used *huperetes*, meaning "under-oarsman." He served on the ancient trireme galley that had three tiers of oars. The *huperetes* was not the guy with the gorgeous tan and the whip. He was way down below, muscling the ship by the sweat of his brow.

We are not to give glory to the under-oarsman, nor to the master of the trireme. The glory belongs solely to the triune God of the oceans. We are to make purposeful use of the whole world. With life and death even our servants, we must rock the boat, not gently row it.

1 Corinthians 3:21-23 ☐ *1 Corinthians 3:18-4:7*

Truly, truly, I say to you, before Abraham was, I am.

The ancient Jew venerated Abraham. His name was invoked in ways that bordered on the superstitious. When Jesus said, "Your father Abraham rejoiced that he was to see my day; he saw it and was glad," His listeners took it as blasphemy. "So they took up stones to throw at him; but Jesus hid himself, and went out of the temple."

Is Jesus quietly stealing away now as we move into place the final props to stage our customary Christmas spectacular? What if we stole away also, to take a trip down memory lane with Him? We can start on skid row. "For God so loved the world that he gave his only Son . . ." City Hall is nearby. "We have a strong city; he sets up salvation as walls and bulwarks." There is a deserted high school. "Behold, a virgin shall conceive and bear a son . . ." Look at the busy intersection teeming with humanity. "Comfort, comfort my people, says your God."

Bethlehem comes alive in the hospital waiting room on the maternity floor. We have everything in common with the strangers floating in and out of there. We long to take these people into our arms and anoint them with the redemption that has come to our joys and sorrows. But we are nothing more than a lonely stranger. "He came to his own home, and his own people received him not."

Tiptoe to the nursery at midnight! Ask the nurse to point out Mary's baby. Forget the golden child of our gilded mangers. This tiny little male appears so bald and shriveled. "Before Abraham was, I am." Have the nurse move him closer to make quite sure. "He had no form or comeliness that we should look at him, and no beauty that we should desire him." Filled with pity, motion to the nurse to lift the baby up and hold him. "And I, when I am lifted up . . . will draw all men to myself." When tears blind your eyes, your song in the night will surely come. "Joy to the world! The Saviour reigns . . ."

John 8:58 □ John 8:48-59

Blessed are the poor in spirit, for theirs is the kingdom of heaven.

Oh, the wonder of the superbly staged Christmas pageant! Wending our way through the maze of props back to the dressing room of our private being, euphoria gives way to a pensive mood. Looking intently into the mirror of our soul while removing the holiday makeup, we wonder about lasting effects. We know instinctively that we must get back to "normal." The image created for the holidays cannot be sustained.

What was it that we sought to project most? Serenity in a world gone mad? We were right to unwrap the lovely traditions from the yellowed tissue paper of yesteryear. These fragile structures make for the temporary festal arches that allow young and old to mingle happily without bumping into the solid stuff of our ordinary, set ways. Nature teaches with her varied "season's greetings" that God smiles on the occasionally showy and extravagantly delightful. He surely created the strawberry — and whipped up the cow — for no other reason than spectacular desserts in May!

Perhaps the image we cultivated more than any other was that of our adequacy. Each year we do a tightrope act across December. Having balanced our way to today's showstopper, we must now consider the encore. How do we gracefully get back down to earth? Now comes the determined free fall that will make or break us. We either land on the fragmenting surface of the nominal-Christian reality, or on the cushioning straw of Bethlehem's manger.

Does that straw not perfectly sum up every inadequacy that is ours by reason of circumstance? The most carefully planned "blessed event" of all times came off like a makeshift affair against a world scene arrogantly staged by Rome. Bethlehem established God's norm of calculated inadequacy. The "normal" Christian is inherently inadequate. Blessed — happy! — are those with an abiding sense of need. Theirs is the makeshift bed of straw. His kingdom is not imposing structure, but substance imparted to the needy — need by need, opportunity by opportunity. Christmas was; the kingdom of heaven is. It "is" ours one day at a time, sharply focused on eternity's own endurance and expectancy.

Matthew 5:3

And the shepherds returned, glorifying and praising God for all they had heard and seen, as it had been told them.

It takes the ordinary to crystallize the extraordinary. "And in that region there were shepherds out in the field, keeping watch over their flock by night." Nearby a host of experts were keeping watch over God's promises of a Messiah. Jerusalem's clergy kept watch; the Roman yoke demanded a Deliverer. There was Simeon, "righteous and devout." There also was the prophetess Anna. None of these saw the angel.

Of the shepherds the Bible simply says that they were on the job. A character profile is best drawn from their response to the stupendous birth announcement, not our pious imaginings. They pretended none of our easy familiarity with God Almighty. When His glory shone around them, they quickly admitted to natural man's affinity for darkness. That sudden, stabbing burst of light revealed in each of them a convict on the run. Stopped cold in their tracks, fearing for their lives, the shepherds were understandably receptive to the announcement of good news. No wonder they made a beeline for Bethlehem to check out the sign. How astonishing that God's solution to their sinful condition was summed up in a vulnerable baby. Did those rudimentary theologians not gasp and blurt out, "Why, He looks just like one of us!"? Now fear gave way to faith, hope and love. The glory of God became internalized. Praise surged forth.

Is the Christ Child that simple and real to us? It is not too late to be arrested and set free forever by the blazing truth that the Light of the World deliberately shone on men sitting in darkness. Feel their fear, follow their footsteps, fall in love with the Savior of their elementary "baby faith."

Above all, return to your ordinary days and duties with this extraordinary distinction: Glorify and praise God for what you have seen and heard of Him. Be a herald angel to someone in darkness. Transform your place of work into one of worship.

Luke 2:20 ☐ *Luke 2:8-20*

"Saul, Saul . . ." Now those who were with me saw the light but did not hear the voice of the one who was speaking to me.

"God told me!" God's spokesmen are swarming all over the divided Christian camp today, some strong on dogma, others exuding personal charisma. Whose ear can we trust? Jesus, Word incarnate, takes us deeper into the mystery of heaven's unmistakable voice. The setting is Jerusalem after His triumphant entry.

"'Now is my soul troubled. And what shall I say? Father, save me from this hour? No, for this purpose I have come to this hour. Father, glorify thy name.' Then a voice came from heaven, 'I have glorified it, and I will glorify it again.' The crowd standing by heard it and said that it had thundered. Others said, 'An angel has spoken to him.' Jesus answered, 'This voice has come for your sake, not for mine'" (John 12:27-30). Calling Himself light, He exhorted the crowd to believe in Him, "that you may become sons of light."

Heaven's authoritative voice centers on Christ and His atonement alone. The supernatural light penetrates to a specific sinner's heart — "Saul, Saul" — and declares his Redeemer's worth. The authentic voice glorifies God, not human astuteness. His high calling draws attention to His exalted character and purpose, not ours. Paul became a chosen instrument to carry Christ's name before Gentiles, Jews and kings. His mark of distinction? "For I will show him how much he must suffer for the sake of my name." The voice that Paul alone could hear offered him the companionship of the cross. He accepted it at the hands of the risen Lord. God in every age shines forth His light and sounds the clarion call that woos the heart — anonymous shepherd, famous religious figure, modern laywoman — willing to glorify His name. "God told me!" If He did, the power of His name will give eloquent expression to the servant's surrendered life.

Acts 22:7,9

So you have sorrow now, but I will see you again and your hearts will rejoice, and no one will take your joy from you. In that day you will ask nothing of me.

That will be the day! We grudgingly learn to go from crisis to crisis, never quite grasping that we are being changed from one degree of glory to another. We prefer antiseptic inspiration to Gethsemane perspiration. We put up with God after a fashion, affirming His lordship, but propping it up between question marks.

We piously learn to say the Lord this and that, never even questioning our sincerity. Few of us are chronically ill, or unemployed, or abused, or exposed to the sordid and sub-human. Few of us know the rugged reality of a discipleship bound for Jerusalem in all its grief and glory.

Could it not be safely said that our Lord would gladly trade 500 politely pliable Presbyterians for 12 plucky disciples whose aggressive questions and petitions develop along Peter's lines, "Lord, if it is you, bid me come to you on the water"? Or, "Lo, we have left everything and followed you," which really means, "Just where do we stand, Lord? We understand your kingdom less and less!"

To such a band of plucky, problematic disciples the Suffering Servant spoke these significant words of consolation, "In that day you will ask nothing of me." *That* day was after Christ's ascension when He was glorified in heaven. The visible sign of His glorification was the outpouring of the Holy Spirit at Pentecost. Now human intellect and emotions became intimately fused with the mind and heart of the risen Lord. Now the strategy of the kingdom became visibly deployed, with persecution, suffering and death the order of the day. Why, God? Why so little genuine joy in the church today? Is it because we want to be baptized into Christ's Resurrection without being baptized into His death?

John 16:22-23

I have fought the good fight, I have finished the race, I have kept the faith.

Paul talks about successful Christian retirement! We beg to differ. There are other attractive options. I have invested wisely, I have quit the rat race, I have firmly held to the success gospel. Or, I have stayed married for fifty years, I have children, grandchildren and great-grandchildren, I have upheld the family ideal. Or, I have studied life, I have developed guidelines for coping with it, I have written a helpful book. But how do these stand up to Paul's introductory remark, "For I am already on the point of being sacrificed; the time of my departure has come."?

With senility more rampant these days than beheadings, the threat of sudden death should not send us scurrying for spiritual reinforcement. What should scare us to death is the question of the "good fight." The minute there is a ripple in our smooth life we petition God to make it go away. Two ripples have us cry "Satan."

Either Paul was an inept Christian and glutton for punishment, or our idea of a good fight needs an urgent update. This is what he lumps in with "good" on top of lashes, beatings, shipwrecks and one stoning: "On frequent journeys, in danger from rivers, danger from robbers, danger from my own people, danger from Gentiles . . . And . . . there is the daily pressure upon me of my anxiety for all the churches" (2 Corinthians 11:26-28).

What nerve we have to go to our nice little church meetings where we praise Jesus for giving us peace and joy — provided these are held at a convenient hour in a safe part of town! What nerve to cry "Satan" when God consistently pulls the rug out from under our complacency! If we are part of His strategy we need to be tested and stretched to the utmost. How else are we going to cry out for His Holy Spirit who alone imparts courageous, victorious faith?

2 Timothy 4:7 □ 2 Timothy 4:6-8

I am praying for them; I am not praying for the world but for those whom thou hast given me . . .

Shocking. The moment we take down the "Peace on Earth" cards we discover that the Prince of Peace is not praying for the world. Time bombs are ticking away all over the globe. Terror might strike anytime and the blood of innocents be shed. Our Lord does not pray that we would rush in with Bibles, beans, grants, birth control aids, helicopters or advisers. Our High Priest simply prays, "Holy Father, keep them in thy name, which thou has given me, that they may be one, even as we are one."

"By this all men will know that you are my disciples, if you have love for one another." Same jarring note. Forget the world. "If you love me, you will keep my commandments. And I will pray the Father, and he will give you another Counselor, to be with you for ever, even the Spirit of truth, whom the world cannot receive, because it neither sees him nor knows him; you know him, for he dwells with you, and will be in you." To the world Jesus Christ was and remains a stumbling block. It was only by His death and resurrection that a new breed of humanity became possible. We belong to that fellowship of His suffering. Because of it, "God's love has been poured into our hearts through the Holy Spirit which has been given to us." We are to exercise that love on behalf of the body that the Head might be honored. Then the Father can send us into the world as servants and disciple makers!

Are we faithfully involved with a Christian education class? Are we willing to pray and grow with the believer with whom we have no natural affinity? Do we demonstrate the love and oneness our Lord offers us in His name and power? If we must worry, let us worry about that first! The world will just have to wait.

John 17:9 □ John 17

Amen. Come, Lord Jesus!

> *On Christ the solid Rock I stand;*
> *All other ground is sinking sand.*
> *All other ground is sinking sand.*

> *My hope is built on nothing less*
> *Than Jesus' blood and righteousness;*
> *I dare not trust the sweetest frame,*
> *But wholly lean on Jesus' name.*

> *When darkness veils His lovely face,*
> *I rest on His unchanging grace;*
> *In every high and stormy gale,*
> *My anchor holds within the vale.*

> *His oath, His covenant, His blood*
> *Support me in the whelming flood;*
> *When all around my soul gives way*
> *He then is all my hope and stay.*

> *When He shall come with trumpet sound,*
> *O may I then in Him be found;*
> *Dressed in His righteousness alone,*
> *Faultless to stand before the throne.*

On May 30, 1979, my life hit rock bottom. At night, in deep discouragement I cried out to God, holding on to the Word for dear life. My eyes fell on Psalm 42:8, "By day the Lord commands his steadfast love; and at night his song is with me . . ." Give me my song, I pleaded. That night I was awakened from deep sleep to the sound of a song. The Spirit in me was singing zestfully, "On Christ the solid Rock I stand . . ." Let us stand together and sing His songs in the night.

Revelation 22:20